"This book is timely and exciting because it takes teachers, their experiences, and their efforts at scholarly inquiry seriously. In an era when teachers are increasingly positioned as anti-intellectual and incompetent, we need books that illuminate teachers' perspectives, struggles, and intellectual curiosity."

Amanda Haertling Thein, The University of Iowa, USA

"A useful integration of theory, research and practice, this book is a call for continuing to press for teacher autonomy and the small and large ways in which researchers, theorists and practitioners can do so when working together and through an inquiry approach to teaching and teacher development."

Wanda Brooks, Temple University, USA

"Understanding global cultures and multiple world views is no longer an optional curricular component, but a necessity for living in a global society.... Global literature, in particular, provides an incredibly rich context for children and teachers to try on ways of living and thinking that take them outside the boundaries of their own cultural identities and communities.... [This book] provides many examples of interactions around global books in which children come to recognize, extend, and critique their own perspectives and are challenged to go beyond themselves to consider alternative perspectives....We can either recreate the status quo in our classrooms or we can take on the challenge [the authors] have given us to take the risk of transformative dialogue."

Kathy G. Short, University of Arizona, USA—*From the Foreword*

"These powerful stories offer hope, not just for teaching and teachers, but also for the future of society. Their examples suggest that because of engagements with global literature, students develop, among other things, better relationships, more productive identities, a stronger sense of agency, and a diminished likelihood of stereotyping. Perhaps more importantly, they develop a stronger sense of equity and justice and a critical awareness of their own role in its production."

Peter H. Johnston, University at Albany-SUNY—*From the Afterword*

TEACHING GLOBAL LITERATURE IN ELEMENTARY CLASSROOMS

Demonstrating the power of teaching global literature from a critical literacy perspective, this book explores the ways that K-6 educators can infuse diverse texts into their classrooms and find support for their endeavours in teacher inquiry communities. Through carefully analyzed, ethnographically informed portraits of classroom life alternating with teachers' own accounts of their teaching and learning experiences, it demonstrates how students are moved to question, debate, and take action in response to global texts. This multivocal work both emerges from and responds to tensions and debates related to the purpose and practice of literature education in a time of Common Core State Standards.

Kelly K. Wissman is an Associate Professor of Literacy Teaching and Learning at the University at Albany, USA.

Maggie Naughter Burns is a Reading Specialist at Delaware Community School, Albany, NY, USA.

Krista Jiampetti is a Literacy Specialist at Lisha Kill Middle School, Albany, NY, USA.

Heather O'Leary is a teacher of English as a New Language in the Schenectady City School District, Schenectady, New York, USA.

Simeen Tabatabai is a Reading Teacher at Southgate Elementary School, Albany, NY, USA.

TEACHING GLOBAL LITERATURE IN ELEMENTARY CLASSROOMS

A Critical Literacy and Teacher Inquiry Approach

Kelly K. Wissman, Maggie Naughter Burns, Krista Jiampetti, Heather O'Leary, and Simeen Tabatabai

Routledge
Taylor & Francis Group

NEW YORK AND LONDON

First published 2017
by Routledge
711 Third Avenue, New York, NY 10017

and by Routledge
2 Park Square, Milton Park, Abingdon, Oxon, OX14 4RN

Routledge is an imprint of the Taylor & Francis Group, an informa business

Library of Congress Cataloging in Publication Data
Wissman, Kelly K.
Title: Teaching global literature in elementary classrooms : a critical literacy and teacher inquiry approach / by Kelly K. Wissman [and four others].
Description: New York : Routledge, 2016. Identifiers: LCCN 2016001816|
ISBN 9781138190252 (hardback) | ISBN 9781138190269 (pbk.) | ISBN 9781315641188 (ebook) Subjects: LCSH: Children's literature–Study and teaching (Elementary) Classification: LCC LB1575 .W57 2016 | DDC 372.64/044–dc23 LC record available at http://lccn.loc.gov/2016001816

ISBN: 978-1-138-19025-2 (hbk)
ISBN: 978-1-138-19026-9 (pbk)
ISBN: 978-1-315-64118-8 (ebk)

Typeset in Bembo
by Cenveo Publisher Services

CONTENTS

FOREWORD

Perspectives as Transformation

Kathy G. Short

Perspective matters. When we are trapped within our own individualistic views of the world and our classrooms, we have no way to outgrow ourselves as educators and as human beings. This book is a compelling and moving demonstration of the possibilities that are created when we have the opportunity to explore multiple perspectives within a dialogic community.

The reflections and stories woven into these chapters describe the ways in which the pressures of tests, standards, and mandates that teachers face on a daily basis can overwhelm and create a culture of compliance. This compliance takes away the joy of teaching, but more importantly, causes teachers to question their own knowledge about how to create the most effective learning experiences for their students. Although facing these pressures alone can lead to uncertainty, the perspectives gained within a community of teachers who are inquiring together provide support for risk-taking and professional learning.

Kelly, Maggie, Krista, Heather, and Simeen share the ways in which their inquiry group positioned them as knowledgeable professionals who gained inspiration, competence, and perspective in a space that felt safe from public critique. They had a place to learn through dialogue with each other as they planned and reflected on practice and gained knowledge about critical literacy and global literature, leading to transformative understandings. By thinking collaboratively with each other, they developed a shared purpose and commitment for change that sustained them in moving forward with innovative practice. They also moved flexibly between theory and practice as they explored the implications of theory for practice and developed theory out of effective practice.

Teaching can be a lonely profession as teachers spend most of the day behind closed doors or in required meetings to conduct the business of schools. Professional development frequently takes the form of delivering the newest mandate or program for implementation. This approach to reform is in direct contrast to the learning experiences that teachers find most powerful. A survey by the National Center of Literacy Education (2013) asked a cross-section of teachers to name the single professional learning experience that had the greatest impact on their practice in the previous year. In-services, conferences, and university courses were on the list, but the experience named by an overwhelming majority of teachers was collaborative inquiry with colleagues that was closely embedded in the day-to-day work of teaching and learning. The stories and the letters that the teachers write to each other in this book speak directly to the power of collaborative inquiry for gaining knowledge and perspective that leads to lasting change, not momentary compliance.

The value of multiple perspectives is also evident in the rich examples of classroom practice and student dialogue included throughout the book. Kelly, Maggie, Krista, Heather, and Simeen are committed to the possibilities that dialogue around global literature brings into the lives of children and teachers and they make these opportunities come alive through describing their struggles as well as successes.

We live in a rapidly changing world where global connections are woven into every part of our daily lives through social media, the internet, global mobility, and economic interdependence. Understanding global cultures and multiple world views is no longer an optional curricular component but a necessity for living in a global society. Intercultural understanding moves beyond political rhetoric or curiosity about a culture to a deep understanding of the values and beliefs embedded in the lives of members of global communities (Short, 2016). This understanding provides the basis for living and working together as global citizens within our own local communities as well as worldwide.

Global literature, in particular, provides an incredibly rich context for children and teachers to try on ways of living and thinking that take them outside the boundaries of their own cultural identities and communities. Through literature, readers are able to move away from a tourist perspective of surface-level information about a cultural community and immerse themselves into living within a story world where they connect and empathize with people in that culture. These experiences help them understand that they each have a perspective that comes out of their own cultural identities and locations and that their way of thinking is not the norm from which to judge all others as "different." This focus on perspective extends to the recognition that there are multiple worldviews and each reflects an alternative way to think and live in the world, not a right or wrong way.

Kelly, Maggie, Krista, Heather, and Simeen provide many examples of interactions around global books in which children come to recognize, extend, and critique their own perspectives and are challenged to go beyond themselves to consider alternative perspectives. The chapters do not just contain lists of books but discussions about *why* a particular book invited children to critically consider local and global issues and cultural ways of being. As teachers, we all know a book that effectively engages one group of children can fall flat with another group, and so the discussions of why and how a book engaged students are particularly helpful.

Another way in which this book highlights perspective is through the focus on critical dialogue around literature. The engagements and context that surround the use of a book in a classroom make a difference in whether that book establishes stereotypes through readers feeling pity or superiority to the characters or challenges readers to engage with issues through an intercultural lens. The chapters contain detailed transcripts of dialogue around literature that show the dangers as well as possibilities in how children engage with each other and a particular book.

Rosenblatt (1938) argued that personal response is essential but never sufficient and that readers always need to move from expressing their individual responses to critiquing those responses with other readers. Rosenblatt valued and provided space for individual voice but never at the expense of group responsibility, which she saw as occurring through dialogue. This dialogue provides the reader with a space to share and to critique his/her interpretation as well as to consider the perspectives of other readers. Readers share their individual responses with conviction and enthusiasm, while keeping an open mind toward alternative points of view as they negotiate meaning with each other. Her balance of emotion and reason, individual voice and group responsibility, and personal response and dialogue provide a powerful context for the experiences shared by Kelly, Maggie, Krista, Heather, and Simeen. They live Rosenblatt's theories in complex ways within their classrooms, struggling to figure out what those theories mean in the lives of children from diverse backgrounds and communities.

Our perspectives as educators reflect the beliefs that guide the decisions we make in our classrooms and the ways in which we view our students as well as the larger global world. Kelly, Maggie, Krista, Heather, and Simeen remind us that broadening and deepening our perspectives opens a world of possibility but also brings uncertainty and risk. It often feels much safer to stay in the known, to live within the confines of the walls that have been constructed around us in schools. Ultimately, however, those walls represent barriers, both professionally and personally, that take away the opportunity for opening our minds and transforming our potential to create a better and more just world. We can either recreate the status quo in our classrooms or we can take on the challenge that Kelly, Maggie, Krista, Heather, and Simeen have given us to take the risk of transformative dialogue.

References

National Center for Literacy Education. (2013). *Remodeling literacy learning: Making room for what works.* Urbana, IL: National Council of Teachers of English.

Rosenblatt, L. (1938). *Literature as exploration*. Chicago, IL: Modern Language Association.

Short, K. G. (2016). A curriculum that is intercultural. In K. G. Short, D. Day, & J. Schroeder (Eds.), *Reframing curriculum: Reading the world through literature*. Portsmouth, ME: Stenhouse.

PREFACE

This book is for teachers and teacher educators interested in how global literature can expand students' horizons, invigorate classroom inquiry, and inspire students to make a difference in the world. It details how four K–6 educators, from a range of urban and suburban schools, infused diverse texts into their classrooms and found support for their endeavors in a teacher inquiry community.

This multivocal book illustrates how English Language Learners, "struggling readers," and academically successful students alike wrestled with a host of social issues, including educational inequities, the ethics of war, and the lived experiences of child migrant workers. We weave together transcripts of class discussions, student writing, and teacher reflections to show how elementary students were moved to debate, discuss, write, draw, and take action in response to global literature and how their teachers were inspired to re-envision their own teaching.

This book makes the case for the teaching of global literature from a critical literacy and teacher inquiry approach to promote social justice and cultural awareness. It is distinctive in the following ways:

- Uniquely located at the intersection of three domains: global literature, critical literacy, teacher inquiry
- Offers a sustained focus on global literature as an entry point for student inquiries
- Creates multidimensional portraits of how critical literacy teaching is lived and experienced by teachers and students amidst an educational landscape full of contradictory policies, standards, and evaluation procedures
- Adds to critical literacy theory and practice by bringing in perspectives on dialogic teaching and sociocultural approaches to emotion
- Connects the work of teacher inquiry communities with the lived realities in classrooms

1

INTRODUCTION

Global Visions, Local Inquiries

Kelly K. Wissman

On a late September afternoon, just as the leaves were beginning to change, four teachers and I gathered after school. Soon, Maggie, Krista, Simeen, and Heather traded stories and concerns about new teacher evaluation procedures, the rollout of the Common Core State Standards, and revamped literacy curricula. Even though this was only the second meeting of our global literature inquiry community, conversation flowed freely and spiritedly. With a mixture of exasperation, genuine curiosity, and light-hearted amusement, the teachers shared their experiences navigating the tangled web of initiatives shaping the English Language Arts. While I continued to make final preparations for the official start of the meeting by distributing a range of picturebooks on the tables in front of us, I took note of short bursts of conversation detailing mandates for the increased use of nonfiction texts and for the incorporation of extensive curriculum guides featuring dozens of questions designed to promote "close reading." As more and more stories began to build upon each other, Maggie proclaimed, "It's hard to see straight!"

In the midst of the staccato-like exchanges describing these sometimes disorienting changes, the visual appeal of the picturebooks surrounding us on the meeting table and the compelling stories housed within them captured our attention and began to focus our discussion on the potential of global literature to infuse teaching with a larger sense of purpose. While the sense of anxiety around the complex educational climate in which this work would occur lingered, it moved a bit to the background as we considered the picturebooks and their possibilities. As often occurred within this group, the books created conversational and intellectual openings for considering the potential of teaching with high quality global literature and for imagining the inquiries the texts could inspire. The picturebooks helped us, in a sense, to "see straight."

Within this book, we endeavor to retain this spirit of exploration and possibility that both the texts and the inquiry community inspired, even as we document and reflect on the obstacles and doubts that also accompanied this work. In the chapters that follow, you may notice that references to "seeing" often emerge. At times, we lamented how educators can sometimes lose sight of children in the midst of high stakes testing pressures. At other times, a group member noted how her own eyes had been opened by the global literature she read as a part of this inquiry group. Overwhelmingly, though, our efforts in this book are catalyzed by our collective witnessing of how students' eyes lit up in response to books that reflected their experiences, that transported them to distant lands, and that inspired them to draw, debate, perform, and take action. Across four very distinct contexts, reading global literature cleared spaces for dialogue, creativity, engagement, and action. Reading and responding to global literature both troubled some of the students' own assumptions and promoted a sense of empathy. While the dizzying amount of pressures, initiatives, and demands rarely abated across the time we spent together, keeping global literature at the center of the inquiry helped shift the focus to the global visions the students were developing.

An Introduction to the Inquiry Community

In the summer of 2012, supported by a grant from the Longview Foundation for Education in World Affairs and International Understanding and the Worlds of Words organization, I invited four educators across urban and suburban districts to explore the potential role of global literature within their teaching and professional development responsibilities. Resulting from my work as a teacher educator within the university in which each teacher had pursued graduate studies, I invited the participants to join the inquiry group based on my knowledge of their interest in children's literature and their teaching commitments. For the next 16 months, I served as the facilitator of the monthly meetings of the inquiry community and as a researcher within the teachers' classrooms. This book explores what happened when this group of K-6 educators shared texts, teaching experiences, and emergent analyses of their practice within the inquiry community and also offers descriptions of the pedagogical practices and inquiries that took place within the teachers' classrooms.

The four teachers included a K-4 reading specialist (Maggie), a middle school literacy specialist (Krista), a fifth grade reading teacher (Simeen), and a K-6 English as a New Language teacher (Heather). They taught in a range of urban and suburban schools and had been teaching between 12 and 20 years. We called our group "Tri-Cities" to reflect the geographic region encompassing three mid-size towns in which this study was located. Our monthly meetings typically started with members sharing their plans for incorporating global literature into their classrooms and seeking out suggestions and responses from the group. A wide array of global literature was also on hand for members to look through and consider. As the school year progressed, members shared teaching experiences, student work, and reflections on their teaching. We also discussed articles or book chapters exploring how other teachers have conceptualized global literature and incorporated global perspectives into their classrooms (see Appendix for a list of children's books and professional resources that were most influential in our inquiries). I approached each of these meetings with particular plans in mind in terms of discussions of readings and dedicated time for each teacher to share her thinking on her practice. Unlike traditional models of professional development, however, I was less concerned with transmitting a certain body of knowledge to the teachers. Instead, I endeavored to honor their rich experiences and thoughtful intellects, attempting to create a context in which we co-constructed knowledge together, followed lines of inquiry emergent from the teachers' own contexts, and carved out the time and space for speaking and listening to the complexities, nuances, and lived experiences of teaching. Characterized by a dialogic and relational ethos, this inquiry community constructed knowledge horizontally (Campano, Honeyford, Sánchez, & Vander Zanden, 2010; Simon, 2015), with and for each other.

This inquiry community was also part of a larger national network of global literacy communities under the leadership of Kathy G. Short. These groups shared perspectives and resources in an online blog, published reflective pieces on the Worlds of Words website, and presented their work at the National Council of Teachers of English Annual Convention. Although our inquiry group met most intensively and regularly for the 16 months of our grant period, we have continued to come together to share insights, stories, and inquiries that build on and extend the experiences at the heart of this book.

Sketching the Educational Landscape

This inquiry is set against a backdrop of considerable educational vicissitude. These changes, while disruptive, often carried many traces of the epistemologies that shaped educational reforms and English Language Arts curricula of the past.

Pedagogy and Purpose

Our inquiry group began meeting during a time when the Common Core State Standards (CCSS) were making their way into classrooms and schools in New York in an accelerated manner. Many of the initiatives within the English Language Arts inspired by the CCSS reflected mid-20th century notions of the New Critics (e.g. Brooks, 1947) who argued that meaning was located solely within the text itself without regard for the beliefs, experiences, and meaning-making processes brought by the reader. Through a series of webinars, publications, and addresses, David Coleman, one of the co-authors of the English Language Arts Common Core Standards, perpetuated many of these understandings. Coleman had a high profile and far reach in New York at the time, an impact felt by many in the inquiry group. Across a range of multimedia and print platforms, Coleman asserted that literature instruction should be guided by the mantra of "staying within the four corners of the text" (Coleman & Pimentel, 2012, p. 4). From this perspective, students' responses and connections to texts are considered extraneous to literary interpretation and meaning-making. In a widely viewed videotaped address in which he characterized students as taking up any opportunity available to avoid engaging deeply in text, Coleman shared the following musings to support the proposed CCSS for the English Language Arts:

> Think about it, right? You're reading a text and you talk about the background of the text, or what it reminds you of, or what you think about it, or all sorts of surrounding issues—kids are genius at this—because anything to avoid confronting the difficult words before them is money. (Coleman, 2011, p. 10)

Further arguing that "when you grow up in this world you realize people don't give a shit about what you feel or what you think" (p. 10), Coleman also critiques teachers' efforts to elicit students' thoughts, connections, and feelings in response to texts. Instead, Coleman (2011) argues that teachers should instill in students a "certain reverence" (p. 23) for written texts. To promote this reverence, he contends, like the New Critics, that instruction should "center on careful examination of the text itself" (Coleman & Pimentel, 2012, p. 1). Echoing these calls to re-center the text, Shanahan (2013) questions instructional practices that focus on previewing the text, providing student background information, and matching texts to students by reading levels. He refers to these practices as "daily rituals [that] increasingly have elbowed the text aside" (p. 11) by overwhelming students with a "veritable flood of extra information" (p. 7). By focusing reading instruction on key ideas and details, text structure, literary devices, craft and structure, and author's purpose, Shanahan sees the potential "to move ideas, and thinking about ideas, back to the center of the reading curriculum" (p. 11).

Many have noted, however, that inviting students to analyze texts in relation to their own worlds *does* involve wrestling with ideas and that this wrestling is central to the humanistic aims of the English Language Arts (e.g. Ohanian, 2013; Short, 2009). Evoking two leading theorists of response to literature, Galda (2013) writes:

> Rosenblatt and Britton were right: If we support readers as they read aesthetically, evoking their own poems, and allow them time to think, write, and talk about their experiences, reading a powerful book can become an event that just might change the world, one reader at a time. (p. 12)

Text-centered approaches also run contrary to decades of scholarship documenting the efficacy of reader-based and inquiry-based classroom practices (Short, 2013; Smith, Appleman, & Wilhelm, 2014) and theoretical understandings of reading as transactional, as situated in the social world, and as a social practice (e.g. Beach, Thein, & Parks, 2008; Ivey & Johnston, 2013; Lewis, 2001; Sulzer, 2014; Sumara, 2002). Furthermore, educators informed by the activist and emancipatory aims of critical literacy (Vasquez, 2010) and critical multiculturalism (Möller, 2012), envision literature classrooms as places where students engage in readings that bring to the surface social injustices and where participants engage in processes of "facing biases and stereotypes and taking action in a student-centered learning environment" (Möller, 2012, p. 23).

In this book, we explore how young readers from across four distinct contexts responded to books with global themes in ways that prompted an affective engagement that went far beyond the actual words decoded on the page. When students were invited to express their thoughts and personal insights in response to global literature, they engaged deeply in texts that challenged them conceptually and ethically. In our experience, students not only "revered" the texts they read but also the interpretive communities in which the texts were read and discussed. In many cases, this engagement not only catapulted them beyond "the four corners of the text" (Coleman & Pimentel, 2012) but also beyond the "four corners of the classroom" as students began to reconsider their own place in the world and their responsibilities to it.

Texts and Identities

In addition to exposing fault lines over *how* texts should be taught and for what purposes, the Common Core also renewed debate regarding *what* texts should be taught. Many note the lack of cultural diversity within the "text exemplars" recommended in "Appendix B" of the standards (Gangi, 2010; Möller, 2013; Short, 2013). As Gangi and Benfer (2014) note, "Of 171 texts recommended for elementary children in Appendix B of the CCSS, there are only 18 by authors of color, and few books reflect the lives of children of color and the poor." While efforts are being made to diversify this list with more multicultural and global texts, it remains a particularly problematic document within our increasingly globalized world in which children's literature is uniquely primed to provide students with the knowledge, dispositions, and understandings necessary for informed and ethical participation within local and global contexts (Choo, 2013; Martin, Smolen, Oswald, & Milam, 2012; Short, 2009).

Although the research literature contains many compelling and thought-provoking studies of how young people wrestle with issues of identity in response to multicultural literature exploring the diversity of experiences within America (e.g. Beach, Thein, & Parks, 2008; Enciso, 1994; Möller, 2012; Souto-Manning, 2013), we have fewer windows into how American students consider their own identities in relation to the world outside America's borders (Loh, 2009; Martens et al., 2015). As Loh (2009) argues, "students must learn to envision self as both American and global citizen and that the worlds and worldviews in literary texts allow for imaginings and conversations about self and self in relation to the world" (p. 288). In response to this call to action, we take inspiration from Allen and Alexander (2012) who explore how K-12 teachers worked together to develop and teach from a critical content framework informed by the U.N. Convention on the Rights of a Child. These teachers engaged students in a range of inquiries in which they questioned social injustices and took responsive action. We take a similar collaborative stance, although we chose global literature as an entry point for exploring how to teach in ways supportive of inquiry, critical literacy, and social change. In this book, we hope that our showcasing of dialogue between students and teachers, students and students, and students and texts will provide perspective on the possibilities of teaching with a broader range of texts than currently appearing on CCSS text lists.

Teachers' Roles in Educational Change

The development of the CCSS and the ways in which those standards were interpreted and taken up in the teachers' districts in a top-down fashion also carried traces of the past. This process reflected the historically marginalized role of teachers in informing and shaping large-scale educational reforms (Zancanella & Moore, 2014). Rather than viewing teachers as intellectuals and "cultural workers" (Freire, 2005) with knowledge and experience to craft the standards, teachers were more often viewed as simply implementers of them. Even though the teachers in this inquiry group had a limited role in the development of the standards, they nonetheless lived them, their ramifications, and their possibilities. In this book, we aim to show how teachers engaged with, spoke back to, wrestled with, and adapted the standards in response to their students, instructional goals, and life histories.

While the Common Core understandably took up a good deal of the intellectual and conversational space during the time of the inquiry group, we also encountered the remnants and legacies of the curricular and testing practices associated with No Child Left Behind, a highly contested and hastily proposed statewide teacher evaluation system, and unique district and school-level policies each teacher navigated in her own way. I name these here as a way not only to suggest the complex educational landscape in which this teaching occurred but also to suggest the remarkable moments of teaching and learning that were nonetheless nurtured amidst and despite them. In this book, we aspire to illuminate the complexities and possibilities of reading global literature within schools and how this literature has the potential to help us "better see ourselves in light of the kind of world we wish to create and the kind of people we wish to become" (Leland, Harste, Ociepka, Lewison, & Vasquez, 1999, p. 71). Leland et al. (1999) compel us to consider how literary engagements can change how we see ourselves, our place in the world, and even the very world itself. As we explore across the chapters in this book, conducting research and participating in the inquiry community while teaching this literature added additional layers to our understandings of the kind of teachers and researchers we wanted to be and to become.

Sight Lines

In addition to this complex education landscape of policy debates and curriculum reforms, this inquiry also took place against a multidimensional backdrop of educational research and theory. Here, I discuss the points of view within the educational field that informed and shaped our perceptions of global literature, literary engagement, and collaborative research.

Envisioning Global Literature

In the early meetings of the inquiry group, we pondered what exactly we meant by "global literature" and how these understandings would shape what books we chose to share with students. While many of us had long incorporated multicultural literature exploring diverse cultural groups within the United States into our teaching, we were unsure how or if global literature was different. At first, our perspectives seemed aligned with Lehman, Freeman, and Scharer (2010) who describe global literature as "world literature" taking place in settings outside the United States, while multicultural literature portrays "parallel cultures within the United States" (p. 17). In contrast, Martens et al. (2015), define global literature as encompassing both international and multicultural literature, including books whose settings, authors, and publication venues are located within the United States and elsewhere. For our group, defining global literature thus became a site of inquiry itself, especially as we considered the experiences and identities of the students across the four distinct settings in which the teachers taught. As members of the group started to share books with the students in their classes, we began to question not only what books were considered "global," but also what books were considered "global" to *whom*. For many of Heather's students who were recent immigrants to the United States and who had extended families within other countries, books about China or Yemen were not "global," to them, but were instead "local" stories reflective of their own histories, lives, and experiences. For Heather's students, then, texts exploring the American Civil Rights movement expanded their horizons and understandings in ways reminiscent of the transformative ways Krista's American-born students engaged with a book about a brave librarian miles away in Basra, Iraq (Winter, 2005).

Our understanding of global literature in the inquiry community and in this book is broadly *inclusive* (reflective of the diverse cultures within the U.S. and cultures outside its borders) and *contextual* (dependent on the identities and experiences the reader brings to the text). In many ways, our understanding and use of the term "global literature" is also *intentional*. We consider it intentional in two primary ways. First, given our awareness of the paucity of books with international settings and themes within U.S. school and classroom libraries, we did make purposeful and concerted efforts to find and incorporate books set outside the United States. Second, as globalization is not an abstract concept but a lived reality of the students with whom we work, we also saw the necessity of breaking down artificial barriers between "global" and "multicultural" literature. We did so as a way to decenter an inaccurate view of a monocultural, monolingual United States as the only axis by which books could take on the mantle of "global." We also did so as a way to decenter the notion that there is a singular notion of what it means to be "American" that is untouched by experiences, lives, and histories from other countries outside America's borders. As Ghiso, Campano, and Hall (2012) contend, students bring with them to schools "braided histories" that reflect hybrid, multiple, and dynamic experiences; children's books have a vital role to play in creating contexts for recognizing and exploring those identities. Both global books and the pedagogical practices associated with them can create opportunities to affirm the uniqueness of students' cultural identities while also highlighting their interconnectedness, showcasing how "communities and individuals are implicated in one another's circumstances, struggles, and progress" (Ghiso, Campano, & Hall, 2012, p. 16). In the chapters that follow, our hope is to provide glimpses of these complex and promising negotiations with global literature across a range of contexts.

Envisioning Literary Engagement

Within this book we work from an inclusive, contextual, and intentional definition of what constitutes a global text. In doing so, we also try to be attuned to the complexities of students' identities as they read and responded to these books. In the process of rendering these experiences in the chapters that follow, we name particularly compelling texts and particularly impactful instructional strategies with the texts, yet our primary focus is on looking carefully at student engagement and meaning-making with these texts. Exceptional resources exist that provide guidance in selecting and utilizing high quality global texts (e.g. Bond, 2006; Lehman, Freeman, & Scharer, 2010; Short & Thomas, 2011) and multicultural literature (e.g. Bishop, 2007; Brooks & McNair, 2008; Fox & Short, 2003). Additional resonant and influential texts detail the theory and practice behind the teaching of children's literature informed by principles of critical literacy (e.g. Leland, Lewison, & Harste, 2013; Lewison, Leland, & Harste, 2015; Souto-Manning, 2013; Vasquez, 2010). We take inspiration from and were informed by these resources, even as our gaze in this book shifts focus to providing rich description and reflection on students' literary engagements with global literature. We also draw on, and in some cases, recast, theoretical perspectives on response to literature and critical literacy, as I explore next.

Transactional and hermeneutical lenses. In our skepticism over the renewed embrace of the New Critics as proposed in some interpretations of the Common Core, we locate our understanding of literary engagement within transactional and hermeneutical lenses. Rosenblatt (1982) explores the relationship between the reader and the text, envisioning reading as "a transaction, a two-way process, involving a reader and a text at a particular time under particular circumstances" (p. 268). She highlights the situated, dynamic, and animated nature of reading, describing the "live circuit" (Rosenblatt, 1986) that exists within the reader's transaction with texts. For Sumara (1996), reading is also an ever-evolving, ever-dynamic act that is deeply contextual and deeply connected to the social context in which the reading occurs. Drawing from Rosenblatt's transactional theories and from hermeneutical understandings of literary interpretation, Sumara (1996, 2002) develops an understanding of reading as an interpretive practice. Further informed by poststructural understandings of identities, Sumara explores how reading provides opportunities for readers to interpret and organize their place in the social world. With this notion of identities as discursively produced, as constantly in the process of becoming, Sumara (1998) describes how reading causes identity negotiations, asserting, "relationships readers form with literary fictions become interesting and generative locations for the interpretation of past, present, and projected identities" (p. 206). In arguing that reading is an "important site for the contestation and negotiation of already slippery and shifting identities" (p. 206), Sumara (1998) thus complicates prevailing understandings that literature provides vicarious experiences in which readers search for affirmations of fully realized selves or an "escape" from their own lived realities. By envisioning reading as an act pursued within a set of social relations and as an act of identity work, reading thus involves the construction and reconstruction of knowledge and identity.

For Sumara, these kinds of literary experiences necessitate "dwelling" within texts, as opposed to "touring." Although not conceptualized specifically with the teaching of global literature in mind, these are particularly apt and resonant analogies that inform the chapters that follow. A tourist may enjoy a visit to a new locale, taking in popular sites, tasting a bit of local cuisine, hearing new languages, enjoying tidbits of history shared by a tour guide, but may not come to a deeper appreciation of how life is lived and experienced by those who live there. A person who reads as a tourist would, therefore, stay on the surface of the book, at a distance from the world conveyed and the characters evoked. This kind of literary experience, Sumara (1994) contends, is promoted by pedagogical practices that include:

> some pre-touring information (a bit about the book); sometimes some research into the pending tour site (background information); some pointing out of the most important sites (notice the character development here); and some general discussion and response, usually led by the tour guide (Any questions? How did you feel about that?). (p. 44)

A person who dwells in a new place, on the other hand, and by extension a book, not only understands more deeply but is also more connected to its people and ways of life. To dwell in a text means to spend time within it, "to be able to learn how to live there" (Sumara, 1994, p. 44). Sumara (1994) contends that by dwelling in texts, reading can become a kind of "meditation, a *caring* about the words in the text, the words of others, and the actions which these words support and announce" (emphasis in original, p. 45). Within this book, we are seeking to recount and to explore the complexities of creating contexts that support this propensity to dwell within texts. We contend, like Sumara, that literary engagements can and should be a matter of "caring," about words, about others' responses to them, and about the world. Engagement with texts within interpretive communities that promote this "dwelling" can invariably leave readers changed, and possibly, as I explore next, also inspired to create change themselves.

Critical literacy and sociocultural theories of emotion

Sumara's work reveals how reading can be a site of complex identity negotiations; opportunities for students to read *across* cultures can be an especially generative practice in this regard. For Loh (2010), reading global literature provides opportunities for American students to reconsider the construction of self as American. To do so, Loh contends, requires careful attention to reading in culturally and critically reflexive ways, which necessitates that students move beyond "aesthetic involvement or identification" and look at the text with some "critical distance" (p. 111). Readers, therefore, need to be engaged in rigorous examination of the social, political, and historical dimensions of the texts, the construction of their own cultural identities, and the presence of ideologies and cultural assumptions within the texts they read (Lewis, 2000).

This kind of critical analysis shares a resonance with approaches to critical literacy in children's literature scholarship. These approaches encourage readers of children's literature to consider how texts are situated within the sociopolitical context, to examine whose perspectives are privileged or marginalized, to look below the surface of the text to tease out ideological assumptions, and to consider possibilities for taking action within and beyond the classroom (e.g. Jones, 2006; Leland et al., 2013; Vasquez, 2010). With a particular focus on multicultural identities, Botelho and Rudman (2009) argue, "Bringing a critical lens to the study of multiculturalism in children's' literature invites the reader to deconstruct dominant ideologies of U.S. society (e.g. race, class, gender, and individualism) which privilege those whose interests, values, and beliefs are represented by these worldviews" (p. xiv). For these researchers and educators, children's literature serves as a resource to engage children in inquiry, analysis, and social action.

Often marginalized in many discussions of critical literacy, however, is a recognition of the emotions that can accompany these processes of deconstruction, critique, and reconstruction. Even though Ivey and Johnston (2013) remind us that "engaged reading is fundamentally about highly consequential dimensions of readers' socioemotional lives" (p. 257), critical literacy scholarship has been critiqued for its "rationalist underpinnings" (Janks, 2002, p. 9) that often overlook these dimensions. In discussing critical literacy pedagogy, Janks (2002) argues that educators should entertain the possibilities of interpretive landscapes "beyond reason," including "the territory of desire and identification, pleasure and play, the taboo and the transgressive" (p. 9). In a related way, Jones and Shackelford (2013) describe the "feltness of literacies" (p. 391), how practices of reading and writing are "saturated with feeling and emotion" (p. 390). These scholars point to the embodied experience of reading, suggesting how the cognitive act of reading is also experiential and emotional. While neither Janks (2002), nor Jones and Shackelford (2013) or others producing thought-provoking scholarship on embodiment, affect, and emotion in literacy studies (e.g. Dutro & Bien, 2014; Enriquez, Johnson, Kontovourki, & Mallozzi, 2016; Johnson & Vasudevan, 2012; Leander & Boldt, 2012; Lewis & Tierney, 2013) are writing specifically about children's engagements with children's literature, we find a resonance with our work. We contend that a focus on the emotional undercurrents and the embodiment of response is particularly illuminating and of particular relevance to a broadening of critical literacy scholarship to be inclusive of the affective realm.

In this book, we consider the embodied, affective responses of students reading global literature from critical literacy perspectives. We consider the human dimension of response, of what it feels like to have worldviews and assumptions challenged, to try on a different perspective, and to go about conceptualizing a new set of understandings. We do so recognizing that this can be a profoundly generative and affirmative process, even as it may also be a profoundly destabilizing one that may cause tensions, anxieties, and fears. As Sumara (1996) contends, "it is much easier and safer to point to what we find in the text than it is to point to what the text finds in us" (p. 235). We also recognize these emotions within ourselves as well, when we felt unsettled or uncertain of the path to take, a response to give, a silence to keep. We document in the book instances of teaching and learning that rarely progressed in a smooth or linear or expected way. We hope to add these layers of indeterminacy, unknowing, and nonlinearity to critical literacy scholarship and teaching.

Envisioning Teacher Inquiry and Collaborative Research

Within this teacher inquiry community (Goswami, Lewis, Rutherford, & Waff, 2009), I began with the premise that teachers are legitimate sources of knowledge on their own teaching and that this knowledge takes on a unique dimension when shared within a community of educators engaged in collaborative inquiry. Our monthly meetings were designed to create opportunities for participants to share dilemmas and emergent understandings. The teachers brought their questions, frustrations, and hopes to share with each other; I aimed to create a responsive, relational community where knowledge was built from the "ground up," rather than received from the "top down." The meetings became venues where "participants narrated and unpacked" (Lytle, Portnoy, Waff, & Buckley, 2009, p. 33) the complexities at the heart of their practice and the difficulties at times of reconciling what they wished to pursue in their classrooms with the external realities of their settings. The teachers also shared the keen insights their students brought to the global literature, as well as books that were proving to be especially generative. In the meetings, participants thus gained support by both "narrating" and "unpacking" these layered stories of practice, providing some measure of clarity as they put their experiences into words for a receptive audience and further insight as other members took up, responded to, affirmed, and sometimes offered alternative viewpoints. For many, the opportunity to have a space in which to engage in this kind of dialogue was rare within their professional lives. As the teachers describe in upcoming chapters, this cleared space for narrating experience to an audience engaged in similar inquiries fostered an appreciation for trying out new or challenging ideas, while also honoring the difficulties and challenges of teaching and learning.

Within their classrooms, the teachers engaged in practices of teacher researchers conducting systematic and intentional inquiry (Cochran-Smith & Lytle, 1993). They wrote about their practice in teaching journals, recorded classroom conversations, collected student work, and reflected upon their teaching within the inquiry community. To gain deeper understandings, I drew upon my training as a qualitative researcher, taking field notes in the teachers' classrooms, audiotaping and transcribing small group and whole class discussions, talking with students, reflecting with the teachers after class, studying student writing and artifacts, and attending school functions. As a participant observer, I took note of pauses and outbursts, quiet intensities and exuberant exchanges; I often became caught up in the meaning-making in the classrooms myself, moved by a read aloud or touched by the incisiveness of students' comments. I experienced firsthand the "remarkable vitality, an aliveness, a level of intellectual engagement that occurs" (Leland et al., 2013, p. 61) when students are captivated by texts and are within learning communities that support that kind of engagement. Within classrooms where bells might ring or kids may come in preoccupied with the science test later in the day or two students may share a secret communication about the soccer game after school, I also gained glimpses into the broader context in which the themes explored in this book sometimes were at the center of students' attention, and sometimes not. My research across these contexts, which I recount in upcoming chapters, provided me with invaluable windows into how the teachers pursued their teaching and added immensely to what I learned in the inquiry group meetings.

Organization of This Book

We have designed this book to be purposefully multivocal. In the chapters I write, I weave together qualitative data, theoretical frameworks, and research studies in an attempt to contextualize the teaching and learning pursued across the teachers' four contexts and to illuminate the unique contributions their teaching makes to current conversations in the literacy/literature field. In their chapters, the teachers write about how incorporating global literature into their teaching created profound moments of professional growth for them as they re-envisioned teaching and learning in their own distinctive contexts. In these "Re-Envisioning" chapters, the teachers also offer their own set of principles related to creating more generative spaces for the teaching of global literature with social justice aims and relay their perspectives on doing so while also meeting local, state, and national standards. A unique feature of the book includes the opportunity for the teachers to write about what they learned in the inquiry community and the specific insights they gained from each other's practice. In these "Learning in the Inquiry Community" chapters, each teacher writes a letter to another to showcase the power of teacher learning in an inquiry community and to provide even more insight into the interrelationships among teaching practices, lived experiences, and collaborative learning.

What This Books Adds to the Conversation

This book aims to provide rich descriptions of how students and their teachers engaged with global literature across a range of urban and suburban settings and how the context of a teacher inquiry community became a generative site in which to explore the complexities and possibilities of doing so. We center the perspectives of students and teachers as they navigate global literature in relation to their lives, the inquiry community, local, state, and national educational policies, and the broader social context. While the teachers in the inquiry group brought teaching philosophies that embraced critical literacy perspectives, each understood and pursued these commitments in distinct ways, in light of their own contexts, as well as life histories. We hope that this combination of descriptions of classroom practice, excerpts from class discussions, and analyses of student writing, alongside reflections from the teachers about their learning in the inquiry community, will provide numerous angles into the layered and complex worlds of critical literacy teaching, teacher inquiry, and teacher learning. Instead of presenting only the "victory narratives" of exceptional critical literacy teaching practices, however, we aim to illustrate the disappointments and false starts, the "messy and unnerving" (Möller, 2012, p. 24) moments, the barriers and the eventual openings, that accompany even the most powerful critical literacy work. To illuminate these stories, we draw upon multiple conceptual frameworks to provide insight, including critical literacy, dialogic teaching, and sociocultural approaches to theorizing emotion in the classroom. By doing so, we hope the book not only provides readers with illuminating descriptions of classroom teaching with global literature but also offers additional dimensions to the theory and practice of critical literacy. As you engage with this book, we hope that the perspectives of the students, teachers, and texts we describe invite you to consider the promise of inspiring global visions through local inquiries with diverse texts in your own contexts.

References

Allen, J. & Alexander, L. (Eds.). (2012). *A critical inquiry framework for K-12 teachers: Lessons and resources from the U.N. Rights of the Child*. New York, NY: Teachers College Press.

Beach, R., Thein, A. H., & Parks, D. L. (2008). *High school students' competing social worlds: Negotiating identities and allegiances in response to multicultural literature*. New York, NY: Routledge.

Bishop, R. S. (2007). *Free within ourselves: The development of African American children's literature*. Portsmouth, NH: Heinemann.

Bond, E. (2006). Reading outstanding international children's books. *Journal of Children's Literature, 32*(2), 70–6.

Botelho, M. J. & Rudman, M. K. (2009). *Critical multicultural analysis of children's literature: Mirrors, windows, and doors*. New York, NY: Routledge.

Brooks, C. (1947). *The well wrought urn: Studies in the structure of poetry*. London, UK: Dennis Dobson.

Brooks, W. M. & McNair, J. C. (Eds.). (2008). *Embracing, evaluating and examining African American children's and young adult literature*. Lanham, MD: Scarecrow Press.

Campano, G., Honeyford, M. A., Sánchez, L., & Vander Zanden, S. (2010). Ends in themselves: Theorizing the practice of university-school partnering through *horizontalidad Language Arts, 87*(4), 277–85.

Choo, S. S. (2013). *Reading the world, the globe, and the cosmos: Approaches to teaching literature for the twenty-first century*. New York, NY: Peter Lang.

Cochran-Smith, M. & Lytle, S. L. (1993). *Inside/outside: Teacher research and knowledge*. New York, NY: Teachers College Press.

Coleman, D. (2011, April 28). Bringing the Common Core to life. Retrieved from http://usny.nysed.gov/rttt/resources/bringing-the-common-core-to-life.html

Coleman, D. & Pimentel, S. (2012). Revised publishers' criteria for the Common Core State Standards in English Language Arts and Literacy, Grades 3–12. Retrieved from www.corestandards.org/assets/Publishers_Criteria_for_3-12.pdf

Dutro, E. & Bien, A. C. (2014). Listening to the speaking wound: A trauma studies perspective on student positioning in schools. *American Educational Research Journal, 51*(1), 7–35.

Enciso, P. E. (1994). Cultural identity and response to literature: Running lessons from *Maniac Magee. Language Arts, 71*(7), 524–33.

Enriquez, G., Johnson, E., Kontovourki, S., & Mallozzi, C. A. (Eds.). (2016). *Literacies, learning, and the body: Putting theory and research into pedagogical practice*. New York, NY: Routledge.

Fox, D. L. & Short, K. G. (Eds.). (2003). *Stories matter: The complexity of cultural authenticity in children's literature*. Urbana, IL: National Council of Teachers of English.

Freire, P. (2005). *Teachers as cultural workers: Letters to those who dare teach*. Boulder, CO: Westview Press.

Galda, L. (2013). Learning from children reading books: Transactional theory and the teaching of literature. *Journal of Children's Literature, 39*(2), 5–13.

Gangi, J. M. (2010, December 11). Children of color and the poor left way behind in the National Governors Association and State Chiefs Common Core Standards Initiative: "Text exemplars" for kindergarten through 5th grade. Retrieved from www.maryann-reilly.blogspot.com/2010/12/guest-blog-children-of-color-and-poor.html

Gangi, J. M. & Benfer, N. (2014, September 16). How Common Core's recommended books fail children of color. Retrieved from www.washingtonpost.com/news/answer-sheet/wp/2014/09/16/how-common-cores-recommended-books-fail-children-of-color/

Ghiso, M. P., Campano, G., & Hall, T. (2012). Braided histories and experiences in literature for children and adolescents. *Journal of Children's Literature, 38*(2), 14–22.

Goswami, D., Lewis, C., Rutherford, M., & Waff, D. (Eds.). (2009). *On teacher inquiry.* New York, NY: Teachers College Press.

Ivey, G. & Johnston, P. H. (2013). Engagement with young adult literature: Outcomes and processes. *Reading Research Quarterly, 48*(3), 255–75.

Janks, H. (2002). Critical literacy: Beyond reason. *The Australian Educational Researcher, 29*(1), 7–26.

Johnson, E. & Vasudevan, L. (2012). Seeing and hearing students' lived and embodied critical literacy practices. *Theory Into Practice, 51*, 34–41.

Jones, S. (2006). *Girls, social class, and literacy: What teachers can do to make a difference.* Portsmouth, NH: Heinemann.

Jones, S. & Shackelford, K. (2013). Emotional investments and crises of truth: Gender, class, and literacies. In K. Hall, T. Cremin, B. Comber, & L. Moll (Eds.), *International handbook of research on children's literacy, learning, and culture* (pp. 388–99). Hoboken, NJ: John Wiley & Sons.

Leander, K. & Boldt, G. (2012). Rereading "A pedagogy of multiliteracies": Bodies, texts, and emergence. *Journal of Literacy Research, 45*(1), 22–46.

Lehman, B. A., Freeman, E. B., Scharer, P. L. (2010). *Reading globally, K-8: Connecting students to the world through literature.* Thousand Oaks, CA: Corwin Press.

Leland, C., Harste, J., Ociepka, A., Lewison, M., & Vasquez, V. (1999). Exploring critical literacy: You can hear a pin drop. *Language Arts, 77*(1), 70–7.

Leland, C., Lewison, M., & Harste, J. (2013). *Teaching children's literature: It's critical!* New York, NY: Routledge.

Lewis, C. (2000). Limits of identification: The person, pleasurable, and critical in reader response. *Journal of Literacy Research, 32*(2), 233–66.

Lewis, C. (2001). *Literary practices as social acts: Power, status, and cultural norms in the classroom.* New York, NY: Routledge.

Lewis, C. & Tierney, J. D. (2013). Mobilizing emotion in an urban classroom: Producing identities and transforming signs in a race-related discussion. *Linguistics and Education, 24*(3), 289–304.

Lewison, M., Leland, C., Harste, J. C. (2015). *Creating critical classrooms: Reading and writing with an edge* (2nd ed.). New York, NY: Routledge.

Loh, C. E. (2009). Reading the world: Reconceptualizing reading multicultural literature in the English Language Arts classroom in a global world. *Changing English, 16*(3), 287–99.

Loh, C. E. (2010). Reading nation and world: Cultivating culturally and critically reflexive readers. *English Journal, 100*(1), 108–12.

Lytle, S. L., Portnoy, D., Waff, W., & Buckley, M. (2009). Teacher research in urban Philadelphia: Twenty years working within, against, and beyond the system. *Educational Action Research, 17*(1), 23–42.

Martens, P., Martens, R., Doyle, M. H., Loomis, J., Fuhrman, L., Furnari, C., Soper, E., & Stout, R. (2015). Building intercultural understandings through global literature. *The Reading Teacher, 66*(8), 609–17.

Martin, L. A., Smolen, L. A., Oswald, R. A., & Milam, J. L. (2012). Preparing students for global citizenship in the twenty-first century: Integrating social justice through global literature. *The Social Studies, 103*(4), 158–64.

Möller, K. J. (2012). Developing understandings of social justice: Critical thinking in action in a literature discussion group. *Journal of Children's Literature, 38*(2), 22–36.

Möller, K. J. (2013). Considering the nonfiction CCSS nonfiction literature exemplars as cultural artifacts: What do they represent? *Journal of Children's Literature, 39*(2), 58–67.

Ohanian, S. (2013). Children giving clues. *English Journal, 103*(2), 15–20.

Rosenblatt, L. M. (1982). The literary transaction: Evocation and response. *Theory Into Practice, 21*(4), 268–77.

Rosenblatt, L. M. (1986). The aesthetic transaction. *Journal of Aesthetic Education, 20*(4), 122–8.

Shanahan, T. (2013). Letting the text take center stage: How the Common Core State Standards will transform English Language Arts instruction. *American Educator, 37*(3), 4–11, 43.

Short, K. G. (2009). Critically reading the word and the world: Building intercultural understanding through literature. *Bookbird, 47*(2), 1–10.

Short, K. G. (2013, January 28). The Common Core State Standards: Misunderstandings about response and close reading. Retrieved from www.wowlit.org/blog/2013/01/28/the-common-core-state-standards-misunderstandings-about-response-and-close-reading/

Short, K. G. & Thomas, L. (2011). Developing intercultural understandings through global children's literature. In R. Meyer & K. Whitmore (Eds.), *Reclaiming reading: Teachers, students, and researchers regaining spaces for thinking and action* (pp. 149–62). New York, NY: Routledge.

Simon, R. (2015). "I'm fighting my fight, and I'm not alone anymore": The influence of communities of inquiry. *English Education, 48*(1), 41–71.

Smith, M. W., Appleman, D., & Wilhelm, J. D. (2014). *Uncommon core: Where the authors of the standards go wrong about instruction – and how you can get it right.* Thousand Oaks, CA: Corwin.

Souto-Manning, M. (2013). *Multicultural teaching in the early childhood classroom: Tools, strategies and approaches.* New York, NY: Teachers College Press.

Sulzer, M. (2014). The Common Core State Standards and the "basalisation" of youth. *English Teaching: Practice and Critique, 13*(1), 134–54.

Sumara, D. J. (1994). Resisting the tourist gaze: Literature reading as dwelling. *English Journal, 83*(8), 41–6.

Sumara, D. J. (1996). *Private readings in public: Schooling the literary imagination.* New York, NY: Peter Lang.

Sumara, D. J. (1998). Fictionalizing acts: Reading and the making of identity. *Theory Into Practice, 37*(3), 203–10.

Sumara, D. J. (2002). *Why reading literature in school sill matters: Imagination, interpretation, insight.* Mahwah, NJ: Lawrence Erlbaum.

Vasquez, V. (2010). Setting the context: A critical take on using books in the classroom. *Getting beyond I like the book: Creating space for critical literacy in K-6 classrooms*, 2nd ed. (pp. 1–22). Newark, DE: International Reading Association.

Zancanella, D. & Moore, M. (2014). The origins of the Common Core: Untold stories. *Language Arts, 91*(4), 273–9.

Children's Literature, Media, and Materials

Winter, J. (2005). *The librarian of Basra: A true story from Iraq.* New York, NY: Houghton Mifflin.

2

READING GLOBAL LITERATURE AS EMERGENT GLOBAL CITIZENS

Mirrors, Windows, Doors, and Maps

Kelly K. Wissman

In a landmark essay, Rudine Sims Bishop (1990) offers three metaphors to describe the potential impact of books on young readers. According to Bishop, books can serve as *mirrors*, reflecting back to readers their own lives and experiences. Books can also serve as *windows* into places, cultures, and worlds previously unknown or unimagined by the reader. Books may also serve as *sliding glass doors* through which readers "have only to walk through in imagination to become part of whatever world has been created or recreated by the author" (p. ix). For Bishop, a powerful transformation can take place as windows become mirrors, as readers see their own lives, hopes, and dreams within once unknown worlds reflected back to them and as they consider their own place in the tapestry of human experience.

Bishop's metaphors have been taken up by many children's literature scholars (Botelho & Rudman, 2009; Galda, 1998; Lehman, 2015; Short, 2009; Yokota, 2015), librarians (Vardell, 2014), teacher educators (Möller, 2014; Tschida, Ryan, & Ticknor, 2014), and book publishers (Lee & Low Books) to argue for the inclusion of multicultural and global literature within classrooms and libraries and to make a case for the place of children's literature within the curriculum when it becomes endangered by commercial reading programs and standardized testing regimes. A popular website, "Mirrors Windows Doors," even borrows its name from Bishop's metaphors and provides resources on multicultural and global literature for children and young adults. In March of 2014, the social media campaign #WeNeedDiverseBooks drew increased attention to the continued scarcity of books published by and about people of color and the resulting paucity of "mirrors" for children of diverse backgrounds (Dávila, 2015). These conversations are building on and adding to Bishop's metaphors, offering both imaginative and tangible calls to action regarding literature as a right, as a guide, as a sanctuary, and, as artist Christopher Myers (2014) contends, as a "map."

Within this chapter, I draw on the metaphors of books as mirrors, windows, sliding glass doors, and maps to highlight how Heather and Simeen incorporated global books into their classrooms in ways that inspired complex identity work and responses from their students. Within an increasingly globalized world, I argue, global literature can play a vital role in inspiring broader cartographies of the imagination and supporting students in considering their roles and responsibilities as global citizens. I highlight not only the possibilities, but also the challenges of incorporating global literature into classrooms as Heather contended with broader contextual factors, such as the prominence of high-stakes testing and the pressures of being under increased scrutiny within a school designated as a "priority" school by the state due to low test scores. I also consider Simeen's challenges of engaging children from more affluent and less culturally diverse backgrounds with texts that did not mirror their own lived experiences and that some students initially viewed with antipathy.

A connecting thread across these two teachers is their commitment to sharing texts to spark an inquiry, to dig deeper into the multiple dimensions of the human condition, to find points of connection, and to expand students' horizons. They were not taking their students on grand tours of various cultures represented in the books they shared, offering them snippets of cultural traditions as a tourist might take in while working through a multistep itinerary. Rather, as Sumara (1994) notes, they were encouraging their students to "dwell" in the texts by inviting them to engage with the human dimensions at the heart of each story, the conflicts, the aspirations, the dilemmas, and the joys of people living all over the world. In response, students took these stories in, registering flashes of connection and sometimes confusions, finding inspiration, hope, and more textured understandings of the paths they wished to travel within the world.

Mirroring and Mapping Their Worlds: Global Texts as Inspirational and Aspirational

Over Heather's 20-year teaching career, she has been both an English as a New Language (ENL) teacher and a Social Studies teacher. Teaching across K-12, Heather has always located herself within culturally and linguistically diverse urban schools. She embraces the richness and rewards of her work and is nationally recognized as a model teacher for both her teaching abilities and outreach to the community, as evidenced by her 2010 receipt of a Milken Educator Award, commonly referred to as the "Oscar of teaching." She nonetheless contends with challenges not uncommon to urban educators in high-poverty districts: limited resources, increasing control over curriculum, additional monitoring by state education personnel, and ongoing pressures to increase test scores. During her time in the inquiry community, Heather incorporated global literature across her classes but focused particularly on one class that included 10 students in grades 3–6 who were from a range of countries, including, China, Mexico, Yemen, and the Dominican Republic.

Upon joining the inquiry group, Heather shared with us that children's literature had not held a prominent place in her classroom in the past. As she explores in Chapter 3, incorporating global picturebooks made a qualitative difference in her teaching and opened her up to a range of new possibilities. In contrast to what she referred to as "throwaway books"—texts written for children that she previously downloaded from an Internet resource for bilingual educators—Heather incorporated award-winning picturebooks that featured rich dialogue, compelling narrative prose, and evocative illustrations. These books and how she presented them had a captivating effect on her students, many of whom were able to see themselves and their experiences reflected in the books they were reading in school, often for the very first time. When a girl from the Sudan read *Golden Domes and Silver Lanterns* (Khan & Amini, 2012), Heather recounted that she marveled at each page because the pictures and words resonated with her so deeply. As she looked at one page completely captivated, she exclaimed, "I can read this! It is written in Arabic and I am learning Arabic at Saturday school!" She was also thrilled to see an illustration of a lacy silver lantern very similar to her own. This text clearly served as a "mirror" for this young girl, giving her an opportunity not only to connect to the book but also to articulate her religious and cultural identities within a school space.

Recasting Language Diversity as an Asset

While some students found very direct reflections of their languages, home countries, and other more visible indicators of cultural practices within the global picturebooks Heather shared, they also found a resonance with the experiences and emotions evoked in the books, including immigration and adjusting to a new country. Allen Say's (1993) *Grandfather's Journey* and Eve Bunting and Ronald Himler's (1997) *A Day's Work* sparked flashes of recognition and extended conversations as students talked about their experiences translating for adults in their families. Students shared stories evoking a sense of pride that they could help their parents at the doctor or at the store, while others described their fear and trepidation at being asked to take on these roles. Many also worried about family members who might need assistance translating when they were in school. One fourth grader from Yemen told Heather, "I worry my mom will get lost and won't be able to ask anyone for help!" By sharing picturebooks and encouraging open-ended discussions, Heather's students processed these complex experiences collectively and publicly within the classroom, conversations that previously often occurred privately and on the margins of school space, if at all.

Many students were eager to have the opportunity to explore the rewards, challenges, and complexities of navigating multiple cultures and languages. Students regularly requested that Heather reread *Grandfather's Journey* (Say, 1993) as they related to the feeling of wanting to live in two places at once like the characters in the book. As the narrator recounts, "the moment I am in one country, I am homesick for the other." Often experiencing the same emotions, Heather's students shared with each other the multiple and sometimes conflicting emotions that resulted from their experiences of having immigrated to America, of missing relatives who lived in other countries, and of speaking multiple languages.

While Heather invited discussion in response to picturebook read alouds, she also encouraged writing. This writing opened up further opportunities for students to recount and reflect on their experiences across cultures and languages. After students read Cynthia Rylant and Diane Goode's (1993) *When I Was Young in the Mountains*, Heather invited them to view the book as a mentor text. Using the stem "When I was young…", students first brainstormed memories from their childhoods. They then created flipbooks in which they included their writing and drew pictures. One student wrote:

> When I was young in Mexico, sometimes we drank water from our hands instead of from a cup. When I was young in Mexico, we spoke Trique and Spanish. Now I speak Spanish and English. When I was young in Mexico, there were bathrooms outside and inside. When I was young in Mexico, my dad and everybody killed a cow and we ate the cow. When I was young in Mexico, I lived with my mom, my dad, my brothers, and sister, and grandma and grandpa.

Another wrote:

> When I was young in Yemen, my grampa always took me to the big park to have fun when my grampa had time. When I was young in Yemen, I was scared to come to America because I didn't want to come to America. When I was young in Yemen, our neighbors invited us to go to the wedding and my mom said yes. We got to see the beautiful lady. When I was young in Yemen, I liked to spend time playing with my friends and also talking about when I was coming to America.

This writing not only encouraged students to bring their lives and experiences into the classroom; these compositions also gave them opportunities to practice descriptive writing and writing in the past tense.

The reading of picturebooks reflective of diverse experiences created focused opportunities for students to discuss and reflect on English language use and learning. These books, the discussions they engendered, and the writing they inspired led some students toward powerful identity shifts as they moved from sheepishly referring to themselves as the "ENL kids" who needed "extra help" to embracing the affordances of speaking multiple languages. After Heather invited her students to interview each other about the different languages they speak, she told the inquiry group she noticed a tangible change in students when they added "bilingual" and in some cases "trilingual" to how they described themselves, even as they were working hard to improve their English proficiency.

Illuminating a Path and Making a Difference

Within global texts, Heather's students often found points of connection, mirrors to their experiences. The students also found in these texts experiences, dispositions, and mindsets quite different from their own; nonetheless, they scrutinized these texts for meaning and for ways to inform their own lives. As Myers (2014) writes about the young people he works with:

> They see books less as mirrors and more as maps. They are indeed searching for their place in the world, but they are also deciding where they want to go. They create, through the stories they're given, an atlas of their world, of their relationships to others, of their possible destinations.

In response to global picturebooks, Heather's students not only recognized that speaking multiple languages themselves was an asset instead of a deficit, they also recognized how facility with multiple languages could enable them to make a difference in the world. Heather's students were inspired by *The Boy Who Harnessed the Wind* (Kamkwamba, Mealer, & Zunon, 2012), the story of a boy from Malawi who worked to bring energy to his village by building a windmill. Within this true story, William Kamkwamba describes his early fascination with how mechanical objects worked and how this curiosity propelled him to take apart household items. A lover of learning, William was disheartened when his family could no longer afford to pay his school fees. During this time, William's village was struck by a terrible drought that resulted in a severe famine. Unfazed by his hunger and his inability to attend school, William sought out a library to explore what he might do in response to these crises. With a Chichewa-English dictionary by his side, William consulted a range of texts to learn how to make "electric wind." Gathering many discarded items, from rusty bike parts to clothesline, he began to construct a windmill on his own, all the while dealing with jeers from villagers who called him "misala" or crazy. William persevered, noting, "A windmill meant more than just power, it was freedom." At the age of 15, he created his first windmill, helping water the crops and bring electricity to his village.

The Boy Who Harnessed the Wind was an engaging and inspirational story to Heather's students. As Heather (O'Leary, 2013) wrote, "Many ESL students marveled that William had the patience and perseverance to painstakingly translate technical directions, written in a foreign language, so that he might be able to find scrap material to build the windmill." They recognized his challenges and were inspired to keep persevering in improving their own language skills as a result. The students were also mesmerized by the illustrations created by Elizabeth Zunon. The students were not only delighted to hear that she was born in and lives in a nearby city but also that she herself speaks multiple languages having grown up on the Ivory Coast of West Africa.

In addition to meeting inspirational figures like William Kamkwamba, students in Heather's class also read a range of additional biographies full of individuals that students connected with and aspired to be like. They read about a range of social activists, including Tomás Rivera and Richard Wright, who made a difference in their communities and in the struggle for Civil Rights. As Heather explores in Chapter 3, the text set that she put together about Wangari Maathai, a Kenyan environmental activist who became the first African woman to win a Nobel Peace Prize, enthralled the students and particularly inspired one young girl to consider her own role in making the world a better place.

For Heather, centering her teaching within books that served as both mirrors and maps, created intensive, layered, and meaningful learning. Despite feeling the pressures of high stakes testing acutely and despite managing the increased monitoring of her classroom as her school contended with being placed on a list of "priority" schools, Heather herself persevered in making children's books essential to the learning in her classroom. As she wrote:

> Making global literature the centerpiece of our year helped keep instruction focused on material that was engaging, challenging, and interconnected. We were armchair travelers as the globe was always on the table while we read, and students looked up the places where the stories took place. Geography started to become ESL students' strength, especially in relation to their peers. They could pick up the globe, find our location, their native country, and locate William Kamkwamba's country in Africa or show the distance Wangari Maathai travelled by tracing their finger on the globe from Kenya to the American Midwest where she studied science. We studied the environment, learned vocabulary for the parts of a tree, from roots to trunk to canopy. We talked about racism, protest, and civil disobedience. In other words, we studied a rich curriculum…. Global literature helped us stay open to the world, look deeper into a variety of interesting topics, and see the connections between them. (O'Leary, 2013)

Many of the global picturebooks Heather read with her students created powerful opportunities for students to make sense of their experiences while also planting seeds for future discoveries and pathways. The books Heather chose embraced the complexity of the human condition and the layered experiences of loss, prejudice, hardships, bias, risk-taking, possibilities, and homecomings that many of her students had already experienced in their young lives. These books also, as Myers (2014) contends, provided evocative images and hopeful narratives to factor into the lives they were building and imagining for themselves. Within Heather's classroom, global books served as mirrors in deeply affirmative and resonant ways while also providing students variegated maps to help them develop even wider vistas of possibility.

Teaching Global Texts to "Disturb the Waters"

Unlike Heather's context, there was not a good deal of cultural diversity in Simeen's school. Because her fifth grade classroom in an affluent suburban district included only touches of cultural diversity, Simeen made explicit efforts to help students make connections to people and countries very much unlike their own. As she explores in Chapter 9, Simeen's commitment to incorporating diverse texts into her classroom and encouraging her students to grapple with multiple perspectives has roots in her own upbringing. Simeen spent her childhood amidst multiple cultures and languages. When her parents settled in Nigeria to practice medicine and to teach, she recalled navigating "differences in cultural attitudes, norms, and behaviors as a matter of course" within her own schooling experiences. Simeen's early adulthood also involved living in Europe and Asia before settling in the United States. Explaining to me that these experiences shaped her broader worldview and teaching practices within a suburban U.S. school, she noted:

> It's really important for [students] to have multiple perspectives. Because for me, I can't see any other way. This is the way I am. I see from the world where I come from. I've learned this Western way of thinking, it is so powerful. Even before coming here.

Within this same conversation, Simeen went on to make direct connections between these worldviews and her teaching, explaining, "I think that's a component of my teaching. I don't feel like I can just come here and say, 'This is what I need to teach today: I'm going to teach main idea.' [laughs]. It's a lot more than that." Simeen envisions teaching as encompassing much more than discrete objectives like teaching point of view or craft features; rather, her teaching practices are embedded in larger aspirations. She explains further that her teaching is guided by desires to expose students from more privileged backgrounds to multiple perspectives and to "disturb the waters for them":

> Obviously because of who I am, where I come from, the experiences I've had, this multicultural aspect is huge for me because I feel we're not just living in our isolated spaces, you know, we're living in the world. We need to examine life with all this stuff. So, that's where it comes in.

Here, Simeen's points of view resonate with Bishop's (1990) contention that if children from dominant groups only see in books "reflections of themselves, they will grow up with an exaggerated sense of their own importance and value in the world—a dangerous ethnocentrism" (p. x). As Bishop (1990) notes, if children only read books that are mirrors of their own experiences, they grow up with a distorted view of the world and miss opportunities to see themselves as part of the wider tapestry of human experience. For Simeen, "disturbing the waters" becomes a way to both disrupt those points of view as well as to bring in multiple perspectives.

Lakshaman (2009) has convincingly argued that in order for multicultural and global literature to have transformative effects on students from majority, dominant groups, then prevalent conceptualizations of mirrors and windows may not fully suffice. According to Lakshaman, for these books to change hearts and minds within an increasingly globalized and interdependent world, students need to read from a stance in which they and their experiences are not centered, but are in fact, actively *decentered*:

> if global literature is to be an effective bridge, our reading should go beyond the mirrored "I" or the framed window. If we are to enhance our knowledge and understanding of the world, we need to hone a habit of reading which is comfortable with a decentered view of the world and be willing to probe the context and complexity of other perspectives (Lakshaman, 2009, p. 14).

For American students accustomed to seeing their experiences and points of view reflected and reinforced across a range of popular culture texts and school curricula, a decentering of those experiences can be profoundly destabilizing. Across her time teaching to "disturb the waters," Simeen told me her students had responded to these attempts at decentering and "disturbing" by expressing some antipathy toward particular texts, laughter at some cultural practices, and even judgment of the characters or persons in the texts. Although her students might initially resist the texts she provides, Simeen perseveres, embracing the understanding that teaching with diverse texts for the cultivation of multiple perspectives permeates her entire approach to her work as a reading teacher. As she explains here, she embraces the notion that this type of teaching takes time:

> It's challenging, also. I've had students come to me and say, "I don't get it. It's boring." Because they don't see themselves. But once we have done it in class and we have talked about it, especially through powerful characters like Sadako [*Sadako and the Thousand Paper Cranes,* Coerr, 1977/1999] and some of these, like Oliver [*Books for Oliver*, Larkin, Rambo, & Brown, 2007], for example, it just moves them. And they empathize so strongly and they get that sense of kind of getting into that character and then it becomes easier to approach other books and to get comfortable going into all these different spaces.

With a firm grounding in the privileging of multiple perspectives that she lived as a child and continues to live within the U.S., Simeen persists in bringing in multiple texts from multiple perspectives, even when those texts do not always engage students with an instant flicker of recognition or interest. She does so with the understanding of the importance of this work and with the flexibility to pursue her curriculum in ways reflective of her focus on inquiry and building knowledge together over time.

Moving Beyond "That's Weird!"

Simeen wants texts in her classroom to serve as windows into other people's lives, not just mirrors of students' own experiences. She also wants her students not only to observe differences but also to engage deeply with the experiences of other people, to see the texts, as Bishop (1990) describes, as sliding glass doors to "walk through in imagination" (p. ix). Simeen tries to interrupt a tendency in some students to offer appraisals or judgments of characters and cultural practices. As she explains, "For me, reading shouldn't be like standing at a distance and, you know, giving a commentary on it, but trying to understand more." She notes that student comments, such as "that's weird" or "gross!" or "odd," are "triggers" for her. Telling me that she tries to keep her visible reaction to these student responses "in check," she noted that she nonetheless tries to engage kids in conversation about these comments in ways that open up, rather than close down, inquiries.

I witnessed this firsthand one morning when students were sharing with the whole class their thoughts on the books they were reading independently in small groups. Jason (all student names are pseudonyms) recounted a scene in *Water Buffalo Days* (Nhuong, 1999) in which a young boy from Vietnam describes the practice of cricket fighting in his village. Explaining his reaction to the class, Jason noted, "I thought it was kind of weird, just putting two crickets on mats and they just start fighting." Along with others in the class, Jason laughed as he continued describing this scene in the book. Looking carefully into the faces of the students, Simeen paused for a moment and then shared the following anecdote with the whole class:

> OK. Let me tell you an experience. You know when I came first to America and my husband took me to watch a game, a football game. Right? And I saw these people with these strange looking things on their heads, right? [laughter] And then they were attacking each other. Human beings, you know? Big guys! [laughter] Running into each and then people were like falling down on top of each other. [laughter] They told me it was a game for fun! [laughter] Back home, in Africa, if people did that, what they would do is they would grab the people who were running into each other and take them to the elders in the village and they would make them sit down and they would play music to calm them down. And they would try to work on their brains, like,

what's happened to these people? [laughter] And what Jason said made me think about that. Come on, people! Like, you used the word "weird," right? What do you think? I thought that was pretty "weird"!

Here, Simeen used storytelling and a touch of humor "to disturb the waters," providing an illustration of how perceptions of what is considered "normal" or "weird" behavior are actually cultural constructions.

After I had spent a couple weeks in Simeen's class, I became very interested in how students responded when she shared personal accounts of her own experiences living in countries outside the United States. I asked Simeen how she made decisions regarding the sharing of these personal accounts, especially given how much emphasis she put on the students' contributions in her class. It was not unusual, for example, for a 20-minute discussion to go by with Simeen not speaking beyond eliciting student responses with only the oft-repeated question, "What are you thinking?" In response, Simeen told me:

Simeen: So, I want them to have multiple understandings because all our understandings are incomplete. I feel like you go with blinkers on if you just think in one certain way. So what I want them to do is look at other ways. So, if they say "weird" or if they say "eww!" that's when [laughs] I feel like I need to say something or I want to say something or share something with them that will make them stop and think. I don't know. Does that make sense?

Kelly: Yeah, of course. It makes perfect sense. But it seems like you do it strategically.

Simeen: Yeah. Because I don't want to rush them, first of all. And, you know, I feel like unless you own it, it really doesn't change much, so I mean there's no point in me bombarding them with this because they're not going to get it. They'll probably end up thinking, "*She's* weird." [laughs] Right? So I just will do it every now and then and then if it's supported by something we're doing in the classroom, it should make sense to them.

As she explains here, Simeen wants her students to come to these realizations themselves, not receive a lecture from her, a practice she sees as not being very productive.

Reading about Child Migrant Workers: Decentering Dominant Perspectives

Teaching with diverse texts to "disturb the waters" was a complex, layered, and emergent endeavor for both Simeen and her students. Across the six-month period I spent in Simeen's classroom, I learned about both the complexities and the possibilities of teaching with texts that may not mirror students' lived experiences and that may provide windows into worlds and experiences that are difficult to comprehend without actively decentering students' own worldviews. To suggest the nature of how this community of learners built knowledge across a range of multigenre texts and with each other, I describe their explorations of child migrant workers. Simeen created multiple pathways for students to engage with texts and each other in ways that attempted a kind of decentering and a reimagining of students' roles in and perspectives on the world. To support students in learning with and from people different from themselves, Simeen prioritized the following: 1) focusing on the experiences of characters in fiction and persons within nonfiction texts; 2) providing students with multiple genres of texts exploring similar experiences; 3) and incorporating the visual mode to enhance understandings.

Across these three dimensions of classroom practice, Simeen continually created opportunities for students to talk about their emergent understandings. She made purposeful choices to read aloud both fiction and nonfiction texts to her fifth graders, a practice than many upper elementary teachers abandon in the pursuit of developing more independent readers. For Simeen, who placed such an emphasis on thinking within her classroom, reading aloud to the students and soliciting their emergent thoughts as they made sense of the information, was vital to her overall purpose of developing critical readers open to multiple perspectives. The students themselves not only paid very close attention to the author's language choices and messages and articulated how they were constructing meaning in response, but they also heard how their fellow students did so as well. This co-construction of meaning was as multifarious, unexpected, and nonlinear as all meaning-making typically is, but the orchestration of multiple and sometimes conflicting viewpoints often led to some key revelations and shared understandings.

Beginning with Experience

When introducing global texts, Simeen often began with a focus on experience. Rather than providing a lecture on the country the characters are from or their unique cultural characteristics, she started with lived experiences, often of children around the same age as the students in her class. As she explained:

> I use experiences because immediately they can connect it to their lives and start thinking about it in that way. I want them to kind of own it and know that the characters or people have value. It's like, 'You have experiences; they have experiences, too.' Rather than just, 'Here's another person: a Vietnamese.'

When she began the inquiry into child migration, she had the students read the powerful, semi-autobiographical short story, "The Circuit" by Francisco Jiménez (1997). In this story, Pancho describes his Mexican family's experiences following the seasonal crops in California's Central Valley. The story opens with vivid description of Pancho and his family's last day of difficult labor in the strawberry fields, followed by a journey to pack up their belongings to move on to another work camp. While Pancho found relief at the end of his 12-hour day, the prospect of moving once again filled him with sadness. At the next farm, Pancho then describes the equally physically demanding labor of picking grapes in a vineyard amidst 100-degree heat with few breaks and little nourishment. He also describes running at the sight of school buses in order to avoid the troubles a truancy charge would bring to his family. At the end of grape season, Pancho has the opportunity to attend school, where he meets a sixth grade teacher, Mr. Lema, who displays kindness and a willingness to help him with his English. Pancho is even more excited when Mr. Lema picks up on Pancho's love of music and offers to teach him how to play the trumpet. Buoyed by this prospect and by this connection to his teacher, Pancho excitedly returns home to tell his family, only to be met once again with the tableaux of all the family's belongings packed up in cardboard boxes, signaling yet another move.

Within the exquisitely crafted story, Jiménez takes the reader directly into the experiences of Pancho, how these lived experiences of field labor, everyday joys, and profound upheaval, register upon his body and his psyche, allowing readers a window into "the subjectivity of a population that has a lengthy history of dehumanization and demonization in popular media" (Serrato, 2011, p. 391). This story's ending had a particularly strong effect on the students in Simeen's classroom, many of whom gasped and called out their sadness at the realization that Pancho would be taken away so suddenly from a place where he had just begun to forge a relationship with his teacher and where he had allowed himself to become excited by the prospect of a creative outlet in music. Pancho's experience became a touchstone, referred to often as the inquiry continued in the weeks to come.

Grappling with Multiple Perspectives Through Nonfiction

For Simeen, responding to the Common Core's emphasis on nonfiction texts complimented her already existing aims and practices related to exposing students to multiple perspectives and having them grapple with the complexities that result. This multigenre approach also complemented her interest in broadening students' awareness of the world around them and considering carefully the experiences of people unlike themselves. As she told me, "A change in genre forces a change in perspective." After the students read and discussed "The Circuit," Simeen shared with them the introduction and two profiles of young people found in *Voices from the Fields: Children of Migrant Workers Tell Their Stories* (Atkin, 2000), a book that features photographs, interviews, and writings of nine Mexican American children. Simeen chose to read aloud the introduction and have the students take notes and respond to the information shared as she read. As the students listened to the contextual information provided by Atkin regarding the motivations and the working conditions of migrant workers, they raised a number of questions and made connections back to Pancho's experience in the Jiménez

(1997) story. In doing so, they paid very close attention not only to the experiences of the migrant workers rendered but also to the language used by the landowners to describe and sometimes justify their treatment of the workers.

In the beginning of the conversation, the students' responses reflected some dismay that the migrant workers would allow themselves to be treated in the way they were, as well as some forthright suggestions for what the workers should do differently. Jason, the boy who used the word "weird" when describing the cricket fighting scene in *Water Buffalo Days* (Nhuong, 1999) described earlier, approached this text with a similar stance. In response to a passage where Atkin describes how many of the pesticides used on the farms where migrants worked were known to cause cancer and were dangerous to workers, Jason asked, "Why wouldn't they stand up to that nonsense? Like, risking getting cancer or bad things?" Katherine offered her take, asserting, "I think that if the worker is being treated like that, being around all the pesticides, that he should go to the government and tell them that they're not following the regulations." Other students also questioned why the workers did not quit or report these instances. In response to a passage in which Atkin describes how some landowners withheld pay from the workers, Jason stated, "Um, I thought it was kind of silly why they weren't paying them when they were younger, when they were forced to work." In many ways, these questions and assertions make sense from the perspective of those who are economically secure and who may have the cultural capital to know about their rights and to be able to assert them. Jason uses language like "nonsense" and "silly" to describe the situation, a stance that seemed to assess the migrant workers from a distance, to render their experiences unintelligible and their actions nonsensical, rather than reaching toward an empathetic understanding and a critical reading of the social context.

As the students continued to listen to the Atkin introduction, to make connections back to Pancho's experience in the Jiménez story, and to consider Simeen's responses to their assertions, shifts began to occur where they seemed to try to think from the perspectives of the migrant workers as well as the landowners. In response to a passage detailing the experiences of very young children, the students took a close look at the language use of the landowners:

Daphne: I thought, like, why is it considered "helping out" when the children are actually working?

Simeen: Interesting question. Why is it called "helping out" and not working? They are working. Elise?

Elise: I think it's because if they're "helping out," then they don't get paid.

Simeen: Ah! Ah. You think? It might be a clever way of wording things.

Katherine: Well, I think they should raise the pay, for the children, because these children are coming in to help you on their own time when they should be in school. And the person that owns the farm can always go outside and do the work themselves.

Here, the students consider carefully how language can obscure certain realities to benefit particular people. Daphne, Elise, and Katherine question this, with Katherine also chiding the landowners for allowing children to do the work that they could do themselves.

The students also questioned the treatment of the workers, further pondering why migrant workers would stay silent about poor working conditions and environmental dangers. Kelsey began with her assertion that the workers should speak out, while others, in response to Simeen's questions, try to grapple with why migrants might not do so:

Kelsey: They should tell the farmer.

Simeen: They should tell the farmer? Hmm? Do you think the farmers know or don't know? What do people think? Do the farmers know that they might get health problems? What are you thinking? Rebecca?

Rebecca: I kind of think that they do, but it's not like they have any options because the farmers don't care.

Simeen: So the workers know and they don't have options, right? What about the farmers who are employing the workers? Like, Kelsey was saying, the workers should tell the farmers so that they know these are the problems they are facing. So, my question to you is, do you think the farmers who employ them, know or don't know about what's going on? So, what do people think? Katherine?

Katherine: I think that the farmers probably do know, but they just don't want to do the work and get the diseases and things so they just have other people do the work for them.

Simeen: Hmm-mm. What are you thinking, Sophia?

Sophia: I kind of think what Elise said, like, they don't really know them so they don't really kind of care what happens to them, more or less. They just want what's best for them, which is getting like more and better crops.

Here, the students wrestle with the farmers' motivations, even while they are considering the migrant workers' reasons for staying silent. While critical of the farmers' behaviors and actions, Sophia and Katherine do try to understand their rationales for their choices. Katherine, though, still questioned why the landowners would persist in behavior that was so potentially detrimental to the workers' health, framing it not as much as a moral issue but as an economic one:

Katherine: Well, I don't get why the farmers do that with the pesticides because if they keep doing that then all the workers are going to start to get sick and other people are going to find about it and then they're not going to want to work on the farm.

Simeen: So, right now you're thinking that people maybe don't know, that this news has not spread about what they do with the pesticide? Kelsey?

Kelsey: I think maybe if they're not paid, they don't quit, because maybe the farmers said, "If you quit, I'll tell that your kids aren't going to school…"

Simeen: Oh, you're kind of connecting it to "The Circuit," right? When Pancho and his brother hid, remember? Where they both hid because the school bus came and it's the law. Kids have to be in school, right? So, they could be using some kind of threats.

Here, the students' discussion reflects a growing critical understanding as well as empathy as they go beyond naming differences and offering suggestions on what the migrant workers should do. Simeen's pedagogy here is very much in alignment with critical literacy aims (Short, 2009). Students begin to undertake a critical analysis of the social context in which inequities and power imbalances exist, shaping decisions and life chances. In addition, the students are not taking at face value the justifications provided by the farmers and language choices that may obscure the realities of what is occurring, e.g. referring to the unpaid labor of young children as "helping out." Finally, the students are trying on different points of view, attempting to get inside the motivations, belief systems, and rationales of multiple people involved.

Bringing in the Visual Mode

Simeen hoped to build on these critical and engaged readings of the texts and the worlds they emerged from and reflect. Within future classes, she continued the inquiry into migrant children by sharing a picturebook called *Migrant* (Trottier & Arsenault, 2011). In this story, a young girl named Anna travels with her Mennonite family as they follow the seasonal harvest from Mexico to Canada. In highly lyrical prose, Anna likens herself on this journey to a bird, a jackrabbit, a monarch, a "feather in the wind." Prior to reading this text, Simeen and her students read and discussed nonfiction texts detailing the beliefs and practices of Mennonites. Before beginning the read aloud of *Migrant*, she reminded the students of these nonfiction texts and mentioned some of the themes they had been exploring across their inquiries into the experiences of migrant workers. Simeen encouraged the students to pay attention to both the illustrations and the words, inviting a rich discussion of various semiotic modes, as well as some intertextual connections to previous readings. She instructed the students:

> Think about the title. Think about the endpapers, OK? Look at the illustrations. That's what we do when we read a picturebook because the story is more in the pictures than in the words, OK? Look at the choices the illustrator has made. Why are they drawing it the way they are

drawing it? The colors they are using, all that. The author's choice of language. And then how the pictures and the language make you feel, together. OK? People will take their notes as I am reading, but you will, you know, talk as I read. So, you have questions, you have thoughts, you will share them.

As Simeen opened the book to reveal its endpages, students immediately began offering observations and interpretations, drawing inferences on their potential meaning:

Henry: It looks like the triangles are actually made of cloth and they're glued on. It looks like almost 3-D, like it's glued on, like they're painted right on there.

Simeen: Mmm. They're painted? Mmm.

Sophia: It kind of like looks because of the arrows and like how they're going one way and then they come back, going the other way…

Simeen: Hmm.

Sophia: Kind of like they're going back and forth.

Simeen: Hmm. Talk some more.

Sophia: Like, how migrants move one place and then they, like, come back, depending on the season.

Simeen: Mmm! It's interesting, guys. Think about what Sophia is thinking about these. Katherine?

Katherine: Well, they sort of look like the tops of houses.

Simeen: Mmm.

Katherine: Like, moving from one house to another.

Here, Sophia and Katherine consider how the endpages are suggestive of the experiences of moving with the seasons that students had read about earlier: going one way, coming back the other, like migrants. Rebecca later added that the triangles reminded her of "patterns," that the experiences of migrants followed a similar pattern. Daphne offered, "I think every triangle represents each house and every place they've been."

As Simeen began to read the story, the students looked closely at a double-page spread showcasing Anna's family members, each holding a suitcase, with a flock of geese in the sky above them. This page prompted the following conversation, full of observations, inferences, and an insight that many saw as a revelation:

Tyler: I think the suitcases show that they have a lot of people in the family and they have to spend a lot of money on each person. So, that's why they have to move so they can get more money and they can survive.

Simeen: OK.

Rebecca: I think the suitcases it means that everybody has to help and like everybody has to carry something.

Simeen: Hmm! Think about what Rebecca is saying. The suitcase she thinks means that everybody has to carry something. They all have to help. If we think back on what we read yesterday [a nonfiction text on the Mennonites]. Remember the Mennonites? What their idea was about hard work and everybody sharing the work? So, I think maybe that's... but, great ideas. OK, Everybody keep thinking. Alex?

Alex: Um, it looks like the shadows of the people are like the flock of birds.

Simeen: Oh, my gosh, Alex! I was wondering what that was.
[Multiple voices: Whoa! Wow!]

Simeen: What does that mean, I wonder? Why are the shadows not like...The shadows are like birds. Is there a meaning in that? [slight pause] Remember, illustrators always make choices. He drew the shadows like birds.

Alex: But, um, like the first page, it's telling you about like the family is like a flock of birds. And then this other page, the shadows are the birds and the people are like the birds.

Simeen: So, I think the illustrator is like carrying the same image through, right? Awesome!

Simeen continued to read the text, which offers the first of many similes in which Anna is compared to the natural world, reading, "When her mother works hard to make a home of yet another empty farmhouse, the rooms filled with the ghosts of last year's workers. Anna feels like a jackrabbit." Pointing to the illustration, Simeen asked the students, "Why do you think the jackrabbit is jumping out of the window?":

Kelsey: I think she's leaving because she wants to just run away and go somewhere where she can be in just one home forever.

Simeen: Where it would be <u>her</u> home, right? Not this place filled with ghosts. Stephanie?

Stephanie: I think it's sad that she's afraid of her own home. Because I would think that would be like a little alarming.

When Simeen came to the end of the book, she read, "But fall is here and the geese are flying away. And with them, goes Anna, like a monarch, like a robin, like a feather in the wind." The students then discussed their response to the book's ending, as well as connections to "The Circuit" and which had a more powerful effect on them:

Sophia: I like how the illustrator showed how she was like the tree, like she was being uprooted and moved to somewhere else.

Simeen: Mmm.

Sophia: In that picture it's like she's kind of like trying to stay back but like her whole family, even her little sister and her brother are like waiting for her, like, waiting for her to come on.

Simeen: Hmm. "Come on." I think she is like beckoning, right? She is saying, "Come on, come on." What do other people think?

Kelsey: I think it's kind of showing that she's thinking of a time where she can just <u>be</u> and not have to leave.

Elise: It kind of reminded me of the end of "The Circuit."

Simeen then asked the students to share more about their connections to "The Circuit" and to consider which text they read about child migrants had the greatest effect on them:

Elise: I feel like "The Circuit." In this one, she was kind of used to it. In the other one, it was so sudden.

Simeen: The suddenness of it was more powerful, you think.

Sophia: Because, um, "The Circuit" showed his emotion more, like how he was, like how happy he was finally. Because in the beginning he was like so sad and everything and then in the end he finally had what he wanted, and I felt happy. And then it came out that he had to leave again and it was going to happen again.... I feel like Panchito had a little harder life because he was actually working in the fields and Anna wasn't really working, but she was trying to help. So, I felt like once he was happy, like, you thought, it makes you glad, because all his work is done and everything, and once he leaves it's like so sad. And once she leaves, it's kind of like she had more family, I think, and she wasn't losing a lot, leaving, like Panchito.

Across the multiple genre texts and across multiple critical literacy engagements with them, the students embraced opportunities to read about the experiences of migrant children, to consider their experiences in the broader social context, to evaluate the choices made by authors and illustrators as shaping of their own understandings and emotions in response to the text. In this way, the multiple points of view enlivened and gave more texture to conversations and understandings about migrant workers.

Challenges of Context and Questions of Purpose

For both Heather and Simeen, incorporating global literature and teaching it from a critical literacy perspective created generative possibilities for their students to see themselves reflected in texts, to read about experiences very different from their own, to think deeply about the lives, experiences, and motivations of other people, and to imagine who they themselves might become and aspire to be.

In many cases, the boundaries between us/them were blurred as students entered into texts rather than appraising them from above. Over time, students realized their own points of view could shift or could stay the same, but they existed in relation to, not better than, another's point of view. In some cases, they formed substantive critiques of inequitable practices and considered their own potential roles in making change.

At the same time, though, both Heather and Simeen contended with their own social contexts and lived experiences that shaped their choices and often caused frustration and sometimes doubt. For Heather, the pressures of testing were ever-present, along with the continual monitoring of her teaching and her students' "progress" as measured by markers outside of her own design or control. In the next chapter, Heather conveys movingly how her students were upset by the marginalization of the global picturebooks during what she called "testing season." The students, recounts Heather, wanted to know when they would be reading "our books," referring to the global picturebooks, again. Even while the students' claiming of these books as "our books" was an extraordinary statement of their own agency and wisdom regarding what should be their rights as students to read socially meaningful and personally transformative literature, they nonetheless could not read that literature for close to a month as they endured state-mandated tests. For Heather, it was also difficult to know that as powerful as these kinds of literacy engagements were, they were not as prevalent or as sustained in spaces outside of her own classroom.

While Simeen contended less with these pressures of testing and surveillance, she did contend with some of her own doubts about the broader purpose of this work within an unjust educational and social system. Even while she recognized she had a responsibility and an opportunity to disrupt some of the insidious ways in which power and privilege can replicate themselves within educational systems, and even while the texts she chose, the questions she asked, and the personal experiences she shared often did help the students call into question socially inequitable practices, she nonetheless wondered often if she was doing enough. At the end of one class as the inquiry into migrant workers was coming to an end, she asked the students to consider what they might do with the information and insights they had gained from the texts:

Simeen: Now, coming back to the three, we read three different forms of writing, right? Yesterday I read to you the interviews, right?, that some newspaper reporters and tv reporters did with the migrants. Then we read the story, which is the author making up a story about that experience and today we read the real story from somebody to whom it has happened. OK? So, I want you to start thinking about how they are presented, OK? How each one, how each author wrote the story, OK? We've seen three different accounts of the same story, and we've seen their point of view. And now you have a point of view about the story, too. What's your point of view? Can somebody sum up? I hear a lot of like questions about it, OK?

I hear a lot of questions about what their life is like. I hear questions about why does this happen? I hear thoughts about how it's different from our life. Right? So, what are you thinking? Do you identify with the child? Do you identify with the experience? A lot of you told me you felt bad for Pancho. [pause] So, what did you think? And you felt bad about it. Sophia?

Sophia: No child should have to go through that.

Simeen: No child should have to go through that, OK. Should we do something about it? Will we do something about it? Can we do something about it? OK? There are three questions I've thrown out at you. Do you want to talk about it in your groups? <u>Should</u> we do something about it? <u>Can</u> we do something about it? Or <u>will</u> we do something about it? Or are we just going to read the story and kind of feel bad about what's going on? OK? So, why don't you talk about…hmm, we're running out of time. So, hold that question in mind, and we'll start tomorrow with that question, OK?

When the bell rang as Simeen was finishing talking and the students packed up their things, she caught up with me and asked me what I thought, asking me very similar questions to what she had just asked the kids, wondering if and how this work mattered. Searchingly, she asked me, "What do we want kids to know? We read and we talk, but is it valid? I know it's important, but what am I getting? Where am I going? Is it enough?" I told her I didn't have an answer, that the same questions animate my thinking about my teaching as well, even as I continue to incorporate critical literacy perspectives into my teacher education classes and even as I seek out teachers like Simeen to learn with and from.

Simeen asks searching questions here that I think confront all educators working from a critical literacy stance and who incorporate diverse texts purposefully into their classrooms to serve as mirrors, windows, doors, and maps. Why do we read about peoples and cultures from all over the world? Why do we read about social injustices? What purpose does it have? Does it matter? To whom? Is empathy enough? Is social action a necessary result of critical literacy pedagogy? Is this teaching somehow "less" critical if a tangible action does not occur? What messages do children receive when inquiries like these are abruptly stopped when statewide tests occur or when local assessments must be given? How will these stories and experiences travel with children of diverse backgrounds and children from dominant groups after they leave our classrooms? We grapple with these questions throughout this book, recounting times when we envisioned and embraced the possibilities of teaching global literature from a critical stance with utmost clarity. We also recount other times when we shook our heads with uncertainty and our eyes welled at institutional prerogatives that seemed very far from being in the best interests of children and their teachers. In the chapters that follow, we describe ongoing efforts to nurture empathetic, critical, and hopeful readers of the world who encounter global texts as mirrors, windows, sliding glass doors, and maps, and who construct new worlds of understanding as they engage with the books and with each other.

References

Bishop, R. S. (1990). Mirrors, windows, and sliding glass doors. *Perspectives, 6*(3), ix–xi.

Botelho, M. J. & Rudman, M. K. (2009). *Critical multicultural analysis of children's literature: Mirrors, windows, and doors.* New York, NY: Routledge.

Dávila, D. (2015). #WhoNeedsDiverseBooks?: Preservice teachers and religious neutrality with children's literature. *Research in the Teaching of English, 50*(1), 60–83.

Galda, L. (1998). Mirrors and windows: Reading as transformation. In T. E. Raphael & K. H. Au (Eds.), *Literature-based instruction: Reshaping the curriculum* (pp. 1–12). Norwood, MA: Christopher-Gordon.

Lakshaman, M. S. (2009). Looking beyond global literature as bridges, mirrors, and sliding doors. *The Dragon Lode, 27*(2), 11–17.

Lehman, B. A. (2015). Reading multiculturally, globally, critically: Incorporating literature of diversity in literacy education. In D. A. Wooten & B. E. Cullinan (Eds.), *Children's literature in the reading program: Engaging young readers in the 21st century* (4th ed.) (pp. 111–126). Newark, DE: International Literacy Association.

Möller, K. (2014). Mirrors and windows through literature featuring Arabs, Arab Americans, and people of Islamic faith. *Journal of Children's Literature 40*(1), 65–72.

Myers, C. (2014, March 15). The apartheid of children's literature. *New York Times.* Retrieved from www.nytimes.com/2014/03/16/opinion/sunday/the-apartheid-of-childrens-literature.html

O'Leary, H. (2013). ESL students find themselves and expand their horizons through global literature. Retrieved from www.wowlit.org/on-line-publications/stories/storiesiv7/4/

Serrato, P. (2011). "What are young people to think?": The subject of immigration and the immigrant subject in Francisco Jiménez's *The Circuit.* In J. Mickenberg & L. Vallone (Eds.), *The Oxford handbook of children's literature* (pp. 389–410). New York, NY: Oxford University Press.

Short, K. G. (2009). Critically reading the word and the world: Building intercultural understanding through literature. *Bookbird, 47*(2), 1–10.

Sumara, D. J. (1994). Resisting the tourist gaze: Literature reading as dwelling. *English Journal, 83*(8), 41–6.

Tschida, C. M., Ryan, C. L., & Ticknor, A. S. (2014). Building on windows and mirrors: Encouraging the disruption of "single stories" through children's literature. *Journal of Children's Literature, 40*(1), 28–39.

Vardell, S. M. (2014). *Children's literature in action: A librarian's guide* (2nd ed.). Santa Barbara, CA: ABC-CLIO.

Yokota, J. (2015). What needs to happen? *Reading Today, 32*(6), 18–21.

Children's Literature, Media, and Materials

Atkin, S. B. (2000). *Voices from the fields: Children of migrant farmworkers tell their stories.* New York, NY: Little, Brown and Company.

Bunting, E. & Himler, R. (1997). *A day's work.* New York, NY: Houghton Mifflin.

Coerr, E. (1977/1999). *Sadako and the thousand paper cranes.* New York, NY: Penguin.

Jiménez, F. (1997). *The circuit: Stories from the life of a migrant child*. Albuquerque, NM: University of New Mexico Press.

Kamkwamba, W., Mealer, B., & Zunon, E. (2012). *The boy who harnessed the wind*. New York, NY: Dial Books.

Khan, H. & Amini, M. (2012). *Golden domes and silver lanterns: A Muslim book of colors*. San Francisco, CA: Chronicle Books.

Larkin, J., Rambo, E., & Brown, D. (2007). *Books for Oliver*. New York, NY: Mondo Publishing.

Nhuong, H. Q. (1999). *Water buffalo days: Growing up in Vietnam*. New York, NY: HarperCollins.

Rylant, C. & Goode, D. (1993). *When I was young in the mountains*. New York, NY: Reading Rainbow Books.

Say, A. (1993). *Grandfather's journey*. New York, NY: Houghton Mifflin.

Trottier, M. & Arsenault, I. (2011). *Migrant*. Toronto, ON: Groundwood Books.

3

RE-ENVISIONING ENGLISH AS A NEW LANGUAGE TEACHING WITH GLOBAL LITERATURE

Heather O'Leary

The English as a New Language (ENL) classroom probably *seems* like the most obvious place in the school to incorporate global literature. After all, ENL students are likely to have had the most direct, intense connections to other languages, places, cultures, and traditions than any other students in the school. The classroom globe is not an abstraction to them. When they pick up the globe, they have very specific people and places in mind. As they trace their fingers across the distance from upstate New York to Puerto Rico, Mexico, Sudan, Dominican Republic, China, Yemen, and Afghanistan, they are identifying places where their grandparents and siblings may still live or places that they hear about from family. They search for places that they long for, even if they themselves have not ever stepped foot there.

I have been a teacher for over 20 years and an ENL teacher for 14 years. My school is considered "high needs" and is deemed "low-performing." In our elementary school of 400 students, 81 percent of the students qualify for free or reduced lunch. Across the multiple classes I teach every day with culturally and linguistically diverse K-6 ENL students, I contend with multiple demands and pressures. If ENL is such a natural place to use global literature, though, why wasn't I making it a focus in my ENL class? Why was the potential of global literature such a revelation once I joined the inquiry group? In this chapter, I explore how incorporating global literature into my curriculum helped me re-envision my teaching of ENL and how this literature helped my students re-envision themselves. Instead of narrowing my curriculum to focus on basic skills and test-taking strategies in response to the insistent pressures to improve student achievement as measured by standardized tests, I decided instead to widen my curriculum by including beautifully illustrated global picturebooks that provided textured and thought-provoking readings of my students' diverse worlds.

Auspicious Beginnings

For our first foray into global literature, our class read *A Day's Work* by Eve Bunting and Ronald Himler (1997) in which the main character, a boy named Francisco, accompanies his grandfather, a newly arrived Mexican immigrant who speaks Spanish, to a street corner in order to help him find work from the trucks that pick up day workers. Francisco is put in the position of interpreting for his grandfather, a situation that resonated immediately with my students as it is a common situation for them. It can also be a difficult situation: the inversion of family dynamics, the responsibility and stress on the child, the awkward conversations which the child may not have the knowledge to interpret accurately, the adult topics they may struggle psychologically and emotionally to handle. And so it was for Francisco who did not have the decision-making skills and experience needed to handle negotiating with an employer on his grandfather's behalf and who tried to shield his grandfather from bad news.

My students stopped me on the very first page, exchanging knowing glances and piping up that they have been interpreters many times. They only had to hear the first page of the book, and they already had a good idea what direction the story would take. I wonder how many of their monolingual peers would have been tipped off to such accurate predictions just from the first page of the book! As we continued to read, Ricardo (all student names are pseudonyms), a student from Mexico, gave a running commentary, happy to hear some Spanish dialogue, contributing, "Abuelo means grandfather…" and "Oh, he just said 'muy bonito.' That means very pretty." Ricardo also enthusiastically verified the accuracy of the book from his experience, noting, "Yup, my dad has done gardening." He later proclaimed, "Yes, we eat tortillas that my mom makes for us, too. Yum!" Other students could not wait to share their own experiences interpreting. Prior to class, I had created a survey and planned for students to interview each other about what it is like to be bilingual. I had hoped the activities would spark conversation about this topic, but the spirited conversation and sharing happened instantaneously in response to the book without my planned activity. After the spontaneous discussion, the students gamely did the survey and eagerly interviewed each other, thoroughly enjoying sharing their many experiences with interpreting.

The students were clearly and deservedly proud of their ability to help their parents, but many also shared stories similar to Francisco's in which they found themselves a bit over their heads translating in grown up situations. For example, Angelina, a third grader from Puerto Rico, said she had translated many times for her mother at the doctor's office and that she worried about her mom's health and what the doctor might say or ask. Fazia, a fourth grader from Yemen said she helped her mother do all the shopping and errands for the family, describing to clerks and salespeople what her mother was looking to purchase or accomplish, and expressed fear that her mother might attempt a trip to the store without her while she was at school. She worried that no one would understand her and that her mother might even get lost without her. One energetic third grade boy from Puerto Rico, José, chuckled that he had to translate for his teacher so she could tell his mother that he was in trouble. During the discussion, Zuleyka, a 6th grade student from Puerto Rico, who often had problems relating with other people, noted, "It's valuable to be able to speak two languages because then you know when someone is talking about you."

This first foray into global literature could not have been a more positive experience. I witnessed my students tapping into their own cultural and linguistic experience and expertise and I witnessed their intense engagement and excitement sparked by connection with a book. The literature invigorated the class. This experience is in direct contrast to the students' reaction to a leveled reader I found online called *Being Bilingual*. The text was quite dry, and it was painful to get through the short book with the same group of students who had found the topic of bilingualism so exciting when reading Francisco's story in the Bunting and Himler (1997) book. The leveled reader didn't spark anything except boredom, frustration, and the feeling that we just needed to endure it. In the global literature inquiry group, I offhandedly described this text as a "throwaway book" because it was printed on paper and copied for each student. After I shared my students' responses to the text in one of our meetings, I more fully understood the contrast between my students' experiences with high quality picturebooks and the texts that can be found in some online packaged programs. I concluded that it was indeed a "throwaway book" not only because of its formatting and the ease with which it could be recycled, but also because it did not elicit connection, emotion, or interest amongst my students.

Exploring Students' "Braided Histories"

As I continued to incorporate global literature into my classroom, I found that I also needed to expand the definition of "global literature." Global literature in my classroom included literature from Africa, Latin America, and Asia. Global literature also included many books from the United States, particularly stories about the Civil Rights Movement. These stories and characters offered students additional dimension to their expanding critical thought about the struggles and inequity that exist in the world and which they experience. In all that we studied, we noticed that there were people of different races, backgrounds, languages, experiences, and statuses who interacted in surprising ways. Ghiso, Campano, and Hall (2012) contend that different groups' histories are not insulated from each other. For example, the Civil Rights movement is often thought of as Black history, when in reality, it is the history of white people, too, both the ugly and difficult to acknowledge stories of violence and racism, as well as the inspiring and uplifting stories of people from both groups working together for positive social change. All of it must be acknowledged in order to fully understand the history and where we are today. None of the groups was in a vacuum but rather were a part of each other's histories. Ghiso et al. (2012) refer to this as "braided histories" and point out that "experiences are interwoven" (p. 20).

The idea of "braided histories" helps describe my students very well, not just as members of groups that interact and affect each other's histories but also as individuals who have "braided histories" themselves. Many consider themselves both American and Puerto Rican (or Afghani, or Chinese, etc.), some are biracial, and they are bicultural and bilingual, or on the road to becoming so. Their identities often defy strict categorization into discrete categories. One of my bicultural, bilingual students, a third grade boy from Yemen, named Yaseer, finished reading Jeanette Winter's (2014) book *Malala, A Brave Girl from Pakistan/Iqbal, a Brave Boy from Pakistan: Two Stories of Bravery* and a newspaper article about the first woman taxi driver in Pakistan. The article detailed the reactions, both positive and negative, she received. When he responded in writing to what he had read, my student surprised me. He wrote in support of the taxi driver who was challenging the norms of her culture. He respected her need to support her family financially even though this challenged his own culture. This boy has a "braided history" in that he has lived in both Yemen and the United States, and he has seen how his mother and older sister negotiate their roles as observant Muslims in the United States. He has witnessed how they sometimes take on roles and responsibilities normally reserved for men in their culture, especially when his father is not immediately available while he is at work or visiting family in Yemen. Braided histories and identities are very apparent and relevant to my students.

Examples of "braided histories" were plentiful in the global and civil rights literature we read. *Tomás and the Library Lady* by Pat Mora and Raul Colón (2000) recounts the childhood of Tomás Rivera, the son of migrant farm workers from Mexico, who later became the chancellor of the University of California Riverside. As a boy, he became friends with a kind librarian, a white woman in Iowa. Initially, when his grandfather suggested that Tomás visit the library, Tomás was frightened that he would be told to stay out, but the librarian was an ally who welcomed him, read to him, signed books out for him under her name, and encouraged him to keep reading and learning. Despite differences in language, culture, and socioeconomic status, the librarian and Tomás's family shared values. They valued stories, books, and education, and the librarian and Tomás's grandfather each encouraged Tomás's literacy through storytelling, reading, and retelling stories in both Spanish and English. Tomás's family worked hard in the fields and had not met the "library lady" until the end of the summer when Tomás's grandfather accompanied him to the library to say "adiós and gracias." Tomás brought her a loaf of pan leche his mother had made, and the "library lady" gave Tomás a book. My students and I saw ourselves in this interaction. Some of the parents rarely come to the school in person, but their children appear in our classrooms proudly carrying lunch prepared by their mother for the teacher (and even the bus driver for a field trip), or a beautiful keepsake from their country, or cold drinks from the store where their dads work, or a hot thermos of chai that their aunt made. When I visit with parents in their homes, I don't go empty-handed. We exchange small gifts and smiles and our relationship grows even though we may have very few face-to-face interactions. Our relationships grow as the students tell me about their families and convey messages and stories from home. Families also come to know me better through their children, as students return home bearing books and projects.

"Braided histories" were also present in another book that made a big impression on the ENL students, *Richard Wright and the Library Card* by William Miller and R. Gregory Christie (1997). The book focuses on an experience Richard Wright (1945) recounted in *Black Boy*. Richard desperately wanted access to books at the library, knowing that books and literacy would somehow figure into improving his life and circumstances. He was barred from borrowing books in the segregated South but took a huge risk in obtaining the use of a co-worker's library card. He carefully thought about who might help him and found an ally in a white co-worker who, as a Catholic, was also an outsider. In making this choice of whom to trust, Wright showed "a high-stakes reading of the world…in order to know where to seek support" (Ghiso, Campano, & Hall, 2012, p. 18). Ghiso, Campano, and Hall made this observation of Harriet Tubman as she found white allies to help her bring slaves to freedom via the Underground Railroad, almost one hundred years before Richard Wright's decision to find an ally at work.

Richard Wright and the Library Card interested my students very much. It gave them new insight into life during the Jim Crow era. They were puzzled by some details in the story like the line, "As long as he kept his head down, as long as he began every sentence with 'sir', Richard was safe." They wondered why Richard hid his library books in a newspaper, and why, when he was leaving for the North, it was such a big deal that he and his ally shook hands in front of everyone in the office. They were impressed by the way Richard averted a suspicious librarian's accusation that he was borrowing books for himself with a quick reply that played into her racist assumptions about Black people. He replied, "No ma'am. These books aren't for me. Heck I can't even read." The students' questions helped me see that although they had learned the definition of segregation and were familiar with the stories of Martin Luther King Jr., Rosa Parks, and Ruby Bridges, this book broadened their understanding of the period.

Students seemed to be under the impression that segregation meant that normally Black and white people did not come into contact with each other, that the groups were mostly isolated from each other. After all, I had taught them that "segregation" meant "separation" and we pushed our hands apart to reinforce this definition. They didn't understand the extent to which Black and white people were in contact and how it impacted the ways in which people were expected to interact. For example, they were not aware of how Black people were expected to show extreme deference to white people and that the slightest perception of disrespect could result in dire consequences. They did not understand the historical, cultural, and societal structure that created the Jim Crow system and seemed to view segregation as being a result of laws imposed rather than as a result of white privilege, beliefs, and values; children's literature created rich opportunities to grow in their understanding of these complex issues.

As a teacher interested in critical literacy, I look back on this experience in a new way after reading Ghiso et al.'s (2012) ideas about using children's literature to study our braided and interwoven histories. They cogently state:

> [C]hildren's literature might provide a resource for students to explore how we are indeed "all in this together."…. [W]e believe that a nuanced understanding of our togetherness is a necessary precondition for the interrelated processes of redressing past injustices, surviving the present, and working toward a better future…. [C]hildren's literature remains a primary vehicle for intellectual and imaginative maturation, and it is thus important to ask whether younger students have the opportunity to transact with books that represent and raise questions about shared experiences and cooperation across social, cultural, and linguistic boundaries. (p. 15)

I am deeply impressed by the way diverse children's picturebooks have fostered my students' deep inquiry into the world. As I continue to incorporate global picturebooks into my classroom, I am convinced that the themes, topics, and books students read have a huge impact on what they learn, how engaged they are, and how deeply impacted they will be by what we teach them in school. I witness my students asking big, important, difficult questions in response to the books we have read. Global books that explore the interaction of people of different races, cultures, and beliefs have done so much to invigorate my teaching and my students' learning. Now, I cannot imagine teaching ENL without global literature.

Students Re-Envisioning Themselves Through Global Literature

When I first started incorporating picturebooks into my classroom during my time in the inquiry community, I noticed that my students began to re-envision themselves in powerful and impactful ways as we became more and more immersed in the literature over the year. Almost immediately, I noticed that they began to see themselves as having specific expertise in language, culture, and experience that their monolingual classmates did not possess, and they were gaining new understanding about the world and their place in it. When I began to incorporate global literature into my teaching, I had not expected the critical abilities of my students to increase in the way that they did. I had hoped that ENL would become a place where students were able to explore their bicultural and bilingual identities as people "who live between two worlds" as Allen Say's (1993) character expresses in *Grandfather's Journey*, but I didn't realize how my students' capacities to look critically at the world would also grow. In this section, I tell the stories of two such students: Zuleyka and José.

Wangari Maathai Inspires Zuleyka

Zuleyka was not an easy student for me. She had transferred from another school where she had struggled with academics and relationships, and she butted heads with almost everyone—with other students, with me, and with other teachers. She often refused to do work and insisted that she couldn't do it. She avoided work by putting her head down and by stirring the pot to create distractions. To me, Zuleyka often seemed depressed, lonely, and defensive. I worried about how to integrate her into our classroom learning community when she didn't want to interact with other students and seemed to preemptively push others away with negative remarks. It was hard for me to stay positive with her because she resisted so much! A change occurred, though, when we read about a confident, courageous woman from another continent who neither of us had heard of before our adventure in reading global literature. Zuleyka found inspiration and connection with Wangari Maathai, the Kenyan environmentalist who began the Green Belt Movement and was the first African woman to win the Nobel Peace Prize.

I assembled a text set which included Jeanette Winter's (2008) *Wangari's Trees of Peace: A True Story from Africa*, Jen Johnson and Sonia Sadler's (2013) *Seeds of Change: Planting a Path to Peace*, Claire Nivola's (2008) *Planting the Trees of Kenya: The Story of Wangari Maathai*, and Donna Jo Napoli and Kadir Nelson's (2010) *Mama Miti: Wangari Maathai and the Trees of Africa*. Through read alouds, the students heard Wangari's story repeated in different ways, illustrated in different styles, and described in different vocabulary. As a result, students became very familiar with her life and accomplishments. They took notice of the author's craft and the similarities and differences in what authors chose to include and emphasize.

I supplemented the rich text set with videos highlighting important events in Wangari's life. Three videos were particularly powerful. The first showed Wangari in a clash with soldiers while trying to save the Karura Forest during which she was injured, hospitalized, and jailed. This video sent the students back to the books, spontaneously, to see how, or if, the various authors had included that in their portrayal of Wangari. Jeanette Winter had drawn a simple but powerful illustration which had alarmed us by showing bloodshed and which gained even more meaning and interest for the students after seeing the video. Students were shocked that peaceful demonstrators were met by violence, and that Wangari, who was trying to reason with police, was struck down with physical force.

A second video showed the president of Kenya mocking and making fun of "that woman," that troublemaker who dared to step out of the expected role of women in her culture by becoming educated and opposing foreign, corporate, and government interests who wanted to profit by deforesting and degrading the land through commercial farming. We looked back in the books, especially Johnson and Sadler's (2013) book, which describes in more detail than the others, how Wangari started on the path of resisting conventional expectations by convincing her parents, with her brother's help, to send her to school even though most girls didn't have that opportunity. We also learned that Wangari challenged traditional gender roles and exerted her independence when she divorced her husband and wanted to keep her husband's last name. He forbade it, and she, in true Wangari style, peacefully resisted by keeping his name but making a minor change to it by adding an extra "a" to it.

A third video was a film clip from *Dirt!: The Movie* (Beneson & Rosow, 2010). This clip featured Wangari Maathai telling a fable about a hummingbird who fought a forest fire alone, trying to extinguish the flames by carrying water in its tiny beak, while other larger animals with the ability to do much more, stood by helplessly, letting the fire burn. These animals allowed themselves to be overwhelmed and pessimistic, believing there was nothing they could do. The hummingbird, on the other hand, refused to be a helpless victim and stated, "I will do the best that I can." We watched this segment repeatedly, at the students' request, listening to the lovely cadence of Wangari's speech and becoming increasingly inspired by her message and example of doing the best that she could, as one person in the world fighting environmental disaster and gender discrimination.

Zuleyka, who had been coming out of her shell as we became engrossed in the important and engaging work of reading and writing about global literature, eagerly wrote a full-page response to the hummingbird video. She summarized the video, saying it was about "a little bird who saw a big fire and the little bird was the only animal that was trying to stop the fire and a big elephant was there with a big nose. He was not doing nothing to help." She added, "The lesson was to never give up. Always keep trying and never give up." She said Wangari was like the hummingbird because, "She never gave up. She fought for what she believed in. She never said no and did not give up." Most importantly, Zuleyka wrote, "One way I can be like a hummingbird is I can help the world with my two hands." That statement showed the sense of agency she desired and felt she could have. She also contributed to class discussions, saying that "it's important to do what's right even if other people don't like it."

Zuleyka seemed to find a kindred spirit in Wangari. Getting to know Wangari through reading books and articles, and seeing her on video, Zuleyka saw someone like herself—someone willful, strong, uncompromising, and controversial but who was also smiling, beaming, and positive. Wangari helped Zuleyka envision a different way to express her willfulness, strength, and ability to stand alone—in a way that didn't isolate her from others, in a way that enabled her to have friends and supporters and more personal connections in her life. Watching Wangari tell the story of the hummingbird, with her smile and warmth, and beautiful message shining through was something that Zuleyka connected with.

Zuleyka seemed to undergo a re-envisioning where she realized that to enact change and to lead requires courage and the ability to stand alone, qualities that she possesses and could continue to cultivate.

Zuleyka's younger sister is currently in my ENL class, and when we come across her sister's work, she proudly shares with her classmates that her sister was "one of Ms. O'Leary's best students." This gives me hope that Zuleyka's year in ENL reading and writing intensely around global literature themes had a lasting effect on her view of herself as a learner.

Civil Rights Activists Inspire José

José, an energetic, self-described "hyper" third grade boy from Puerto Rico, became a legend the first year we focused on global literature. Even though two years have passed since he moved away, students still remember him for a special role-play of the Greensboro Lunch Counter Sit-ins he spearheaded in ENL. It all started with an anticipation guide focused on the concept of civil disobedience which asked students to indicate whether they agreed or disagreed with statements like:

> It is always wrong to break the law.
> We should always follow rules and laws.
> Regular people like us cannot do anything to change laws.
> Only government leaders can change laws.
> All white people wanted segregation.
> No white people wanted integration.
> We can always trust authority figures like police officers, presidents, and teachers to do what is right.
> Authority figures will always protect us.

In the beginning, students overwhelmingly agreed with the statements, despite knowing some basic facts about the Civil Rights Movement.

My next step was to teach the concept of civil disobedience with two wonderful books about the lunch counter sit-ins. The first was *Freedom on the Menu: The Greensboro Sit-Ins* by Carole Boston Weatherford and Jerome Lagarrigue (2007), and the second was *Sit-In: How Four Friends Stood Up by Sitting Down* by Andrea Davis Pinkney and Brian Pinkney (2010). We took a careful look at a famous photograph showing angry white demonstrators dumping ashtrays, ketchup, mustard, and salt on the heads of protestors, both Black and white, peacefully sitting at the lunch counter while trying to get served. We also watched video of protestors getting trained in civil disobedience and began to realize how much courage it took to be nonviolent. We saw film footage of Martin Luther King Jr. protesting at a lunch-counter sit-in and heard about the feelings of solidarity and pride of protestors who spent time in jail trying to change unjust laws.

While trying to sort out all the important and surprising details of the lunch counter protests, like the fact that the police were called to arrest the peaceful protestors rather than the people who were threatening and assaulting them, the students, led by José, initiated a role-play that synthesized their new understandings. Students took on the roles of police, protestors, and the angry crowds that surrounded them to show that the "law-breakers," sitting peacefully at the lunch counter, did not deserve punishment. José boldly stated that he should take on the role of Martin Luther King Jr. because he looked most like him. The class unanimously agreed. We spent a good hour role-playing, and I expected we would move on the next day, but José said he would bring his "Sunday clothes" the following day to *really* play the role of Martin Luther King Jr. right. He came in the next day carrying a plastic grocery bag with his dress shoes, vest and matching slacks, button-down shirt, and tie. His friend cut out a mustache from construction paper as a finishing touch. We spent another hour role-playing, honing the performance and taking turns acting out different roles. I noticed that much of the improvised dialogue came from what they remembered from Weatherford's book. José in particular showed a clear understanding of civil disobedience and the willingness of the protestors to go to jail in order to put the injustice of the segregation laws in clear relief. At one point, José, playing Dr. King, put his wrists forward as if offering them to the police for handcuffs, to show his willingness to be arrested and go to jail. This reflected part of Weatherford's book in which the peaceful protestors refused the help of their families in procuring their freedom. They chanted, "Jail, not bail." When refused service at the counter, José improvised that he would not "spend [his] money…" in a place that did not respect him, thus displaying his understanding of boycotts, another part of our global literature study. Through these role-plays, students came away with a vivid idea of what it meant to be civilly disobedient, that it is a courageous choice, and one in which the protestor takes on considerable risk physically, as well as to their reputation. I sensed that they were also experiencing a deep engagement in academic learning that many had not experienced before.

José developed a great sense of audience and discovered ways to harness his energy and dramatic skills. He seemed to re-envision himself as someone who earned people's respect and their attention because he had something interesting and important to say. José's self-perception as a student seemed to undergo a transformation. His interest and progress in writing, his focused and outstanding participation, and the respect his peers showed for him were evidence of his transformation. Even though José moved away the following year, he is still remembered for his writing, his acting, his enthusiasm and ideas, his performances, and for being the driving force behind the Martin Luther King Jr. lunch counter sit-in role play. Through the study of authentic literature rooted in the theme of social justice, this student was able to channel his energies, talents, and growing insights in such a way that he, and all around him, both students and teachers, began to re-envision him as a special talent, as someone truly gifted in reading, writing, and the arts.

Re-Envisioning Advocacy in ENL

Just as my students re-envisioned themselves through studying global literature, I also re-envisioned ENL and my role as an ENL teacher. My top priority has always been advocacy for my students and their families. I strive to provide the "safe nest" that Cristina Igoa (1995) describes in her book *The Inner World of the Immigrant Child,* and I try very hard to be the "cultural broker" Mary Pipher (2003) exemplifies in her book *The Middle of Everywhere: Helping Refugees Enter the Country.* Being an advocate has included everything from attending meetings and audits at the Department of Social Services with students' parents, to securing scholarships to camp and acting as the liaison between camp and parents. It has included making sure everyone in ENL has a project to bring to the science fair and has Valentines to send to all their classmates at their class celebrations. This kind of advocacy is important because the ENL students and their parents want to participate in school fully, but they often are not familiar with the expectations or existence of cultural constructs like science fairs, class parties, dances, and talent shows. My efforts to advocate for my students and families have been focused on helping them navigate the culture and language in their adopted home.

My instruction has been similarly oriented toward helping my students learn English and helping them adjust and become knowledgeable about American culture. I try to be very sensitive and respectful of my students' experiences, feelings, and cultures, but before using global literature, my instruction lacked connection to the complexity my students' cultural identities. Nonfiction texts were in abundance in my classroom, even before the Common Core made them a priority. Children's literature, however, did not have a central place in my teaching, and I was not very familiar with quality, authentic, global literature. I literally did not know what we were missing with its absence! Using global literature through the inquiry group helped to widen the curriculum during a time when we have seen a detrimental narrowing of the curriculum with so much focused on test preparation. With its focus on "close reading," the introduction of the Common Core has narrowed the type of reading that is done in school. The primary goal of reading has become to analyze nuanced language in complex texts with the goal of determining the author's intent and purpose. The test-makers do not seem to realize that for most of my ENL students, who are faced with the daunting task of learning the English language while simultaneously learning grade level skills and content, developing the language in order to successfully do this type of inferential reading will take years to develop. My students often have difficulties connecting with the passages they are asked to read "closely" again and again.

Anchoring our learning in global literature counteracted this confining environment. I have been amazed by how my students' writing and ideas developed as we read more and more books that they connected to. In *The Writing Thief*, Ruth Culham (2014) contends that "writing is thinking" (p. 13). When we write, we aren't just writing down or transcribing our thoughts, we are actually clarifying, modifying, expanding, and creating new ideas and understandings as we write. Writing helps us generate deeper thought. As we read more authentic literature and wrote to more open-ended, authentic prompts, opportunities were created for my students to put their lives and their experiences into words both in discussions and on the page. Students expanded their thoughts by connecting books and characters' experiences to their own culture, language, and feelings. Now I see culturally responsive instruction as a new avenue of advocacy for my students as it enables them to experience and see themselves as capable, engaged learners with habits, knowledge, and skills that will enable them to fulfill their potential. The intense engagement that global literature offers my students helps them see themselves as a valuable, indispensable resource in understanding and interpreting the text. The literature facilitates and welcomes this sort of response and self-confidence.

"Our Books": Concluding Thoughts

My students affectionately refer to the global picturebooks in our room as "our books," making it evident that they clearly recognize the difference between test-prep passages and authentic literature. This point was made clear to me soon before "testing season" began. Students and teachers alike were tired, bored, and cranky from a month of test practice, and I was delighted to hear one of my students lament, "When will we be getting back to *our books*?!" Indeed. Test passages and leveled readers feel disposable and disconnected from us, whereas "our books" make a lasting impact on us by bringing to our consciousness inspiring characters and people, problematic and relevant issues, and heartbreaking and heartening stories, all of which change us. Through "our books" I found a new way to advocate for my students. While I don't have the linguistic expertise to help them develop vocabulary and literacy in their home languages, I can create a space for them to talk about their experience as bilingual and bicultural members of the school and of the wider community. I can bear witness to their expertise and experience. In turn, I can help them understand the unique perspective they have, and the things they can teach others, including me, and other adults. Above all, I hope I can support them in taking pride in and being brave about expressing their unique perspectives and experiences.

References

Culham, R. (2014). *The writing thief: Using mentor texts to teach the craft of writing*. Newark, DE: International Reading Association.

Ghiso, M. P., Campano, G., & Hall, T. (2012). Braided histories and experiences in literature for children and adolescents. *Journal of Children's Literature, 38*(2), 14–22.

Igoa, C. (1995). *The inner world of the immigrant child.* New York, NY: Routledge.

Pipher, M. (1993). *The middle of everywhere: Helping refugees enter the American community.* New York, NY: Mariner Books.

Wright, R. (1945). *Black boy: A record of childhood and youth.* Cleveland, OH: The World Publishing Company.

Children's Literature, Media, and Materials

Benenson, B. (Producer) & Rosow, E. (Director). (2010). *Dirt!: The movie* [Motion picture]. New York, NY: Common Ground Media.

Bunting, E. & Himler, R. (1997). *A day's work.* New York, NY: Houghton Mifflin.

Johnson, J. & Sadler, S. (2013). *Seeds of change: Planting a path to peace.* New York, NY: Lee & Low.

Miller, W. & Christie, R. G. (1997). *Richard Wright and the library card.* New York, NY: Lee & Low.

Mora, P. & Colón, R. (2000). *Tomás and the library lady.* New York, NY: Dragonfly Books.

Napoli, J. & Nelson, K. (2010). *Mama Miti: Wangari Maathai and the trees of Kenya.* New York, NY: Simon & Schuster.

Nivola, C. A. (2008). *Planting the trees of Kenya: The story of Wangari Maathai.* New York, NY: Frances Foster Books.

Pinkney, A. D. & Pinkney, B. (2010). *Sit-in: How four friends stood up by sitting down.* New York, NY: Little, Brown and Company.

Say, A. (1993). *Grandfather's journey.* New York, NY: Houghton Mifflin.

Weatherford, C. B. & Lagarrigue, J. (2007). *Freedom on the menu: The Greensboro sit-ins.* New York, NY: Puffin Books.

Winter, J. (2008). *Wangari's trees of peace: A true story from Africa.* New York, NY: Houghton Mifflin.

Winter, J. (2014). *Malala, a brave girl from Pakistan/Iqbal, a brave boy from Pakistan: Two stories of bravery.* New York, NY: Beach Lane Books.

4

READING GLOBAL LITERATURE ABOUT WAR

The Role of Emotion in Constructing Meaning

Kelly K. Wissman

In this chapter, I explore how a unique collaboration between Krista, a literacy specialist, and Toni, a sixth grade teacher, created a context in which sixth grade students considered global perspectives on war through multiple texts, genres, and pedagogical approaches. Although an inquiry question framed and gave focus to their explorations, emotions also played a catalytic role in how students constructed knowledge and made meaning during the unit. Through the three episodes of teaching and learning that I describe and analyze in the chapter, I consider how Krista and Toni's professional investment in this unit of study, text selection, pedagogical choices, and language in the classroom reflected and reinforced the centrality of the role of emotion in constructing knowledge about war and made possible a range of realizations shaped by the varied ways in which they approached the inquiry. This chapter draws upon field notes taken in 16 classes, two interviews with Krista and Toni, numerous informal conversations before and after class, transcripts of whole class and small group discussions, and analysis of curricular materials.

As I analyze and write about the teaching and learning within this unit, I am informed by sociocultural understandings of emotion. Rather than locating emotion as an unmediated expression of an individual's "true" feelings, sociocultural points of view consider how emotions emerge from and move across the social context of the classroom and the social practices embedded within it (Thein, Guise, & Sloan, 2015). Emotions are, therefore, not "anchored" to individuals but instead circulate and are mediated by objects, bodies, and signs (Lewis & Tierney, 2013). Like other scholars taking on a similar sociocultural view, I see emotion as pervasive and as "always already" (Thein et al., 2015, p. 202) present in shaping, limiting, and opening pathways for making meaning and building identities within literature classrooms. In this chapter, I endeavor to show not only how emotion was ever-present within this classroom but was also a desired outcome of the engagement with literature. Given the uniqueness of their teaching styles, however, Krista and Toni created contexts that welcomed emotion and responded to its expression in quite distinct ways. These contrasting examples help exemplify the diversity of ways teachers welcome and respond to emotion in the classroom. Krista and Toni also illustrate how the purposeful use of targeted reading strategies can be employed not simply as ends but as *means* toward enhancing students' opportunities to delve deeply into global texts, connect emotionally, think critically, and consider complexly the human dimensions of war.

Background to the Unit and the Teachers

When Krista joined the inquiry group, she had an already-established professional relationship with Toni, a fellow teacher in her building, and had collaborated with her numerous times to design, plan, and co-teach a unit on World War II (WWII). As Krista explores in Chapter 5, this professional relationship was quite meaningful to her and allowed her to pursue the kind of practices that she most valued as a literacy specialist: to work in collaborative, dialogic, and ongoing ways with teachers to enhance the literacy learning opportunities for all students. When Krista and Toni discussed the unit with me, it was evident that theirs was a collaborative endeavor. Both teachers frequently used the words "we" and "our" and often finished each other's thoughts, as evidenced in this exchange during a conversation with me after class:

Krista: Toni and I will have conversations about books, and the kids will be watching and listening, and then we move on. Just kind of always doing those things to show…

Toni: Because we lead a readerly life. That's what we want our students to do and that's what we model.

Krista and Toni both brought to their collaboration a deep interest in World War II and both had pursued advanced degrees in literacy. Toni was very open not only to learning with and from Krista but also to having her co-teach with her within her classroom. Although Krista had taught this unit with Toni before, her teaching of it at the time of the study was shaped by the pressing and dynamic demands of the broader educational context of standards as well as the additional perspectives she gleaned from her own professional development experiences. In inquiry group meetings, Krista mentioned to us how she wanted to make more explicit the already embedded ways in which the unit reflected Common Core priorities. Furthermore, she was informed by her participation in a workshop in which the facilitator presented ways to utilize picturebooks with middle school students to explore the topic of war. This experience, along with ongoing conversations with Toni, helped shape the inquiry question at the heart of their unit: "How do the views and experiences of people around the world support the statement that 'War is never a good idea'?"

Krista also drew upon her experiences in our global literature inquiry group to inform her teaching of the unit in two main ways. First, she was inspired to broaden even further the range of texts available to students for independent reading to include more global perspectives on the war. Second, she was deeply engaged by our readings in the inquiry group of scholarship by Kathy Short (2009) that broadened understandings of "culture" beyond surface level features such as food, festivals, and holidays. Krista drew upon Short's (2011) curricular framework for intercultural understanding in which students explore the meaning and embodiment of "culture" across many dimensions. Krista was also inspired by our reading and discussion of the work that Jewett (2011) accomplished with first graders when they were given structured opportunities to explore culture as the beliefs and values of a group of a people, or "what matters" to them. Krista and Toni drew on this conceptualization of culture and this expression of "what matters" throughout the unit. "What matters" became a kind of through line in the unit, shaping questions on graphic organizers and response sheets, as well as often spoken verbally to students. The students themselves often used the language of "what matters" when discussing characters in both small and whole group discussions. By focusing on "what matters" to the characters in the novels they read and historical persons they encountered in nonfiction texts, Krista and Toni focused the students' attention on the human dimensions and consequences of the war for all involved. As they explained:

Toni: It's not just the facts of World War II, it's how the characters are struggling and surviving and living. That is, I think, our main focus.
Krista: How it affected them.
Toni: Everyone!

Here, Krista and Toni articulate a focus on the experiential and affective dimensions of the war, a focus that will become further evident in my discussion of the three episodes of teaching and learning below. By orienting the students toward "what matters" to the characters and persons of diverse backgrounds they would meet in the texts, Krista and Toni encouraged the students to focus less on the outward differences in language, customs, or attire but on the internal workings of the people and their complicated responses to war.

An Introduction to Toni and Her Classroom

A sixth grade teacher, Toni described herself as an "avid reader." Her room was filled with multigenre books, colorful posters, and student work, including many materials specific to this unit of study, including, student-created timelines of key events in World War II and calendars in which students added personally significant cultural holidays, such as Eid, that were not officially recognized by the school district. On numerous occasions, Toni also described to me how teaching this unit was very important to her and that it stirred many emotions as well. As we talked one day after class, she told me for the past week she had been "buried in picture-books," in preparation for the students' picturebook study, and noted, "I've been crying like nobody's business." Describing herself as an "emotional wreck, but in a good way," she contrasted her current teaching of this unit with an experience earlier in her teaching career in which she decided to share a picturebook about the Vietnam War with her students:

> [The students] didn't have that emotional connection. Nobody cried. I'm sure when I read *The Wall* (Bunting & Himler, 1990), I was emotional. I don't think I was a stone face. I don't know. I know I've changed a lot over the years. I know I've become a more compassionate person. But the stu-dents didn't have that connection. It was also pre-9/11. I think a lot of our attitudes have changed since then…We didn't have the 'changing the world in a more positive way' as an end result like we do now. It was just a unit that we talked about. I gave them some background, but it didn't fit into the curriculum. It was probably just something I was taking in my grad classes that sparked an interest and I thought this would be cool.

As Toni notes, her approach to including emotionally complex texts has evolved since this initial experience, shaped by world events like September 11 and her own professional growth. Here, Toni touches upon themes central to this chapter: the primacy of emotion in meaning-making and the emphasis on an integrated purpose across all facets of the unit.

In what follows, I explore three episodes of teaching and learning involving three texts: *The Quilt* (Paulsen, 2005), *Faithful Elephants: A True Story of Animals People, and War* (Tsuchiya & Lewin, 1997), and *Shin's Tricycle* (Kodama & Ando, 1995). In these episodes, emotion was a dynamic force that shaped interpretive possibilities with global literature in generative and distinct ways.

Introducing the Unit: *The Quilt*

Krista and Toni began the unit by shifting the location of the class to the library in order to facilitate their presentation of a slideshow meant to provide background to *The Quilt*, a book by Gary Paulsen (2005) that they chose to start with because it provides perspectives on WWII from family members who were affected by it. For Krista and Toni, it was important that students had a shared experience of one text to ground the inquiry, to introduce key terms and events to build background knowledge, and to provide opportunities for students to think about and explore some of the essential themes in the unit with the support of the entire class before pursuing similar inquiries on their own and with each other throughout the month-long unit. Both Krista and Toni were very deliberate in modeling and introducing reading strategies for the students; however, these strategies were not ends in and of themselves. Instead, previewing the text, highlighting new vocabulary, and inviting students to make personal connections were pursued in the service of inviting students into a deeper exploration of the central lines of inquiry in the unit related to how war affected people, animals, and the environment.

As the students sat at long tables with room for about five students, Toni and Krista took turns presenting information and asking questions of the students. As the following field notes suggest, Krista and Toni both approached this presentation as a way to construct knowledge with the students and to locate themselves within the inquiry as well:

> Toni explains to everyone that they're starting a new unit. She asks if anyone has ever read a book about another time period and got really confused. (This is a pattern throughout of asking kids direct questions about themselves/their experiences before introducing a new concept or idea). Many hands go up. Toni tells them today they'll find out more about the time period in a book, *The Quilt.* Krista stands and notes that the book they'll be exploring takes place in a time when they were not alive yet. She reminds them of the term "background knowledge" and says they will be introducing vocabulary, images, and sounds to "set the mood" for reading. She then tells students they will be exploring historical fiction and asks students if they know what that means. One boy says, "It happened in history, but it's fake." Krista goes on to talk about how history matters and affects today, giving the example of airport security because of 9/11 (many kids nod with recognition) and also talks about freedoms we have in this country because of what has happened before. She notes that she "loves" historical fiction because it provides insight into "what really matters today." She notes her own grandfather was in WWII and that she has seen his uniform and other documents. Toni asks the students, "Can you make a connection to Social Studies?" A couple students call out, "Artifacts!"

Toni then provided a brief synopsis of *The Quilt,* a semi-autobiographical tale in which a young boy goes to live with family on a farm in northern Minnesota while his mother works in an ammunition factory in Chicago. At the farm, the boy observes how the women in the family have taken over daily operations while the men are fighting the war. After reading a short passage from the book, Toni pointed to key ideas within it, noting, "it's not about a soldier, but the people left behind." Here, she drew students' attention to the unit's focus on the human dimensions of the war. As the presentation continued, Krista and Toni built on this focus, and at times invited students to make connections to their own lives, as these field notes attest:

With a new slide, Toni begins a discussion of how important radio was for news. Toni tells the students that people during this time would go to movies for news reels "rather than Channel 6." She asks, "Who wants to see one?" Kids respond with excitement. Krista plays the clip. Toni says she loves to see students writing things down on the graphic organizer in front of them. The footage uses the word "Japs." After the clip plays, a student asks, "Where was that?" Toni says, "the South Pacific." She notes that she noticed the announcer "talked different" and that she would never use the term "Japs," that it's "not socially acceptable." She also talks about the music, noting it was dramatic. A boy says, "like Bugs Bunny!" Krista asks the kids how would they feel if they had a brother or uncle or father fighting in the war and watched that footage? Kids say, "sad," "worried."

By focusing on the human dimension, and on emotions, as a way to build knowledge, Krista and Toni are also laying important groundwork here for an understanding of other cultures the children will meet in future readings. Throughout the presentation, Krista and Toni talked through the various ways people during this time period ate, worked, what kind of music they listened to, popular movies at the time, etc. By doing so within an American context with American students, they were developing understandings of culture not just as something people "out there" have but something that they also have.

In addition to inviting students to consider their own emotions in relation to what they were learning, to consider the human dimensions of the conflict, and to reflect on the cultural dimensions of the characters' lives, Krista and Toni also encouraged students to ask questions, a practice that would continue throughout the unit. While the students were listening to the presentation, they were jotting notes on what was striking to them and questions they had. As class was wrapping up, Toni instructed the students: "Pick one thing to share that's a first impression or that you didn't understand." A sampling of what the students shared:

- "Were people forced to fight?"
- "Why were movies so cheap?"
- "Wouldn't a wood burning stove start a fire in a house?"
- "Did kids have to go to war?"
- "How did the war affect people?"

As I explore next, these invitations for students to take an inquiry stance continued throughout the unit, complementing and extending the teachers' aims to have the students attend to the human and emotional dimensions of the war and their own responses to it.

Faithful Elephants: A True Story of Animals, People, and War

For Krista and Toni, picturebook read alouds were of critical importance in this unit. They devoted four classes to whole class read alouds of picturebooks, a significant time commitment within a unit lasting one month and a significant point of departure for many students who were more accustomed to this practice occurring primarily in the younger grades. During these read alouds, students gathered on the floor in a semicircle and directed their gaze toward either Krista or Toni who conducted the read aloud. Students could respond at any time during the read alouds, without raising their hands; Krista and Toni regularly encouraged them to share "thoughts, questions, feelings."

Yukio Tsuchiya's (1997) *Faithful Elephants*, a story based on the real-life experiences of zookeepers in Japan during World War II, explores the ramification of the Japanese Army's order that all large animals be killed to prevent the damage that could occur if they escaped during the anticipated bombing of the Ueno Zoo in Tokyo.[1] Tsuchiya's story opens on a beautiful, bright day with the cherry blossoms blooming and the elephants performing in front of a delighted audience. The narrator turns away from this scene, however, to tell the story of the zookeeper who years earlier was faced with a much more dire circumstance. Tsuchiya narrates the story from the zookeeper's perspective of his close relationship with three elephants who would be poisoned and ultimately starved to death.

Throughout the read aloud, Toni and Krista integrated three approaches to shape the meaning-making within the room: 1) offering students invitations to share their emotions and making explicit their own; 2) naming the reading strategies they were employing while reading the text and asking students to do the same in response to their questions; and 3) drawing upon the students' emotional investment in the story and their comprehension of it through the reading strategies to offer analytical responses to the text. These three approaches provided a layered way to make multiple meanings with this text. At the same time, however, the particular nature of this text and the lived experiences of one girl, Melissa (all student names are pseudonyms), resulted in an emotional outburst that punctuated this read aloud and precipitated a momentary state of crisis in the class.

Situating the Text in the Broader Inquiry

Once the students were gathered on the floor, Toni informed the students that one student, Alexandra, had asked to share a thought that emerged for her after the previous day's read aloud of *Feathers and Fools* by Mem Fox and Nicholas Wilton (2000), an allegory depicting a conflict between peacocks and swans. Reading from a Post-it® Note where she had jotted down her idea, Alexandra offered the following insight: "[The birds] were definitely looking at the outside, not the inside." In response to Toni's request that she elaborate on her idea,

Alexandra continued, "Like, they were just looking at the differences between darker hair and darker eyes. They couldn't see that she was like really nice and really fun." Toni then asked the students if they knew of times in history when similar things had happened. A couple students mentioned "bullying," while others named segregation in the American South, the response to Muslims after September 11, and Hitler.

Even though Toni conducted the read aloud, Krista also made key contributions before and after the read aloud as well. Before Toni began reading *Faithful Elephants*, Krista invited the students to reflect on the inquiries they had been pursuing throughout the unit:

Krista: If I asked you for one sentence, what would that be about, for yesterday?

James: How, uh, how much damage war can do. What war does to people who live on the planet and what it does to the planet.

Krista: And long-term effects. The ripple effect, maybe?

Melissa: People had to be more protective of each other because of the war.

Toni: Can you be more specific?

Melissa: Women had to be supportive and support each other. So they could feel everything was better.

In this conversation, Toni and Krista created a context for students to make connections back to previous texts read and inquiries explored. Initially, Alexandra's discussion of a central theme in *Feathers and Fools* and Toni's response opened up conversational space for students to name historical events and situations that shared a resonance with the unit's broad inquiries. Krista's question also prompted Melissa to make an intertextual connection when discussing broader themes of the unit as she recalled how the women in *The Quilt* bonded together to provide support while the male members of the family were at war.

Grappling with Ethics in a Time of War

As Toni began to read *Faithful Elephants*, students listened intently, while also looking carefully at the illustrations. Noting her own mounting concerns at the information that the zookeeper had begun to add poison to the elephants' food, Toni invited the students to share their own feelings, thoughts, and connections. Students shared a range of responses, questions, and alternatives, including considerations of a recent event in the local news:

Toni: Anybody wrinkling their foreheads like me right now? What thoughts are you having? Share them with me.

Melissa: Why would they poison them and not tranquilize them? You know that time when bears got loose in that backyard? [Melissa references a

	story that was prominent in the local news at the time in which police tranquilized and relocated bears that entered a suburban community.]
Toni:	OK. So you're wondering why did they jump right to killing them? Could they have done something to preserve the animals' lives? What do you think?
Alexandra:	Why did they kill them? Why not move them to another part of the world?
Toni:	OK. All right. So, why didn't they just move them? Do you see why this is a problem, though? Do you all agree that this would have been a problem? Can you imagine living in Tokyo, having a bomb hit in the wrong place, and then having all these animals running around? So, it is a problem they had to solve, but you're coming up with some other solutions: bring them someplace else; tranquilize them.
Aneesa:	I think they should take them to a quieter place.
Toni:	Like out in the country or something?
Aneesa:	Yeah. I think they should take them to countryside instead of the city where the bombs are always falling.

In this exchange, the students draw from personal experiences and details in the text to share their responses and to propose alternatives to the points of view and actions taken by the zookeepers.

As the story progressed, the emotional quotient continued to build as the zookeeper wrestles with his decision not to feed the elephants and the effects on the animals are detailed. In the following exchange, Toni references her own emotions and personal experiences multiple times as background knowledge that she is bringing to the text, even as she also encourages the students to pay attention to details in the story:

Toni:	I know from personal experience that starvation is probably one of the most horrific –
Students:	Painful
Toni:	– ways to go. It's very painful. Remember I told you my grandfather had a stroke and we had to put a feeding tube in him? I'm connecting the fact that this elephant is starving to death, connecting to what I know about humans starving to death. That's a horrible way to go.

Toni continues to read from the text, asking the students to consider the feelings of the zookeeper:

Toni:	What do you think this guy's feeling right now?
Matt:	Like, like dying inside.
Toni:	What detail did you hear in the text that shows how much he loves them?

Melissa: It says they were "like his kids."
Toni: Yeah. Can you imagine not feeding your children? So I'm trying to imagine how he's feeling right now.

Here, Toni not only prioritizes the role of attending to emotions and feelings in making meaning about a text but also asks students to support their assertions about the characters' emotions with details from the text. Unprompted by Toni, Melissa then provides a close reading of the title, adding:

Melissa: I think the title means the zookeepers and elephants are not giving up faith, they are putting up with everything, hoping for a better day. I think they're just hoping, hoping for a better day.
Toni: Do you think that was common throughout the war? Not just in Japan but maybe in Europe and other places too? People kept just trying to have faith that this war will end soon and things can go back to the way they were supposed to be? Good connection, Melissa.

Toni then continues to read from the book:

Toni: Can you tell I'm getting a little emotional? Yeah?
Matt: I think the zookeepers didn't go because I think they would be tempted to feed them and give them water.
Toni: OK. So maybe they didn't want that temptation. Why else would they stay away? Alexandra?
Alexandra: I think the elephant trainer didn't want to see his precious elephants die.
Toni: Yeah. Can you imagine watching them waste away, little by little, how much that must hurt? Maybe they're protecting themselves from feeling the pain, too.

In almost every speaking turn, Toni either references her emotions and experiences or encourages the students to imagine what the people in the story were experiencing. In response, the students very often refer back to key details within the text. Melissa, in her close reading of the title, took the opportunity to reflect on its meaning in relation to the content of the story, repeating the word "hoping" three times to describe the zookeepers' state of mind. Both Matt and Alexandra also use details from the text to ascertain the zookeepers' states of mind and their actions.

A Rupture

Within the read aloud to this point, the students were primarily engaged in responding to the text, describing the characters, and offering up their thoughts related to injustices or inconsistencies they were noticing. Aside from Toni's voice slightly quivering at one point while she read, both the teachers' and students' facial expressions did not show overt concern or sadness and their voices were relatively controlled, the pitch and register of their comments similar to typical classroom discourse. In response to a particularly charged moment in the text when the final elephant died, however, Melissa cried out, "Oh!" in such a way that was markedly different and that created a kind of rupture in the classroom, even one such as this that valued discussions of feelings and emotions. The other students became very still and looks of concern flashed across their faces. For a moment, it seemed everyone was holding their collective breath. While Melissa softly cried, Toni continued to read from the book, and paused to say, "It's OK, Melissa." Toni also motioned to Krista to stand closer to Melissa while she finished reading the book. After finishing the reading, Toni stood up and walked over to where Melissa was sitting. Putting her arms around her shoulders, she leaned down, and told her, "It's OK to cry. That's what I appreciate about you—how you respond to the books and care so much." She stayed in this position for a few more minutes, even while eliciting additional thoughts and responses about the book from other students.

Within the field of trauma studies, these "ruptures" are often created during what Felman and Laub (1991) call the "crisis of witnessing" in response to the representation of historical traumas in film and literature. It is noteworthy that even within a classroom that values emotion, Melissa's exclamation and crying was markedly different and caused a moment of destabilization and a tangible change in the tenor and tone of the class, even as both teachers were able to continue on with the read aloud and with facilitating discussion about it. As I explore next, this moment also brought to light the differences in Krista and Toni's response to and analysis of the role of emotion in their teaching.

Krista and Toni's Response to Melissa

Following the read aloud of *Faithful Elephants*, I sat down with Krista and Toni to gain their perspectives on what occurred. Our conversation sheds light on the different approaches they took but with a focus on a similar end goal: to create opportunities for students to have deep engagements and connections with texts:

Kelly: What was it like for you when Melissa started to cry in response to *Faithful Elephants*?

Toni: It was really hard. Because I'm a hugger, I'm a toucher. I will cry if I see you cry. I'm really firm. I'm really fair, but I'm very compassionate.

Krista: I'm not. [said in a joking manner]

Toni: She's not a hugger!

Krista: I'm not a hugger, but I'm compassionate.

Toni: I don't know if you heard me, but I said, "Can you take care of her?" And Krista sat by her. I wanted to go hug her and hold her and tell her it was going to be OK, but I continued on. For me, that was a real challenge. I don't want everybody to cry just because they think that's what I want, either. Do you know what I mean? But I didn't want her.... Melissa's got some tough issues that she deals with on an everyday basis, from bullying to people not understanding her, but she's one of the most beautiful people in this classroom. She is.

Krista: And that's what we're trying to get at.

Toni: She is a gorgeous person inside. She would do anything for anyone. Compassion at that age is just, you know, it's not cool. She'll thank you for everything. She's just an amazing person. I didn't want her to suffer by herself.

Krista: Right. But, on the other hand, my view was I don't want to disturb her –

Toni: It's OK to be sad.

Krista: It's OK. And I was not glad she was upset; I was glad we got some kind of response from them because kids at this age, things kind of pass them by and they're like "OK, whatever" and they don't get it. So, for somebody to cry or get angry and maybe mad about the book or yell: that's what we wanted. To see her emotional like that, it's not like I didn't feel bad, it was like, "She got it." She got it and the kids noticed.

Later on in the conversation, Krista clarified how and why she saw the importance of emotion in constructing meaning with texts:

Krista: One thing I always tell kids, if you've never cried at a book, that's one thing you should do in your lifetime. They think I'm crazy, but they get it when they finally let themselves. Like, they saw you [Toni] getting emotional and the looks on their faces were like, "What's going on?" And then Melissa got upset and I think that even woke them up even more.

Toni: …and they got to hear me talking about crying on my treadmill reading last night's book!

While Toni was more forthcoming than Krista with her own emotions, she was also more direct with the students about their own. Here, she describes how she followed up with Melissa after class:

Toni: And what made Melissa cry, because I asked her afterwards, was, I said, "Was it the domino effect, you saw me cry and you lost it?" She said, "No, I had an experience where I had to put down an animal and it killed me a little inside." So, for her, that was the connection she was making: the death of these innocent creatures. Did she understand it was probably better for the people that they did it? Yeah, but it didn't take away that pain and that connection she had to her own life.

Kelly: And your [Krista's] point was, you didn't want her to feel like she had to stop crying?

Krista: Exactly.

Kelly: You wanted her to feel like she could just have the emotion and not take her out of the room?

Krista: Yeah.

Toni: We balance each other very well. We don't plan it. It's just the way we work.

Here, Krista and Toni both underscore the centrality of emotion in their teaching practice, even while they recognize their distinctive approaches to responding to its expression. By "balancing" and complementing each other, they also make available to students a range of ways to engage with and respond to texts.

Shin's Tricycle

Following the picturebook read alouds and before the students' independent reading of World War II novels, Krista and Toni created an opportunity for students to explore additional global picturebooks about World War II in pairs. Toni asked the students to read their book at least two times. The first time, they were asked to read for understanding of the text, the context, and the characters, to get the "gist" of the story. For the second reading, Toni asked the students to read for deeper understandings of the characters and themes in the book. To assist them, Krista and Toni developed a handout with questions to guide their responses and places to jot notes. On this graphic organizer used during paired discussions of picturebooks, the students were asked to write notes in response to these three prompts: "1) What Really Matters to the Main Character, 2) What Surprised Me or Worried Me About This Story and 3) What I Still Wonder/Questions I Still Have." Toni clarified that when students were considering "what matters" to the character, they should think about the character's "heart's desire, what he or she wants more than anything." She asked the students to consider carefully "what the characters are going through, how it affected their lives."

In their study, Thein, Guise, and Sloan (2015) argue that different participation structures and pedagogical practices such as literature circles "unbound and unstuck emotional rules for literature interpretation" (p. 215). In Toni and Krista's classroom, the paired work with picturebooks also provided opportunities for different and deeper engagements with the texts and themes in the unit, prompting even more elaborated discussions of emotions and responses to texts. Whereas in the whole group read aloud and discussion of *The Quilt* (Paulsen, 2005) and *Faithful Elephants* (Tsuchiya & Lewin, 1997) students built knowledge across affective and analytical domains through discussion, not all students spoke during whole group discussions. For those who did speak, their speaking turns might consist of a phrase or a sentence or two at most. Within these paired groups, many of the conversational turns were much longer, filled with more continuous emotional undertones, and inclusive of additional connections to issues in the world and in their own reading lives. In this section, I draw from a conversation between Aneesa and Derek who were discussing *Shin's Tricycle* (Kodama & Ando, 1995), a picturebook set in World War II Japan in which a young boy and much of his family were killed as a result of the Hiroshima bombing. The title of this historical fiction text comes from the description of Shin's excitement at receiving a tricycle for his birthday and his father's enormous sadness at finding the tricycle amidst the death and destruction that killed his son.

"I Really Want to Write Down 'Why?'"

In order to gather a range of student perspectives within this unit, the teachers and I placed audio recorders on students' desks to capture their paired discussions. The following conversation is transcribed from one of those audiotapes. As documented in my exploration of the teaching and learning involved with *The Quilt* and *Faithful Elephants*, the approach students take here is a combination of traveling across both analytical and affective domains, of drawing on academic language and reading strategies alongside prioritizing emotional transactions with literature. For Aneesa and Derek, their roughly 30-minute conversation traversed many themes, texts, and personal experiences and contrasted with their whole class participation. While Derek did not speak at all during the whole group read aloud of *Faithful Elephants*, Aneesa did on two occasions. In the first, she offered her perspective on moving the animals to the countryside instead of killing them. In her second contribution, she used academic language to frame her response, even without a specific prompt to do so, asserting, "Maybe the author's purpose was to show that war doesn't just affect humans, but the animals, too." Her contributions in the whole group discussion were insightful, yet brief, while also focusing primarily on the text and the author, rather than her own emotions about them. In this conversation with Derek, however, she spoke at length during her speaking turns and expressed her ideas with a good deal of passion.

As they sat down together with *Shin's Tricycle* in front of them, Aneesa mentioned how deeply the texts read in this unit affected her, exclaiming to Derek, "When we read [*Faithful Elephants*] I felt myself in that person's, the elephant keeper's, shoes. I was like, I felt like crying in my mind. I was like, 'Oh my God. I can't believe that!'" Derek agreed, stating that he found the book "incredibly sad." Derek and Aneesa then read *Shin's Tricycle* together. As they settled into their conversation about the book, they considered the handout in front of them. In response to the prompt "What Surprised or Worried Me About This Story," Aneesa expressed her surprise that Shin's father would feel guilty in response to his son's death. This surprise became a springboard for both Derek and Aneesa to explore many complicated ideas related to the morality of war and the responsibilities of those who pursue it:

Aneesa: I wanted to add to what surprised me was why does the author feel guilty? It's not his fault. Why is he feeling guilty when other people are the ones who should be feeling guilty? They're killing these innocent people's lives. Why is he the one? That's really surprising me.

Derek: Well, can I just say this one thing?

Aneesa: Yeah.

Derek: Well, you know, everybody, like, I think it was because…

Aneesa: I'm saying, why aren't the people who are hitting them feeling guilty? Why are they so happy because they are winning and everything? They're killing each other.

Derek: I don't think that all of them are happy. I just think that maybe they wanted to win and they just wanted to feel the winner.

Aneesa: But I really want to write down "*Why?*" *Why* can't the people who are fighting in the war, why aren't *they* feeling guilty?

Derek: Well, I think they kind of feel guilty, but they had no choice.

Aneesa: But why aren't the *leaders* feeling guilty? Like the president? They're the ones that started the war.

As the conversation builds, Aneesa becomes more and more adamant as she articulates her argument that the leaders of the principal countries in the war should feel guilty, not Shin's father. Even though Aneesa is very forthright in her declarations about the book and Derek at first struggles to find his footing in the conversation, Derek eventually raises questions and tries to add additional nuance to her assertions that the leaders of the war were "happy" and that they enjoyed "winning." It is apparent here that the students are listening to each other given that they often use each other's words in response to the other.

Throughout the conversation, the prompts on the handout seemed to guide the students' conversation, but did not limit it. Instead, Aneesa and Derek keep digging deeper into the story, often using academic language to support their inquiries:

Aneesa: What else can we add to "What Really Matters to the Main Character?"

Derek: Well, we could think of the father as the main character, too, because he's kind of narrating it, too. So, we should like line that out and then write the narrator first on top. And then write what the narrator feels because the narrator is just as important as Shin…Something's that really important to the narrator is his family. So let's write that down. Also, well, let's…. Let's write down what the narrator feels because I think that's really important how the narrator feels. Because the main character, I want to see how, I want to write down how he feels, like that will come in handy. So we can create another column and then just write he feels guilty.

Here, Derek adds his own take on the handout, shaping it to his own purposes to highlight how important it is to make clear that the father is the narrator of the story.

Aneesa then builds on Derek's discussion of Shin's father and brings in a connection to her own family, discussing how she would feel if this happened to her. In an extended speaking turn, Aneesa also expands the conversation to reference current world events, what she calls a "text to world connection," and discusses various books she has read on her own that were not a part of this unit:

> I just can't imagine my family. Like, if that really happened to my family and like, my own children, I would be so mad that I would just want this war to end like really quickly. All these things that are happening: people are dying, people are getting injured, people's families are getting lost. Like, because of this one war and relating this thing to another thing.... So, I have a text to world connection. The war that is happening now in Egypt and everything, you know, like, the war in Egypt? A lot of kids there, you see in the news, like a lot of little, little kids who don't even have their mom and dad anymore. I'm connecting this to this because this father, his children are dying in front of his eyes and he can't save them. And these children in like Egypt, their family members are dying, people are getting like stressed out because they don't have anybody to care for them.

After referencing the strife in Egypt and the connections she sees between the anguish experienced by Egyptian families and Shin's family, Aneesa then goes on to discuss two books in relation to *Shin's Tricycle*:

> I read a book. I can't remember this title, but it's a different book. It's not the book you read. It's this girl, her mother died because there was this bomb attack. It really made me cry out because this daughter, this baby, who was just born, and her mother dies because of this bomb attack. They were going home and she was the only one saved. Her father, her mother, her grandmother died. So she had to go live with her uncle. It's kind of like *The Secret Garden* — that's in another book. She had to live with her uncle and her uncle is like a shadow in a shadow. He can't come out of this room and there's no light and nobody goes in there. He can't go in there because his wife died and he just feels like it is all his fault and everything. He had the room locked up. And that's how I feel like this person [Shin's father] is. Like, inside his heart he is locked up. He can't go out. He just keeps thinking about this thing. He feels guilty and thinks it is all his fault.

Within this speaking turn, Aneesa begins with trying to imagine her own family in a situation similar to Shin's. She then references the turmoil in Egypt and makes intertextual connections to two books. She brings all these threads together with a poetic assertion, comparing Shin's father's to a character in *The Secret Garden* who is "like a shadow inside a shadow" and "inside his heart is all locked up."

As the conversation continued, both students' speaking turns became lengthier and more inclusive of their own personal experiences and emotional reactions:

Derek: I mean, if this was a situation where my family was in the same position as Shin's family and him, I wouldn't be able to live anymore.

Aneesa: I would be like crying all my eyes out. I would want to die with them. Like now when I read these books and I think about like when the world is going to end, I just feel like crying. Like, my parents, would I be able to meet them again? Would I be able to meet you again? There's just like a dark feeling in my heart. Like, all these things going on in the war. Why can't everyone be happy? Why can't everyone be friends? Why does Hitler have to kill all these people? Why can't they all just be happy together in this one place?

Aneesa builds on this emotion to circle back to her earlier emphasis on larger questions of morality and accountability in war.

For Derek and Aneesa, the opportunity to talk together about this picturebook opened up a space to articulate a range of responses to the book and to make connections to the broader inquiry. The students seized the opportunity to make meaning together and to direct their own conversation. The prompts provided by Krista and Toni served as touchstones to provoke and give direction to their conversation, but both Derek and Aneesa also felt free to adapt the questions to their own needs. Even though their conversation traversed many different topics, the story's powerful portrayal of the pain and loss of Shin's father due to war resonated throughout.

Conclusion

Krista and Toni welcomed in their students' thoughts and feelings into the classroom as "texts" of significance and importance, rather than as asides that get in the way of literary interpretation and analysis. Across many pedagogical spheres, Toni and Krista illuminate how centering emotion complimented other key objectives within literature study: understanding character traits and development; ascertaining the author's purpose; noticing key details; identifying larger themes. The students engaged in numerous and layered readings of multiple texts to construct meaning, make connections across texts, and consider the complexities of the human condition. In doing so, their work stands in contrast to some of the arguments put forward in documents arguing for shifts in English Language Arts instruction in the Common Core State Standards (e.g. Coleman & Pimentel, 2012) toward text-centered pedagogical approaches and away from reading strategies. The graphic organizers, the slideshow activating background knowledge, and the multiple read alouds were far from the empty "daily rituals [that] increasingly have elbowed the text aside" (Shanahan, 2013, p. 11); instead, they were thoughtfully designed to provide multiple pathways back into the texts. Furthermore, Krista and Toni's efforts illuminate how students embraced the opportunity to share their thoughts and feelings as conduits for, and complements of, literary understandings. In contrast to Coleman's (2011) assertion that students engage in these types of discussions of connections and feelings to avoid close readings of complex texts and new vocabulary, the students in this classroom repeatedly attended to key ideas and details within texts for the broader purpose of making meaning. Krista and Toni also illuminate how prioritizing the role of picturebooks in this unit opened up vital pathways toward understanding on a more visceral level the experiences of war due to their visual components, the brevity of the text, and the connections students could form to characters and events that they could see, hear, and take in together as a community. Finally, as Krista explores next in her chapter, their work exemplifies how keeping the human dimension at the heart of teaching with global texts—and at the heart of her professional relationship with Toni—made possible a range of insights and learning.

Note

1 It is important to note that Tsuchiya's rendering of this event is seen as historically and culturally inaccurate by some historians and literary critics. In a comprehensive review of the controversies associated with the content, title, and illustrations within *Faithful Elephants*, Kawabata and Vandergrift (1998) point to evidence that the purpose of euthanizing the animals was not, as the book suggests, to prevent disorder if the zoo was bombed and the animals escaped. Instead, the Japanese government ordered the animals' deaths as "part of the army's propaganda effort to encourage people to prepare for the worst and, more importantly, to encourage their (especially children's) hatred of the enemy" (Kawabata & Vandergrift, 1998, p. 7). The authors go on to describe how Tsuchiya made particular choices to communicate strong antiwar and animal rights messages, themes further reinforced when the English translation included a subtitle attesting to the book's veracity and provided no mention of the numerous controversies surrounding the factually accuracy of the book in Japan. Although Krista and Toni did not incorporate these perspectives into their discussion of the book, adding in these perspectives could open up space for the development of critical perspectives on authors' intentions and of the role of myth-building versus historical accuracy within cultural narratives and historical fiction texts. As I explore in Chapter 8, reservations of a similar nature are also levied at the book *Sadako* (Coerr, 1977/1999), thus creating possibilities for a range of critical engagements with students. As Kathy Short notes, "The inaccuracies do not take away from the power of those books in supporting dialogue, but add an important dimension of critical literacy" (personal communication).

References

Coleman, D. (2011, April 28). Bringing the Common Core to life. Retrieved from http://usny.nysed.gov/rttt/resources/bringing-the-common-core-to-life.html

Coleman, D. & Pimentel, S. (2012). Revised publishers' criteria for the Common Core State Standards in English Language Arts and Literacy, Grades 3–12. Retrieved from www.corestandards.org/assets/Publishers_Criteria_for_3-12.pdf

Felman, S. & Laub, D. (1991). *Testimony: Crises of witnessing in literature, psychoanalysis and history*. New York, NY: Routledge.

Jewett, P. (2011). "Some people do things different from us": Exploring personal and global cultures in a first grade class. *Journal of Children's Literature, 37*(1), 20–9.

Kawabata, A. & Vandergrift, K. E. (1998). History into myth: The anatomy of a picture book. *Bookbird, 36*(2), 6–12.

Lewis, C. & Tierney, J. (2013). Mobilizing emotion in an urban classroom: Producing identities and transforming signs in a race-related discussion. *Linguistics & Education, 24*, 289–304.

Shanahan, T. (2013). Letting the text take center stage: How the Common Core State Standards will transform English Language Arts instruction. *American Educator, 37*(3), 4–11, 43.

Short, K. G. (2009). Critically reading the word and the world: Building intercultural understanding through literature. *Bookbird, 47*(2), 1–10.

Short, K. G. (2011). Building bridges of cultural understanding through international literature. In A. W. Bedord & L. K. Albright (Eds.), *A master class in children's literature* (pp. 130–48). Urbana, IL: National Council of Teacher of English.

Thein, A. H., Guise, M., & Sloan, D. L. (2015). Examining emotional rules in the English classroom: A critical discourse analysis of one student's literary responses in two academic contexts. *Research in the Teaching of English, 49*(5), 200–23.

Children's Literature, Media, and Materials

Bunting, E. & Himler, R. (1990). *The wall*. New York, NY: Clarion Books.

Fox, M. & Wilton, N. (2000). *Feathers and fools*. New York, NY: Houghton Mifflin.

Kodama, T. & Ando, N. (1995). *Shin's tricycle*. New York, NY: Walker and Company.

Paulsen, G. (2005). *The quilt*. New York, NY: Yearling.

Tsuchiya, Y. & Lewin, T. (1997). *Faithful elephants: A true story of animals, people, and war*. New York, NY: Houghton Mifflin.

5

RE-ENVISIONING THE ROLE OF THE LITERACY SPECIALIST AS COLLABORATING TEACHER

Krista Jiampetti

What does it mean as a Literacy Specialist to act in the role of "collaborating teacher"? Is it giving guidance, answering questions, modeling lessons, and providing materials to other colleagues? One component in the description of "Reading Specialist/Literacy Coach" as defined by the International Reading Association (2010) reads:

> These professionals, often known as literacy or reading coaches, provide coaching and other professional development support that enables teachers to think reflectively about improving student learning and implementing various instructional programs and practices. (p. 50)

To me, the role of the Literacy Specialist is also one that endures constant evolution and change. As I dig deeper into the notion that a Literacy Specialist *enables teachers to think reflectively*, I find that relationships play an integral part in the effectiveness of the Literacy Specialist. The teachers I work with may not reflect or attempt new challenges or improve instruction if they do not feel valued and heard from the point at which they are. For me, building trust, having a genuine interest in teachers as people, and initiating dialogue from where teachers feel most comfortable are the starting places that allow for the flow of discussion and ideas. I feel it is important for me to really *see* teachers I'm working with, their hopes for their students and their challenges in their teaching. The confidence gained from these interactions inspire teachers to trust in me and themselves and move forward, not only for their students but for their own growth as well. I believe it is these underlying relationships that drive the professional path of teacher collaboration and ultimately student success.

As a Literacy Specialist, I work with many teachers. With one teacher, Toni, I worked hard to build a foundation of trust and a positive relationship that allowed for constant collaboration. We re-envisioned our working relationship as a partnership and a learning opportunity for both of us. At the time I joined the global literature inquiry community, I was fortunate to have had worked with Toni previously and she welcomed the possibilities of including additional global texts into our work together. Toni and I share certain beliefs about maintaining a classroom that encourages success, such as providing extended amounts of time for students to read books at their levels, offering book choice based on the topic, creating opportunities for discussion that encourage everyone's thoughts to be heard, and promoting an understanding of why what we're reading matters in our lives. Our goals as teachers are to show students how the information we learn in school really does impact our lives outside of school and to provide students a chance to take on other people's perspectives all over the world through books.

A Place to Start

The global literature unit that Toni and I taught centered on books set during the time of World War II, which happened to be some of our favorite books as teachers. It was clear to our students that we shared a passion for these books and they seemed to feel our excitement. In front of the class, we would often turn to each other and talk as if we were in our own private book group, asking, "Did you read…?", "What did you think of…?", "Did you know this really happened?" Our conversations served not only to demonstrate our commitment and engagement in this topic but also revealed some of our goals and desires for students without handing out a worksheet or just giving direct instruction. We were models for how we wanted them to engage in the books and in discussion with each other. This was most successful because of that underlying relationship Toni and I had even before this unit began: one of respect and trust.

Because of time restraints, we had to choose carefully what we would cover within this expansive topic. One way we did this was to frame the unit around a central question: *How do the views and experiences of people around the world support the statement that "War is never a good idea"?* In order to meet the needs of all students in the class, the materials we used consisted of one novel as a read aloud, several picturebooks, historical fiction novels at various reading levels, and informational articles. Part of our collaboration included information acquired from the Grade Six New York State Common Core Learning Standards for English Language Arts and Literacy, which stated that students should be able to, "Respond to literature by employing knowledge of literary language, textual features, and forms to read and comprehend, reflect upon, and interpret literary texts from a variety of genres and a wide spectrum of American and world cultures." With these ideas in mind, Toni and I moved forward in our collaboration, setting up an outline of the unit as well as a timeline to ensure we would cover everything involved in this experience. Although we needed to follow the outline and time frame of the Common Core English Language Arts (ELA) unit, we chose to utilize the standards as support from which we would begin our work. We already had the books, the ideas, and the motivation to present this unit to students. When we read the above statement from the standards, we thought, "Oh, this fits perfectly with what we want to do!" As experienced readers and teachers, we realized we did not need to throw out all that we already had in order to adapt to Common Core—just the opposite. We were already doing great things with and for our students, so the standards reinforced and validated our concepts. I have seen other teachers hesitate to take risks and dive in to the units to embrace what Common Core presents. Our collaborative effort allowed us to take educated risks and cover all our bases while implementing our ideas.

One strategy I use with the teachers with whom I work is to "chart" the Common Core Standards to be addressed for a particular unit of study. In a two-column chart, the left side would be filled in with reading and/or writing standards specific to the unit. For example, in regards to the standard mentioned above, Toni and I knew we would utilize novels, informational texts, and picturebooks with our students. We would analyze and discuss the perspectives on WWII from people throughout the world and how it affected them. Our strengths in this area easily adapted to how the standards were guiding us and we wrote these notes on the right side of our chart. In this way, we continued to input and read the standards specific to this unit, and often there would be a standard that made us think and add to or alter our instruction. Even the first Reading Standard for Literature, "Cite textual evidence to support analysis of what the text says explicitly as well as inferences drawn from the text," made us stop and think. This not only made us think about if or how well our students could reach this standard, we also questioned our own methods and instruction in getting them there. This drove us to consider the ways in which we showed students how to make inferences and then evaluate our own types of assessments for ensuring their success.

One way we addressed this standard during our War Unit was with the use of picturebooks. We were inspired by Lester Laminack (2009) who encourages teachers to build conceptual understandings with students before tackling content. Before students even began reading the WWII novels, we selected four picturebooks that addressed the concept of war in different ways. We read one each day and used whole class discussions as the catalyst for asking questions, making inferences, and using text evidence to support opinions. In doing this, our hope was to build those necessary reading skills but also to continuously refer back to our central question of why war is never a good idea. The picturebooks helped us see war from different perspectives and helped get students ready to read the novels. The chart we used helped us as teachers to analyze our instruction and guided us to a more well-rounded experience for students, while at the same time addressed the standards in a relevant, up-to-date way.

Choosing appropriate books at various reading levels takes time and effort. Gary Paulsen shares this advice with all young people, "Read like a wolf eats" (Green, 2010, p. 21). Toni and I discovered our passion as we read World War II books voraciously. When the Common Core asked us to work with "texts from a variety of genres and a wide spectrum of American and world cultures," we saw it as an open door to exploring and experiencing books from a wide range of viewpoints across the globe. Our war unit offered books that dealt with events that affected innocent people, soldiers, animals, and the environment. What happened in the past affects how we live today. It is through our experience with books that we lived and felt another's pain, joy, and became more empathetic.

Collaborating Across Differences

Just as students have varying learning styles, teachers also have varying learning/teaching styles of their own. As our collaboration began, it was clear to see Toni and I had our own ideas of how to proceed. As a Literacy Specialist, I pushed into the ELA class and provided as much assistance and materials as I could, both to the teacher and ultimately to the students. Because I did not give grades on what I taught, I could focus on cultivating and learning about students' processes of discovery. I wanted students to build background knowledge about the time period, read picturebooks and articles, and then dive into the WWII novels. I took an inquiry-based approach and liked to be open to where our conversations and explorations would take us. Toni liked to have a set plan, not only in her mind but also on paper. She wanted to be as prepared as she could be and had to work some grading into the unit as well. Even though we both wanted the most for our students, our ways of getting there were quite different. Again, the underlying relationship we had allowed us opportunities to listen to each other and make compromises.

Throughout the unit, Toni and I worked in reminders and guidance for students about using reading strategies, acquiring new concepts and words, embracing the value of writing in knowledge making, and reflecting on what they learned. We understood each other's approach to teaching and learning, so even though we had a written plan for each day, the nature of our collaboration allowed us the freedom to stray from that if a teachable moment arose at any time. On one occasion, I found a quote by Edmund Burke in the epigraph to *Hitler's Canary* by Sandi Toksvig (2007) that applied to our central idea: "The one condition necessary for the triumph of evil is that good men do nothing." I typed the quote and posted it in the classroom. I showed the class what I found, and we discussed how it applied. From then on, I was flooded with quotes students found such as this one from *Sadako and the Thousand Paper Cranes* by Eleanor Coerr (2004), "This is our cry, this is our prayer; peace in the world." Each quote students found was typed, hung in the classroom, and added to our understanding of the perspectives from each book. It is this type of day-to-day adjustment during the unit that allowed it to grow and expand with the needs and interests of the students. Collaboration between teachers is imperative to effective planning, but it also requires the flexibility to add or change materials and instruction and the ability to listen to one another's ideas about making these changes.

Another example of the way we tried to build responsiveness and openness into our work together occurred as a result of current events. Toni and I encouraged students to watch the national news at night to gain their own perspectives of the world around them and also to make connections to what we discuss and learn in school. At the time of this unit, Malala Yousafzai, an activist for girls' education in Pakistan, was shot by the Taliban. The news reports and articles about Malala encouraged discussions in relation to our central question and also overlapped into social studies themes and topics. Often times, these discussions would emerge during social studies class and the connections students made became more cross-curricular and had more real-life relevance to them. Did our unit carry on past the allotted time frame of the unit? Yes. Did we meet the expectations of the Common Core Standards? Yes. Do we believe that students had meaningful discussions and experiences while learning about things beyond the realm of the classroom? Absolutely.

Toni and I also worked out a way to bridge my interest in students constructing knowledge together through class discussion with Toni's need to have concrete products for assessment purposes. In addition to having rich discussions about the books and the topic, we arranged for students to do some written responses that would be handed in for a grade. One of our final assessments was in the style of a critical lens essay, wherein students responded to this quote: "After all this is over all that will have really mattered is how we treated each other." We asked students to write about changes in their thinking throughout this unit, new appreciations they may have for other people in the world, connections to WWII information they learned, and how the quote applies to their own lives. Students' responses provided us with insight about their thinking, while also providing a solid and multi-faceted basis for assessment.

Loving What You Do—And the People, Too

As a Literacy Specialist, I have the benefit of working with and observing many different teachers and their interactions with students. I find a direct correlation between the reading and writing attitudes and habits of teachers to how students develop their own attitudes and habits. Toni loves to read and will often talk with her class about the books she discovers. She becomes excited when book sequels come out and she is expressive and engaged during read alouds with her class. She is an excellent writer and can articulate her thoughts and processes she goes through while writing. She sets a firm yet fair classroom atmosphere where the students take an active role in maintaining the classroom structure. When these components are in place, beginning a unit such as the one we worked on is that much easier.

During the unit, we read several picturebooks involving the concept of war, which provided seeds of thought that built our discussions. One picturebook, *Faithful Elephants* by Yukio Tsuchiya and Ted Lewin (1997), recounts the suffering of elephants at a Tokyo zoo during WWII. As Kelly explored in Chapter 4, Toni is an avid and expressive reader, as well as a true animal lover, and when she read this book she had tears in her eyes. The class listened intently. Near the end of the story, we noticed one of our students was crying as well. Toni sat with this student, consoling her and validating her emotions and compassion for the elephants. The rest of the class then began devising alternatives for the elephants, including things the people could have done differently to save them from suffering. This was not only one of those moments that could not be graded or assessed or planned for, but it also provided us a different route back to our central idea that "war is never a good idea." This time it was from the perspective of the animals in the zoo, and it was a way to develop and expand students' knowledge while revealing that what has happened in the past really does affect their thoughts and opinions today. What Toni did and how she expressed her own concern had a direct effect on her students.

Re-Envisioning Literacy Coaching: Relationships, Dialogue, and Love

A component of literacy coaching that often goes unaddressed is the type of relationship a coach develops with teachers. Here, I am not referring only to the working relationship but the underlying relationship that offers growth and development professionally because of the very existence of what lies beneath. In the following excerpt from a conversation we had with Kelly about our unit, Toni describes our collaboration, showing evidence of a trust and a devotion that only strengthened the working relationship: "We balance each other very well. We don't plan it. It's just the way we work. I'd be crushed if there was a year that went by that I didn't get to work with Krista." Wall and Palmer (2015) draw upon Paulo Freire's understandings of dialogue to illuminate how coaches might communicate with teachers. According to Wall and Palmer (2015), Freirean dialogue "is much more than a simple conversation between two people. Rather, true dialogue is the honest exchange of ideas between people who, 'by naming the world, transform it' (1993, p. 69)" (p. 629). My work with Toni was not only a collaboration but also a transformation. It was a strengthening of a bond that had its roots in common interests, beliefs, and trust. This unit succeeded partly due to the fact that there was a partnership that would not allow it to fail! One of the conditions that Freire asserts for dialogue to occur is love. To Freire (1993), love is defined as a "commitment to others" (p. 70). From this point of view, "love" was present within the dialogue and within the mutual respect Toni and I built over time that allowed the students the space and the opportunity to learn as much as they could.

Dialogue also comes at times when teachers and coaches are at a point of spontaneity. With the love that has developed comes an understanding of who we are as well as our strengths, of how we teach, and the support we give to students. When Kelly included in Chapter 4 a portion of the transcript of my discussion with Toni about one of our student's tearful responses to *Faithful Elephants* (Tsuchiya & Lewin, 1997), it was clear we had very different approaches and reactions to the sharing of emotion in the classroom. In our discussion about those differences, though, we were not reprimanding each other for acting in a way that did not reflect our own individual beliefs. Rather, this conversation reflects a comfortable space in which we could say… "this is how I felt"… and not need to be defensive. It was a space in which we could learn from each other's perspectives. Only in an environment where, in Freire's (1993) view that "love is a commitment to others," can collaboration and co-teaching promote student discovery in the ways we hoped in this unit.

What's the Secret?

Ralph Fletcher, author of many books and a writing mentor to numerous teachers and students, asserts, "Here's the secret of writing: there is no secret" (cited in Sentz, 2013, p. xi). With that concept in mind, the principles of literacy coaching are not necessarily absolute. The skills lie within each person—in order to be a good Literacy Specialist you must love your job and love the people with whom you work. You must be capable of having sincere dialogue, and you must also be willing to listen. You will come across many teachers with varying pedagogies and values, but you must not judge. Each relationship you have with numerous teachers will be different, even within the same school. You can give your advice and guidance, but you must let teachers evolve at their own pace. When you observe a classroom, look with generous eyes. Be patient, be kind, but keep the success of your students in the forefront. As far as your own growth as a collaborating teacher, find someone with whom you can work that shares your interests and your passions. Start small and take a risk. Work together to create an amazing experience for your students and then build on that in the years to come.

References

Freire, P. (1993). *Pedagogy of the oppressed*. London, UK: Penguin.

Green, J. (2010). *How bullets saved my life: Fun ways to teach some serious writing skills*. Portland, ME: Stenhouse.

International Reading Association. (2010). *Standards for reading professionals—revised 2010*. Newark, DE: Author.

Laminack, L. (2009). *Unwrapping the read aloud: Making every read aloud intentional and instructional.* New York, NY: Scholastic.

Sentz, L. (2013). *Write with me: Partnering with parents in writing instruction.* New York, NY: Routledge.

Wall, H. & Palmer, M. (2015). Courage to love: Coaching dialogically toward teacher empowerment. *The Reading Teacher, 68*(8), 627–35.

Children's Literature, Media, and Materials

Coerr, E. (2004). *Sadako and the thousand paper cranes.* New York, NY: Puffin.

Toksvig, S. (2007). *Hitler's canary.* New York, NY: Roaring Brook Press.

Tsuchiya, Y. & Lewin, T. (1997). *Faithful elephants: A true story of animals, people, and war.* New York, NY: Houghton Mifflin Company.

6

LEARNING IN THE INQUIRY COMMUNITY

A Letter to Krista

Heather O'Leary

Dear Krista,

When I was first invited to the inquiry group, I did not foresee the powerful impact it would have on my teaching and on my vision of what I could be as a teacher. I predicted it would have an impact on which books I chose to read with my students and on the activities I would plan for them, but beyond that, I was not sure what to expect. I didn't feel worthy to join the group, and I worried that I lacked the expertise to be a positive contributor. In addition, I was used to being self-sufficient since I am a "department of one," the only English as a New Language (ENL) teacher in my school. However, I found that the shared purpose, sustained effort, and genuine collegial support of our inquiry group magnified my learning. I also found that the group continues to help sustain my motivation and optimism for teaching. You, Simeen, Maggie, and Kelly are models of the kind of teacher I hope to be. You, in your role as Literacy Coach, hold tremendous interest for me and provide a positive counterpoint to my prior experiences working with coaches and observers. Your calm demeanor, kindness, knowledge, and philosophy of building trust with your colleagues and students are qualities all coaches should aspire to.

Many times, when coaches and observers have come into my classrooms over the years, they seemed to be on fact-finding missions. Often arriving in response to our school being identified as a "low-performing" school, they entered into a context already filled with anxiety, stress, and disappointment. Instead of building trust, helping me reflect on my practice, exchanging ideas, working with students, or modeling lessons, many came bearing professional texts, the latest buzzwords, checklists, rubrics, improvement plans from the state education department, and laptop computers. Many times, it seemed like their focus was on system-wide change rather than on classroom-level change. My students were often puzzled by the presence of observers and coaches in our room. They asked, "Why is he here?" or "What is she typing on her computer?" I often wondered the same things, and their visits were a source of anxiety for me. While I knew they were doing the job assigned to them, there were times when the title "coach" seemed misapplied to their positions. In my experience, sharing my classroom with coaches and observers has involved power imbalances, a lack of collaboration, and a lack of trust. This made me fearful of working with coaches.

The peace and support at our inquiry meetings bolstered me. During that time, I admit, I sometimes thought I did not have the time and energy to make the meetings, and I was not sure it was a good time to take risks in trying a lot of new things. I worried how to fit in benchmark testing, progress monitoring, district practice exams, and monthly pre- and post-tests tied to the curriculum maps. I also felt I would disappoint the inquiry group and that my original concern of not being a worthy contributor would be a self-fulfilling prophecy. However, the interaction with our group was inspiring and supportive and helped me gain some perspective and equilibrium. I often came into the meetings needing to unload all of the worries and pressures I felt. One important discovery for me began to emerge right away. What I found was that you, Simeen, Maggie, and Kelly—all amazing teachers—also experience, at times, feelings of anxiety and doubt, but you use these uncomfortable points as prompts for deeper exploration. You use challenges to push to deeper reflection and you also speak up so that situations can be improved, rather than wait passively, hoping things will change. I began to reframe my concerns and doubts and see them as possible directions for deeper thinking rather than as a shortcoming or dire weakness in myself, and I began to gain confidence in using my voice.

Krista, you played an important role in helping me see what true collaboration and support can be and what it can accomplish. You acted as a powerful counterexample to the coaching I had experienced. You build trust with your colleagues, and you root your work in cultivating positive relationships with the teachers you work with. Your relationships with teachers are long-term, a real investment on a personal and professional level. I share your belief that relationships and trust are the foundation that supports people in learning. It motivates people and sustains them through the times when learning is not coming easily. With my students, I see that they will persist because they do not want to let me down and because they trust that things will be better once we struggle through, and the struggle will have been worth it. The same principle applies to adults. Just as you wrote so movingly:

> building trust, having a genuine interest in teachers as people, and initiating dialogue from where teachers feel most comfortable are the starting places that allow for the flow of discussion and ideas. The confidence gained from these interactions inspires teachers to trust in me and themselves and move forward, not only for their students, but for their own growth as well.

The human aspect of teaching and learning cannot be discounted. The trust and relationship you and your co-teachers have is the safe place from which the forays into learning and reflection can begin and the place where all can fall back for some support and recharging. Without the trusting bond you and your teachers develop, the benefits and magnification of learning and teaching that you bring as a coach would not be realized.

Krista, you are in the work, doing the work, and sharing the responsibility with the teachers and students rather than offering a critique from behind the desk. Ideally, that is how collaboration should work with both teachers sharing responsibility and having a stake in the outcome. It goes a long way with a teacher if the coach is in the trenches along with her, helping with the work of selecting inspiring themes and the best texts to engage the students, and is sharing the heavy lifting involved in implementing the lessons and units, evaluating students' work, and thinking about what is working and not working from the perspective of someone who is in the classroom teaching. Because you are a player-coach rather than a coach from the sidelines, you know the students and how they are responding to the books and lessons. You and the teachers both support the students and figure out ways to help them progress. So many times, it seems like the help teachers get with their most challenging and needy students comes from people who have not spent much time with the student, and who don't know them as learners as the teacher does. They are a bit too removed from the situation. The solutions offered in those situations may be rooted in "best practices" but sometimes do not seem to fit the challenges the student is facing. Many times, the teacher would appreciate having the perspective of someone else who truly knows the student. Because you actively plan, teach, and reflect with the teachers, you witness exactly what the teachers are witnessing.

I am inspired by how your presence in the classroom contributes to the students' realization that the learning they are doing is important, interesting, and valuable. Your conversations with your co-teachers model the curiosity and excitement that we feel when we are really learning. One beautiful example of your participation as a co-teacher and fellow learner in the class was when you came across a quote in one of the World War II books the class was reading that resonated so strongly with you that you posted it and shared it with the class and your co-teacher, Toni. The students were obviously inspired by this because they began to share quotes that resonated with them, and the wall began to fill up with ideas that were meaningful to the students and showed their connection to the books they were reading. This example also taught me that it is good to be flexible and in the moment when teaching.

As much as being a co-teacher and fellow learner is important to being an effective, supportive coach, the term "coach" does imply a difference in perspective in that a coach offers assistance, advice, guidance, ideas, and knowledge. There is a mentoring or leadership aspect to the role. The player-coach has to take on additional responsibilities and exercise additional skill. This requires a tremendous amount of experience, knowledge, reflection, and skill on the part of the coach. The coach must have a deep well of expertise to tap into in real time, and I see this in you, Krista. On the one hand, you have the ability to see things from the bird's eye view, the patchwork of goals, mandates, standards, best practices, and the curriculum. On the other hand, you have a deep working knowledge of teaching and all that goes into managing a classroom. You understand the impact all of these aspects of education have on the teacher. During our inquiry group meetings, when I felt I was getting bogged down and my efforts to use global literature were stalled even before I got started, you were a model for me of a way to get started, and you also directly addressed my situation. For example, the Common Core Standards were in their first years of implementation, and with them had come a testing system which districts added to by creating practice tests, progress monitoring, and benchmark tests. I was feeling overwhelmed. I felt like I didn't have time to add one more thing. You see a lot of possibility in the Common Core standards, and helped me begin to tease apart the standards from the testing system. I began to see that the standards are not so limiting and that I had the freedom to choose really good books and to help my students think deeply, and that I didn't have to start from scratch. I could keep all the best things about my classroom and instruction. The testing mandates are a related but separate issue. It is an issue that is not easily changed, but I still had (and have) a tremendous amount of power over my instruction. It just took me time and reflection, and you and the inquiry group helped hold up the mirror so I could do that. Looking back, on our discussions in the inquiry group, I can see that I was experiencing what your co-teachers experience. You took me from where I was, which was a state of near paralysis, fear, and anger with all the changes going on, and slid the door open just a bit until I realized it would not be difficult at all to walk through the door.

The big changes in education and teaching continue. This year, state regulations have changed and ENL is going from a mostly "pull-out" model to an "integrated content" model where ENL teachers will collaborate in the mainstream classrooms. As with many of the recent changes, there was little lead-time, and little support in making this change happen smoothly. Yet, I have a vision of how I would like to be as a collaborating teacher because I have gained insight through the inquiry group and through you, Krista. I know I want to establish trust and personal relationships with the teachers I work with. I want to be an equal partner in the heavy lifting, and I want to be well prepared and well informed so that I bring ideas, support, and the ENL perspective with me as I become a partnering teacher and participant in the classroom learning community. So much of the vision of the kind of co-teacher I want to be, and how to be that co-teacher, comes from you, Krista!

With gratitude,
Heather

7

LEARNING IN THE INQUIRY COMMUNITY

A Letter to Heather

Krista Jiampetti

Dear Heather,

In our daily lives, as well as in our teaching lives at school, we can get so wrapped up in the day-to-day procedures and routines that we sometimes forget to reflect upon our successes and what motivates us to do more. This inquiry group provided that space in which we could all step back and see the world around us. Not only could we discuss our own projects, questions, and doubts, we also had the opportunity to go into each other's teaching lives and explore. Discussions that occur in groups such as this enable me to use parts of my brain that may not be utilized every day: the parts that help me see another's perspective and that help me think in ways that I had not before. Learning more about the role of the English as a New Language (ENL) teacher, understanding the struggles of teaching in an urban setting, and widening my vision of being a culturally responsive teacher are just a few of the lessons I learned from the amazing people in this group. I also learned that it is ok to celebrate something we've done right—there is too much self-doubt or fear of judgment among teachers.

There are people in this world who somehow always seem to be positive, upbeat, and encouraging. Not only are these people a pleasure to be around, they also make excellent teachers. Heather, you are most definitely one of these people, and I am inspired by the work you do. I'm sure there are people like me who have misconceptions about what ENL teachers and students do. Forgive me for saying so, but for a long time I believed your goal as an ENL teacher was just to acclimate your students to American culture. I thought teaching vocabulary was your main focus and exposing students to terms and ideas they might not know would help them survive in school. My interactions with you in our inquiry group, along with what you have written in this book, have educated me and inspired me to open my eyes to another world!

You must give yourself credit for the progress you made with your students. The books you chose were outstanding, and your desire to immerse your students in the literature and the concepts presented were key to their success. I love when you state that "nonfiction texts were in abundance in my classroom, even before the Common Core made them a priority." That is a point I stress with my colleagues: that we are already doing great things. The Common Core is validating what we do! You also had the intuition to know that the leveled readers were not engaging your students at all. The books and the role-plays brought everything to life and had relevant meaning and purpose for your students. This seemed to be the case when you read the picturebook, *A Day's Work* (Bunting & Himler, 1997). You didn't just pick this book randomly; you thought about your students and their backgrounds and used literature to help them see themselves through these characters. Just the fact that they stopped you after the first page to discuss reflects their engagement and desire to relate. Even throughout the book, I can imagine how your students must have felt. Your insight in choosing this book made all the difference for them!

I have to say, if I worked with you as a Literacy Specialist, I would not only be proud of what you are doing, I would pick your brain to decide what our next steps would be! My hope for you is that you continue to take risks and not follow the norm that everyone expects of an ENL teacher. Your students may not know it yet, but you will be the source through which they come to understand their lives here and merge their worlds. It is evident that the experiences you are giving them are ingrained in their minds. You may never realize the effect you have had, but I know that won't stop you from doing the best you can for your students.

Learning in this group alongside you has been a pleasure. It is no wonder you are asked to sit in on meetings and on committees, because I believe it is the smile on your face and the desire to make life better for your students that attracts people to you. Thank you for sharing your joys, your struggles, and your successes with the group—it has made us all a little richer.

Taking risks is the right thing to do with and for students. I encourage all of my friends in this inquiry group to keep taking risks because I see the outcomes and rewards that are happening!

Sincerely,
Krista

Children's Literature, Media, and Materials

Bunting, E. & Himler, R. (1997). *A day's work*. New York, NY: HMH Books for Young Readers.

8

READING GLOBAL LITERATURE AT THE INTERSECTION OF CRITICAL LITERACY AND DIALOGIC TEACHING

Kelly K. Wissman

In this chapter, I describe and analyze Simeen's perspectives and teaching practices as she explores with her fifth grade students global literature from a critical literacy stance, through dialogic means, and with social justice ends. My purpose is to illuminate both the tensions and possibilities of doing such work with students in an affluent suburban school with little cultural diversity and to tease out the complexities that emerged when Simeen attempted to reconcile the sometimes competing aims of dialogic teaching and critical literacy.

Perspectives on Reading Global Literature with U.S. Students, Dialogism, and Critical Literacy

Embedded within the decades-long arguments for the inclusion of multicultural and global literature into English Language Arts curricula are assertions that this literature can promote cross-cultural awareness, empathy, and understanding (Dressel, 2005; Short, 2009). Incorporating this literature, however, is not without challenges (Montero & Robertson, 2006). Studies have shown that in response to multicultural and global literature, some students have difficulties engaging with the books due to a lack of comprehension of the unfamiliar experiences of the characters and social practices embedded within them (Bond, 2006). Other studies have chronicled how teachers, prospective teachers, and students may struggle with feelings of resistance or guilt in response to racist, colonialist, or violent actions taken by white and/or Western characters in the books (Lewis, Ketter, & Fabos, 2001; Trainor, 2005). Additional challenges emerge when pedagogical approaches leave students with reductive and superficial understandings of other cultures (Fang, Fu, & Lamme, 2003) and when the books themselves perpetuate stereotypical or distorted representations of other cultural groups (Crocco, 2005).

Furthermore, Lewis (2000) notes the tendency of readers from dominant groups to overidentify with characters who are actually quite different from themselves, often in an attempt to forge connections with the characters, thereby universalizing the experiences without attention to the broader social, historical, and political context in which the differences matter.

In arguing for the need for teachers to work carefully to provide instructional guidance to students in reading this literature, Loh (2009) argues:

> [H]abits of the mind (Purves, 1993; Thein, Beach, & Parks, 2007) have to be *learned*, and in order to help students acquire such habits, teachers need to keep the goal in view and ask the right questions. Cultivating critically and culturally reflexive reading dispositions allows for critical dialogue to take place in the multicultural classroom. (emphasis in original, p. 293)

Given the complexities documented in the research on student engagements with global and multicultural literature, the questions and dilemmas that lie at the heart of this chapter concern *how* to promote these habits of mind and dispositions in response to global literature. These dilemmas come into sharper focus when considered in light of the particular teaching practices of Simeen, whose teaching was strongly shaped by principles of both dialogic instruction and critical literacy.

Dialogic instruction prioritizes student talk and whole class discussion as fundamental components of learning. According to Juzwik, Nystrand, Kelly, and Sherry (2008), key features of dialogic instruction include "those discourse moves (e.g. authentic teacher questions, student questions, and uptake) that incorporate, probe, and honor students' multiple voices in the classroom" (p. 1116). Aukerman, Belfatti, and Santori (2008) emphasize how "dialogically organized reading instruction" decenters the teacher as the "primary knower" (Berry, 1981) by positioning all classroom participants as knowledge-makers. This kind of instruction shifts the burden of evaluating the "correctness" and value of responses from the teacher to the entire classroom community and prioritizes multiple and contextual interpretations as opposed to one predetermined answer. As they argue, "Understanding students' thinking and purposes matters more than the traditional goal of reaching a conventional textual understanding" (p. 243).

Literature instruction informed by principles of critical literacy places a similar emphasis on centering student experiences to shape classroom discourse and on positioning students as active agents of their own learning (Souto-Manning, 2009). At the same time, practitioners working from this point of view also seek to encourage their students to question the status quo; deconstruct the assumptions and ideologies embedded in texts; consider how identities shape how texts are produced and interpreted; and advocate for social change (Jones, 2012). Rather than focusing on specific instructional practices or specific texts, Vasquez (2010) refers to critical literacy as a "way of being" (p. 2) or a "frame through which to participate in the world" (p. 2). For Vasquez, no text is ever neutral; therefore, the choice of children's books in the curriculum is important primarily in terms of how books can prompt students to consider the messages relayed to readers and how texts position readers. As she argues, critical literacy is "about creating opportunities for critical conversations and making available different social positionings for students as they engage with texts" (p. 11). For Vasquez and for many educators teaching from a critical literacy stance, children's books serve as entry points for children to engage in conversations related to the socio-political context within broader instructional goals to promote thinking and action toward a more equitable and just world. This kind of teaching often does elicit intellectual unrest, a necessary condition, as Möller (2012) contends, to pursue literary study in the service of social justice: "Educators and their students must be willing to examine systemic prejudice and privilege and to raise issues that might cause dissent in the hopes of moving to new levels of self- and group-reflection" (p. 33). As I explored in Chapter 2, Simeen approached her teaching with an explicit objective to "disturb the waters," an approach that caused some moments of uneasiness and discomfort within the students' discussions.

Simeen's efforts to teach global literature was informed by intertwined perspectives from dialogic teaching and critical literacy. This created opportunities for wide-ranging and often searching classroom discussions; however, these approaches also caused her some moments of doubt and frustration as the discussions at times lacked the critical perspectives and questioning dimensions promoted by critical literacy.

Simeen's Classroom in Context

At the time of the study, 85 percent of the students within Simeen's school identified as white. Out of the 22 students in the class at the center of this chapter, three students were students of color, including one African American girl, one Indian American boy, and one Latina. Within this school, 7 percent of students qualified for free and reduced price lunch. This chapter draws from the work I conducted as a participant observer within Simeen's classroom over a six-month time period that included observations of 14 classes that lasted approximately 60 minutes each. I also draw from transcripts from 11 of those classes, with a particular emphasis on the class discussion of *Sadako* (Coerr, 1977/1999). Drawn from the true-life experiences of Sadako Sasaki, this historical fiction book tells the story of an 11-year-old girl who contracts leukemia due to radiation poisoning from the dropping of the atomic bomb in Hiroshima.[1] Additional data sources that shape the analysis in this chapter include two one-on-one conversations with Simeen that took place directly after her teaching of *Sadako*, student journal entries and artwork, and Simeen's participation in the monthly inquiry community.

In this chapter, I present an instrumental case study designed "to provide insight into an issue or to redraw a generalization" (Stake, 2008, p. 123), particularly the teaching of this literature from intertwined perspectives of both dialogic teaching and critical literacy. Simeen's teaching of *Sadako* brought to the surface the possibilities and the tensions of supporting students in making meaning of texts that explore experiences and cultures different from their own, particularly texts that have the potential to challenge students' own systems of belief and understandings of themselves as Americans and America's role in the world.

Simeen's Teaching of *Sadako*

As I explored in Chapter 2, Simeen's lived experiences and perspectives profoundly inform her teaching practice, an endeavor in which she aims to expose students to a range of texts from multiple cultures and to promote critical thinking on students' place in the world. In interviews and in the teacher inquiry community, she often discussed her responsibility to create these kinds of learning opportunities for young people and to create moments where their own frames of reference can be "disrupted." As she explained to me, "If they don't know and they're just swimming in this, everything is just normal for them… my work is to disrupt that a little bit." Along with these lived experiences, Simeen also brings to her teaching extensive study of critical literacy pursued within her doctoral program. Simeen's literacy instruction within her fifth grade reading classes includes a range of pedagogical practices reflective of these principles, including multidisciplinary units, guided reading lessons, book clubs, and independent reading.

Simeen's teaching of *Sadako* occurred near the end of the school year. Throughout the year, Simeen had incorporated a range of literature set in countries outside the U.S. and exploring a range of social issues and world events, from child migrant workers to the Vietnam War. Simeen chose to read *Sadako* aloud to the students. During this time, students were invited to write their thoughts in their journals. She stopped frequently during the reading to ask students the ubiquitous question, "What are you thinking?" Students both talked in small groups (their desks were arranged in groups of four where students faced each other) and with the whole class. Near the conclusion of the book, Simeen also provided the students with nonfiction texts, including one piece exploring the making of the atomic bomb and another that provided students with a first person testimonial of a survivor of the bombing.

As Simeen approached the end of *Sadako*, she framed the penultimate read aloud with the following questions that were posted on chart paper at the front of the class and repeated at times during the discussion that followed: "What are our thoughts about Sadako? What is happening to her? Why is it happening to her?" Simeen stopped reading at various parts in the book to hear from students and to ask them directly, "*Why* is this happening to Sadako?" Below, I describe and analyze the students' responses as they unfolded across two periods of class discussion, with students offering their emergent responses, sometimes building on each other's ideas, sometimes taking the conversation in entirely new directions. Simeen's responses to the students' contributions are key here as well, as she endeavors to draw out their thinking, revoice their perspectives while trying not to evaluate them, and invite other thoughts and speakers into the conversation.

"You Have to Change Your Fate": Themes of Individualism, Emotion, and Blame

On the first day of the two-part discussion I will analyze, Simeen opened the conversation this way (all student names are pseudonyms):

Simeen: So, let's look at what we're thinking about [Sadako], what's happening to her, *why* is it happening? Yeah? *Why* is it happening and what do we think about that? Yes.

Jason: Well, usually, sometimes, a lot of things happen for a reason, but I don't really get the reason of why this happened to her.

Here, Jason invokes a common aphorism, "things happen for a reason," and uses it as a frame to ponder his own confusion regarding Sadako's situation. Other students also drew upon aphorisms, words of wisdom from family members, and their own personal experiences to make sense of what happened to Sadako. Throughout the conversation, students tended to draw on these frames of reference in ways that placed blame on Sadako herself for contracting leukemia and the individual choices she made. Chelsea noted, for example, "I think that maybe if she told her parents the first time when she was dizzy she might have been better. Like, when she was running, she got dizzy, but she still didn't tell them." David also considered Sadako's own role in causing her illness, saying, "I think that maybe she ran too hard and she may have gotten too tired." While David considered if Sadako's physical exertion was the cause of her illness, Tom asserted, "If I heard that they had leukemia there and that's where the bomb was dropped, I would move out of there as fast as I could. I wouldn't stay there." By placing himself in her situation, Tom proclaimed he would make a different choice, assuming the autonomy and means to do so.

While Tom and others critiqued Sadako's actions, others commented on her state of mind. One student, Sophia, posited that Sadako believed too strongly in the idea of "bad luck," asserting that instead, "you have to change your fate… like, you have to go out and do it yourself, instead of relying on other things." Here, Sophia revoices a prominent strand of Western individualism and belief in personal responsibility. Other students critiqued Sadako for not being more optimistic in the face of her illness. In addition to criticizing both Sadako and a fellow patient for lacking hope they would get better, some students also faulted Sadako for not making the paper cranes quickly enough (according to the legend described in the book, if Sadako was successful in making 1,000 cranes, she would live). These range of responses are rooted in beliefs that individuals can take control of their own lives through rational decision-making, common sense, and positive thinking.

As the conversation continued, students began to share their feelings in response to *Sadako*. To Simeen's surprise, many students commented that they were frustrated by the sadness of the book. After Simeen read aloud a section in which Kenji, a fellow patient of Sadako's, passes away in the hospital, Henry let out an exasperated sigh and said, "I can't believe Kenji died. This story is so sad." With a similar tone of irritation in her voice, Daphne noted that it was difficult for her to think about Simeen's question about why this was happening to Sadako because she "was trying to make this story a little bit happier. They're just talking about dying children. It didn't seem very happy." Daphne continued, "It shouldn't have a happy ending, but it still should be happier in it. Because, if you, like, read it…and you don't understand it, you will cry and just be sad." After a few conversational terms, Daphne then added, "I'm thinking that they should make a sequel to this book and make it about how when she isn't alive anymore, when she's dead, and looking over her family. They should do that to make it happy." As Daphne spoke, many students nodded their heads, murmuring their thoughts on the sadness of the book. Katherine agreed that the book was "too sad," noting, "Like, I can't even. I can't really imagine her parents, looking over at her while she's sleeping and then she dies." In her comments, Kelsey picked up on both the elements of sadness in the book, as well as earlier comments related to the necessity of having a positive attitude in the face of adversity, saying, "I just think it's really sad because [Kenji] died because he didn't have any hope and maybe if he would have had hope, he would have lived." The tone of these exchanges was in marked contrast to the conversation I recounted in Chapter 4 between two students who were discussing *Shin's Tricycle* (Kodama & Ando, 1995), a book in which children also died as a result of bombing. Although those students also commented extensively on the book's sadness, they did so in such a way that suggested they were engaged by the emotional quotient of the book, not put off by it.

While many students commented on the sadness of the book, others commented on its literary qualities, reflecting on the author's characterization of Sadako and the dynamics of the plot. At one point in the read aloud, after the students were uncharacteristically reluctant to share their thoughts on the book, Simeen said to the class:

> Boy, that's hard book to read, huh? What do you think? Is it a hard book to read? It's a hard book for me to read. So, let's kind of think, go back and think about, how many people felt as though what was happening to Sadako was happening to them? How many people felt like they were part of the book? [pause]
>
> [Almost all hands go up]

Simeen: So, let me ask the people that didn't feel that they were part of the book, what were you thinking? How were you, how were you reading it? [pause] What do you think? [pause] Come on, Jeremiah. [some laughter]

Jeremiah: I guess I could have been reading it as if someone was like watching the whole thing.

Simeen: So, you're at a distance from it?

Jeremiah: Yes.

After a couple more students shared, Jeremiah rejoined the conversation, assessing Sadako's illness from a characterization perspective, noting that the author was "rounding out" the character, explaining, "Well, I think she had everything good, like, the rice and the kimono. I think it's time for her to get something bad." Jason and his small group then decided to think ahead toward how the author might make choices in the plot development to add drama to the story:

Jason: Well, I'm kind of looking… that she'll have 999 [cranes] and then her life will end.

Simeen: Right, right there?

Jason: Like, right when she does the last one.

Simeen: You think so? Hmm-mm. What did other people in the group think or talk about? Elise or Alexandra?

Alexandra: We just mostly talked about that.

Simeen: Hmm?

Alexandra: We just mostly talked about that.

Simeen: Mostly about that? Like, you guys are trying to deepen the tragedy, right? Right there, at the point where she's getting there and…? OK.

In the conversation I had with Simeen directly after the class, she noted her disappointment with this class discussion, as well as her dilemma as someone who does not want to "interfere" in the students' meaning-making. To Simeen, the students' responses this day that focused on Sadako's actions, the sadness of the book, and the plot, caused some frustration as well as confusion. She had anticipated that the students would be well-positioned to engage productively in a free-ranging conversation about the broader social context in which Sadako contracted leukemia. Throughout the year, Simeen had found her students to be highly adept at asking questions of texts and providing critical insight in response to such books like *Migrant* (Trottier & Arsenault, 2011), *Inside Out and Back Again* (Lai, 2011), *Blue Jasmine* (Sheth, 2004) and *Water Buffalo Days* (Nhuong, 1999). Expressing her dilemma, she told me, "But I don't know how, I don't want to push it too much, or lead it, or just have them just say it and have them following me. It should come from their own…so I don't know whether it just needs more time or…" Later in the conversation she expounded on this, noting that she already felt she was imposing too much in this conversation with the third guiding question, noting:

For me, I thought this was leading enough, like, "Why is this happening?" But, they don't get that in the broader picture. And, I don't know why. I'm reluctant to just push that agenda on them. I'm thinking if it comes to their mind, they will question it, you know? I don't know....

As someone grounded both in critical literacy principles and dialogic teaching practices, this day's class discussion was particularly difficult and Simeen continually questioned her approach that reflected her strong interest in valuing students' thoughts and responses as they emerge. In this class, however, the students did not on their own raise the critical questions she had anticipated, nor did they discuss the "broader picture" of power, war, and America's role within it, as she had hoped.

"I Feel Like We're Linked to Everything That Happened in the Story": *Themes of Collective Responsibility and the Ethics of War*

The next day, prior to reading aloud the final chapter of *Sadako*, Simeen decided to share with the students a nonfiction first-person testimonial from a survivor of the Hiroshima bombing. After then reading aloud the final chapters of *Sadako*, she invited the students to talk together in their small groups and opened up the conversation to the whole class. In this day's class, students continued to offer responses with echoes of the themes of taking individual responsibility and staying positive in the face of adversity; however, some students began to offer perspectives that attended to the broader context of the war, that questioned American culpability within it, and that weighed the deaths of soldiers against civilians, among other considerations. Interestingly, the conversation was characterized by a darting away from—and then a circling back to—the responses that carried these more critical perspectives.

Early in the whole group conversation, Sophia offered an insight that emerged in her small group, noting, "What we were thinking is like, our ancestors like back then, that maybe like, in way, they killed Sadako." As she said this, a student in another group gasped and other students in the room turned quickly to look at her. Elise, a member of Sophia's group, then quickly added, "Not on purpose, but maybe." While the atmosphere in the room was a bit unsettled by this assertion, other students continued to share with the whole class the thoughts that emerged in their small group conversations, with students commenting on the symbolism of the dove in the ending of the book and another group asking questions related to other wars Japan participated in before and after this one. Simeen then directed the students back to Sophia's initial statement regarding "our" culpability in Sadako's death:

Simeen: Well, I'm interested in what Sophia was thinking first and I want to hear from people what...Because she made a strong statement and she said, "Maybe we did kill her." So, what do you think? What about it? Why do you cringe, Katherine?

Katherine:	Because it's just, like, thinking about all the pain her and her family went through…thinking that we killed her it's just…sickening.
Simeen:	It's sickening? What other words come to your mind? Or, I mean, how does it make you feel?
Kelsey:	Well, it makes me hope that we didn't do it.
Simeen:	Makes you hope that we didn't do it?

Here, Simeen draws the students' attention back to Sophia's earlier comments and asks them to think about them again, picking up on students' nonverbal reactions of surprise, confusion, and a bit of shock both when Sophia first spoke, as well as when Simeen restated her perspective.

When Katherine cringed and said the thought of having had some measure of responsibility for this "sickened" her and Kelsey expressed her strong hope that this wasn't the case, both girls at that moment seemed open to allowing consideration of America's broader role in the war. This thread was dropped, however, as Chelsea immediately brought the conversation back to Sadako's and her parent's responsibility within the situation:

Chelsea:	I was thinking that if she told her parents earlier, like, how she was having pains and how she was dizzy, then they would have helped her…
Simeen:	Hmm. So, what do you think, Chelsea? In your mind, are you holding her responsible?
Chelsea:	Well, kind of, but, like, not really because her parents should have, like, asked her…because, if, it was her…. She liked running. They should have asked her if she was OK.
Simeen:	So you think the parents are responsible? I don't know, guys! [addressing the whole class] I have no clue about these things. My mind is also, like, struggling with it, like, responsibility. These people are saying, "She didn't say anything." Sophia is saying, "Maybe we did it." Did she do it? Did the parents do it? What, what are you thinking?

Here, Simeen continues to ask questions, asserting that her mind is also "struggling" with these ideas. Her comments attempt to leave as many interpretive pathways open as possible, while also inviting the students to extend and support their points of view.

In their response, students again circled back to Sadako's actions. Stephanie drew on advice she had heard from her mother to question Sadako's choice in response to her illness, telling Simeen, "When you were reading that Sadako went to bed, um, I was hearing my mom, like, 'No, you shouldn't do that.' Like, my mom told me that like sometimes when you're really sick and like if you hit your head, you shouldn't go to bed, you might die." Tom made an even more direct assertion of blame, asserting, "I think [Sadako] kind of brought it on herself because she didn't use her better judgment. Because she was getting like a head-ache and she didn't tell…." Simeen responded:

Simeen: Hmmm. What do other people think? She brought it upon herself. She didn't use her better judgment, is Tom's idea. Which is, you know, Sadako didn't tell. That's a fact. In the book, she didn't tell, in the begin-ning. Elise, what do you think?

Elise: I think she didn't tell in the beginning because she didn't know it was that bad. And so she didn't think that it mattered that much.

Here, Elise adds a bit more nuance to this contention, suggesting the reasons why Sadako might have kept this information to herself.

As Simeen continued to gather multiple student perspectives, she turned to Andrew, who had not spoken in the discussion yet. His comment shifted the tenor of the conversation yet again, but this thread was sustained for the remain-der of the class period:

Andrew: For some reason, I feel like *we're* linked to everything that happened in the story.

Simeen: How?

Andrew: Because *we* dropped the atom bomb and then that caused people to die. And then caused Sadako to start folding paper cranes and so on and so forth.

Simeen: Hmmm. What do people think to what Andrew is saying? Raj?

Raj: I agree with what Andrew is saying that it is our fault. If we never dropped the bomb, then no one would have radiation poisoning and it wouldn't spread to Sadako and she would be, like, all right.

Here, Andrew and Raj echo Sophia's earlier assertions and use of the pronoun "we," yet they extrapolate on the point by specifically naming the atom bomb and radiation poisoning. These assertions moved beyond the realm of individual choices made by Sadako and her family. Sadako's death is contextualized into a broader history, rather than being reduced to her individual actions.

In response, Katherine broadened the conversation to all the participants in the war, noting, "if Japan and Germany and the U.S. wouldn't have gotten into war, then they wouldn't have dropped the atomic bomb and Sadako wouldn't have gotten sick." Stephanie picked up on this thread of the aftermath of war on indi-viduals and added, "Sometimes when I think of war, I think it's kind of immature to just kill innocent people who didn't have anything to do with the war." Other students continued to discuss these themes of the larger consequences of war yet from different points of view. These students reflected on their emotions and tried to take on the perspectives of those in the book. Maya said that the book inspired her to think about "if another country, like, dropped a nuclear bomb here, how would we feel?" Other students shared similar thoughts, with Elise noting, "We were talking about what would happen if one of *our* siblings got leukemia…We were saying how *we* would feel" and Alexandra added, "We also did, like, parents' point of view, like if we were the parents, how would we feel?" Daphne then offered, "Um, I'm thinking, if the war was still going on, and if we were in the Japanese people's shoes, we wouldn't feel good because we might have got radiation poisoning, maybe, like Sadako."

In the midst of these conversations related to shifting points of view and the innocent victims of war, Alexandra brought into the conversation an issue that would be picked up and never quite resolved over the remainder of the day's class, asserting quite plainly, "If we didn't drop the bomb, um, then the war would still be going on. So, at one point, um, the U.S. or Japan would have to do something." Alexandra both empathized with Sadako's parents at the loss of their daughter, as noted in her quote above, while also taking on the perspective of the necessity of "do[ing] something" to end the war by dropping the very same bomb that gave Sadako leukemia. In her comments, it appeared that she was able to hold in tension both of these seemingly contradictory ideas.

Alexandra's contributions led to additional conversation about the ethics of war, with students offering their perspectives on the sensibility of the choices made and their effects on civilians. Some did this through the lens of taking on the perspectives of those involved, while others drew on the nonfiction texts shared in class to inform their thinking and assertions. After a couple conversational turns in which these various lines of thought were pursued, Jeremiah then jumped in to counter Alexandra's earlier point, indicating that there was a different choice available than dropping the bomb to end the war:

Jeremiah:	It's, it's, in my opinion, it's like all *our* fault, meaning us, because we could have done it another way, kind of like, not just drop the bomb and kill like, like, an entire city, entire families. And then, to do it again.
Simeen:	So, we did it one time and we did it again. What other way could we have done it?
Jeremiah:	Well, they said in that first passage [referring to the nonfiction text shared at the beginning of class] that we read that they were thinking about just bringing in soldiers and going through the country.
Simeen:	They were thinking of bringing soldiers, that's true, in the first thing that we read. They said it would have taken maybe a million more American soldiers dying. Was it a million more or was it 100—
Multiple Student Voices:	100,000!
Simeen:	100,000 more soldiers dying. So, it was a choice between 100,000 of our people or like the 300,000 of

	theirs. What would you choose? [slight pause] Is that even a choice that we should have?
Multiple Student Voices:	No!
Simeen:	I think that's a very, uh, like, crazy question for me to ask, right? [student laughter] The wrong kind of.... But, what do you think? We, if, let's say, let's say, that we have that awful choice, what would you do? Jeremiah?
Jeremiah:	Uh, I would sacrifice our soldiers because their country is, like, a lot smaller than ours. Our country is big and we have more people in it.
Simeen:	[slight pause] That's interesting. Jeremiah is saying that we would sacrifice our soldiers because we have more people, basically. I don't know.

Simeen's "crazy question" prompted a great deal of student response and talking both at their small group tables and with the whole class. Interestingly, the question emerged from interaction with a range of texts in the classroom: *Sadako*, nonfiction texts, as well as the students' own perspectives shared over the course of their engagement with the group. After pondering this for a moment, Elise raised her hand and said to Simeen, "I don't get why we would even make choices like this. Like, we should talk it out." While many students in the room nodded in agreement and seemed to wish to extend this line of thinking, David oriented the conversation back to the exploration of the role of soldiers and civilians in wars:

David:	I think we should sacrifice the soldiers. I think we should sacrifice our soldiers because they are the ones with the weapons and they can kill. If you drop the atom bomb, then there are thousands of innocent people who get killed.
Simeen:	So, we have more weapons and we have back up, you think?
David:	Yep.
Simeen:	OK. Raj? Last comment.
Raj:	I think, uh, we should put our soldiers there because they wanted to join the army, it's not like they [Japanese people] were drafted...
Simeen:	So, the soldiers were not innocent. Is that what you were saying?
Raj:	Well, we killed innocent civilians.

While Simeen would have liked to continue the conversation this day, she was very pleased with the tenor and topics of the students' responses, telling me after class with a large sigh of relief, "They got there!" Over the span of the students' engagement with *Sadako*, Simeen was keen to elicit their multiple points of view, while also being committed to creating a classroom environment where students could explore issues from a critical perspective. For Simeen, for students "to get there" she needed to have them do so mostly of their own accord, without explicit intervention from her. This process, however, of sustaining a classroom community open to students' emergent points of view and responses, while also working toward critical literacy aims, was not a simple or linear process and Simeen was often left with a number of doubts about her own practice. These conversations were filled with what at first appear to be watershed moments—using the pronoun "we," for example, in discussing responsibility for Sadako's illness; however, these incisive comments would then also be followed by a range of perspectives that located all responsibility within Sadako herself and without a consideration of the broader context of war. The nonlinearity of knowledge construction in this context is striking, a compelling indication of the sometimes conflicting and contradictory puzzle of bringing together principles of dialogic teaching with critical literacy.

Bringing Forth a "Co-Emergent World"

Within the discussions highlighted in this chapter, Simeen kept dialogic instruction and critical literacy principles in a productive and dynamic tension. As a result, I would argue that the students came to deeper understandings that may not have been possible if Simeen's pedagogy was informed by only one framework or the other. I see the richness and complexity of these conversations emerging from the choice of an engaging narrative with a main character close to the students' age; nonfiction pieces that were carefully chosen and purposefully introduced when they would further students' meaning-making; offering substantial time to talk both in small groups and the whole group to come to understanding; the risk-taking involved in one student's first use of the term "we" to consider America's role in the war; and Simeen's patience and trust that the students would "get there" given time, materials, and discussion.

As the students had additional time for discussion, for talking and listening to each other, for considering the questions posed by Simeen, and for reading multiple texts, additional meaning-making opportunities emerged. They took on multiple perspectives and considered the broader sociopolitical context of the book. Drawing on these key principles of critical literacy, they were able to shift positions as readers of an individual tale about someone far away who may be at fault, to readers who not only have empathy for Sadako but who also consider their own roles and responsibilities as global citizens. In this way, their experiences more closely resembled Sumara's (1996) contention that "reading requires moving, locating, and relocating one's self in relation to a co-emergent world" (p. 78) and involves a "continual bridging of newly opened spaces—gaps—that make themselves present in the ever-emerging intertextual fabric of lived experience" (p. 78). Simeen's consistent request for the students to share their points of view were central to the meaning-making in this classroom but these processes were not ends but *means* toward shared knowledge building and deeper considerations of the complexities of the human condition and our roles and responsibilities to each other. In the process, there were certainly moments of discomfort and unease for both Simeen and her students; Simeen was able to welcome and build on those disquieting moments to lead her students toward deeper understandings and interpretations.

Even within these possibilities, tensions and questions persist, however, related to how to pursue this kind of layered, unpredictable, and uncertain work within these trying times of standards, accountability, and testing. At the time of the study, Simeen's teaching could exist productively in the spaces between critical literacy and dialogic teaching and she had the time and space to work through some of those tensions and frustrations for many reasons: her esteemed stature in the school, her record of producing students who scored highly on state tests, her own life experiences that strengthened her commitments and abilities to articulate and pursue her social justice stance, among a constellation of other reasons. Since this time, though, in many places, the pressures associated with testing have only increased and the interpretations of the standards have only narrowed. Current emphases in Common Core on text evidence and argumentation, as well as the increasing link between students' test scores and teacher evaluations, can constrict and undermine the creation of these kinds of exploratory spaces for inquiries of this depth and complexity that need time and trust to develop (Möller, 2012). Books like *Sadako* are rich with potential to engage students in thoughtful consideration and to weigh multiple perspectives. As Apol, Sakuma, Reynolds, and Rop (2003) contend, even more potential for critical readings may emerge in close analysis of the various—and culturally distinct—versions of the life story told about the person at the heart of *Sadako*, the ideologies that these various versions reflect and promote, and the ways in which they position the reader. In order to match this potential, though, children need fluid and emergent pedagogical spaces in which to ponder, relate, consider, and wonder in response to global texts, and their teachers need professional contexts in which to find support for their pursuit of these kinds of complex and unpredictable teaching endeavors.

Note

1 As I alluded to in Chapter 4 when discussing *Faithful Elephants*, *Sadako* has also been critiqued for historical and cultural inaccuracies and for co-opting Sadako Sasaki's story for ideological purposes. Apol, Sakuma, Reynolds, and Rop (2003) detail the resistance of preservice teachers in entertaining these critiques and factoring them into their teaching of the book, holding close to the Western ideologies reflected and reinforced in the book. As with *Faithful Elephants*, scholars of critical literacy and children's literature advocate not for the exclusion of these books from the curriculum but for a critical interrogation of them. As Apol et al. (2003) note, "In order to recognize this kind of power in text, readers of historical fiction must learn to identify the ideology at work – the overt messages and subtle agendas contained in a piece of literature. One way readers can begin to identify and negotiate these ideologies is through critical reading – that is, through choosing to read in a way that looks below the surface of a text to interrogate the assumptions and question the ideological positions contained within it" (p. 431).

While Simeen's teaching of the book did not highlight its cultural and historical inaccuracies, her efforts were directed at decentering and questioning some of her *students'* responses to the text that reflected Western ideologies of individualism, personal responsibility, and meritocracy.

References

Apol, L., Sakuma, A., Reynolds, T. M., & Rop, S. K. (2003). "When can we make paper cranes?": Examining pre-service teachers' resistance to critical readings of historical fiction. *Journal of Literacy Research, 34*(4), 429–64.

Aukerman, M. S., Belfatti, M. A., & Santori, D. M. (2008). Teaching and learning dialogically organized reading instruction. *English Education, 40*(4), 340–64.

Berry, M. (1981). Systemic linguistics and discourse analysis: A multi-layered approach to exchange structure. In M. Coulthard & M. Montgomery (Eds.), *Studies in discourse analysis* (pp. 120–45). London, UK: Routledge.

Bond, E. (2006). Reading outstanding international children's books. *Journal of Children's Literature, 32*(2), 70–6.

Crocco, M. S. (2005). Teaching *Shabanu*: The challenges of using world literature in the US social studies classroom. *Journal of Curriculum Studies, 37*(5), 561–82.

Dressel, J. H. (2005). Personal response and social responsibility: Responses of middle school students to multicultural literature. *The Reading Teacher, 58*(8), 750–64.

Fang, Z., Fu, D., & Lamme, L. (2003). The trivialization and misuse of multicultural literature: Issues of representation and communication. In D. L. Fox & K. G. Short (Eds.), *Stories matter: The complexity of cultural authenticity in children's literature* (pp. 284–303). Urbana, IL: National Council of Teachers of English.

Jones, S. (2012). Critical literacies in the making: Social class and identities in the early reading classroom. *Journal of Early Childhood Literacy, 13*(2), 197–224.

Juzwik, M. M., Nystrand, M., Kelly, S., & Sherry, M. B. (2008). Oral narrative genres as dialogic resources for classroom literature study: A contextualized case study of conversational narrative discussion. *American Educational Research Journal, 45*(4), 1111–54.

Lewis, C. (2000). The limits of identification: The personal, pleasurable, and critical in reader response. *Journal of Literacy Research, 32*(2), 253–66.

Lewis, C., Ketter, J., & Fabos, B. (2001). Reading race in a rural context. *International Journal of Qualitative Studies in Education, 14*(3), 317–50.

Loh, C. E. (2009). Reading the world: Reconceptualizing reading multicultural literature in the English Language Arts classroom in a global world. *Changing English, 16*(3), 287–99.

Möller, K. J. (2012). Developing understandings of social justice: Critical thinking in action in a literature discussion group. *Journal of Children's Literature, 38*(2), 22–36.

Montero, M. K. & Robertson, J. M. (2006). "Teachers can't teach what they don't know": Teaching teachers about international and global children's literature to facilitate culturally responsive pedagogy. *Journal of Children's Literature, 32*(2), 27–35.

Purves, A. C. (1993). Towards a reevaluation of reader response and school literature. *Language Arts, 70*, 348–61.

Short, K. G. (2009). Critically reading the word and the world: Building intercultural understanding through literature. *Bookbird, (47)*2, 1–10.

Souto-Manning, M. (2009). Negotiating culturally responsive pedagogy through multicultural children's literature: Towards critical democratic literacy practices in a first grade classroom. *Journal of Early Childhood Literacy, 9*(1), 50–74.

Stake, R. (2008). Qualitative case studies. In N. K. Denzin & Y. S. Lincoln (Eds.), *Strategies of qualitative inquiry* (pp. 119–49). Los Angeles, CA: Sage Publications.

Sumara, D. J. (1996). *Private readings in public: Schooling the literary imagination.* New York, NY: Peter Lang.

Thein, A. H., Beach, R., & Parks, D. (2007). Perspective-taking as transformative practice in teaching multicultural literature to White students. *English Journal, 97,* 54–60.

Trainor, J. S. (2005). "My ancestors didn't own slaves": Understanding white talk about race. *Research in the Teaching of English, 40*(2), 140–67.

Vasquez, V. (2010). Setting the context: A critical take on using books in the classroom. *Getting beyond I like the book: Creating space for critical literacy in K-6 classrooms,* 2nd ed. (pp. 1–22). Newark, DE: International Reading Association.

Children's Literature, Media, and Materials

Coerr, E. (1977/1999). *Sadako and the thousand paper cranes.* New York, NY: Penguin.

Kodama, T. & Ando, N. (1995). *Shin's tricycle.* New York, NY: Walker and Company.

Lai, T. (2011). *Inside out and back again.* New York, NY: Harper Collins.

Nhuong, H. Q. (1999). *Water buffalo days: Growing up in Vietnam.* New York, NY: Harper Collins.

Sheth, K. (2004). *Blue jasmine.* New York, NY: Hyperion Books for Children.

Trottier, M. & Arsenault, I. (2011). *Migrant.* Toronto, ON: Groundwood Books.

9

RE-ENVISIONING CRITICAL LITERACY TEACHING WITH GLOBAL LITERATURE IN CULTURALLY HOMOGENOUS SETTINGS

Simeen Tabatabai

It is late in the fall. I circulate around the classroom taking notes, listening to the voices of my fifth grade students who are deep in conversation. They are in their book club groups, thoroughly engaged in conversations around the picturebook, Books for Oliver (Larkin, Rambo, & Brown, 2007):

> *"I was thinking, can't he share with somebody who actually has a book?"*
> *"How strong he must be! He is very courageous!"*
> *"It is a very big, sticky situation…"*
> *"Here we have computers, but there they don't have any."*
> *"It made me sad!"*
> *"He really wants a bright future…he wants to learn."*

I have taught reading to fifth graders at a suburban school for the past decade and a half. The school is located within a predominantly white neighborhood; however, the demographics have started to change in recent years. What used to be a community with sprinkling of different ethnicities, including African American, Arab, Chinese, Korean, Indian and Pakistani, now has a much more diverse face. Within this largely affluent suburb, populated with professional and wealthy families, there are now pockets of poverty in the community. Most students in my classes, though, continue to live what many would consider sheltered lives, isolated from poor people and from the realities of poverty. When these students first come to my class, they can seem cocooned in their own comfortable realities, with critical thinking around identity, privilege, and power not a central aspect of their previous schooling experiences. Cultural diversity can also be a novel concept for many. Understanding and accepting differences, which is at the core of critical literacy, can be strenuous for students when they are being brought up in predominantly homogenous environments. Like many people, they are not used to examining their own thinking or reflecting in deep and sustained ways on how their lives and experiences are different from others. To them, their culture and ways of being are natural and legitimate, while other ways may be "odd," "strange," or "weird."

Within my students' previous educational experiences, opportunities to engage in critical literacy or in meaningful explorations of multiculturalism are few and far between. My experience with teacher-based or school-based activities around diversity is that the focus of such activities is minority students, especially immigrants and language learners rather than mainstream or privileged students. The emphasis is on helping these students get exposed to and adjust to the majority white culture rather than being a true two-way exchange. There are other multicultural activities in various forms: sometimes different ethnic backgrounds are celebrated in assemblies and festivals; parents or families may be invited into the classroom to share; different world holidays and observances may be a part of the curriculum, touched upon in class when the topic comes up in the curricular framework. These are interesting and fun activities for students, but they do not always lead to deeper levels of exploration or understanding of differences.

A Curriculum of Questioning: Critical Literacy and Global Literature

Working from a critical literacy stance, I have different goals: I want learning for my students to be more than just a set of facts that they learn from me. I want them to care about social issues that are outside their immediate experiences; I want them to question life, look at possibilities and alternatives, and position themselves differently so that they can transform their lives and their worlds. I want them to become independent and critical thinkers. I see critical literacy as a way of thinking that is rooted in the principles of questioning, analysis, resistance, and action toward social justice and equality (Lewison, Flint, & Van Sluys, 2002). In my fifth grade classroom, I build on the concept of questioning through classroom conversations as a fundamental aspect of a critical literacy curriculum that is based primarily on reading global literature. Through questions and conversation, I want my students to challenge their assumptions, to explore multiple perspectives, to look closely at relationships (especially those involving power and difference), and to reflect upon how they can take action for social justice in their world (Dozier, Johnston, & Rogers, 2006; Freire, 2004).

In a world that is increasingly multicultural and global, lack of exposure to diversity and critical thinking is a serious disadvantage. It is important for all students to have a deeper global awareness and understanding of other cultures because understanding, communicating and collaborating across languages and cultures are the real-life skills needed for today's global world and economies. Learning about other cultures and becoming able to explore new ideas and prospects make options available to us that would not exist otherwise in our lives. As Kathy Short (2012) notes:

> Many of our students gain their world knowledge through television, video games, and popular movies, many of which focus on catastrophe, terrorism, and war. Their understandings are superficial and grounded in fear and stereotypes, leading to ethnocentrism, a lack of understanding about global cultures, and a stance of pity and superiority over the "poor and unfortunate" in the world. Global literature is an important resource for challenging these views and exploring interculturalism, because it provides an opportunity for children to go beyond a tourist perspective in which they gain only surface information about another country. (p. 13)

Knowledge and understanding of others makes us question our own assumptions about how the world works and can lead to deep and lasting changes in our beliefs. Changing our beliefs is often the first step in changing our behaviors and actions to change the world.

I learned this early in life: that each individual perceives the world around him or her in quite different ways than everybody else does. I am a little different from the other teachers that my students have had. I grew up in Africa at a time when African nations were gaining their independence from their colonizing countries. My parents joined the influx of people from all over the world that came to Africa to bridge the gap in manpower resources that were needed as these nations reorganized their institutions. As a child, I remember being in a class where the 35 students all spoke different languages at home, some speaking multiple languages! I grew up in a truly multicultural environment and had to navigate differences in cultural attitudes, norms, and behaviors as a matter of course.

Because I understood at a young age that people experienced the world differently, I accepted that what was the norm in my context could be strange to someone else. Having this ability is a challenge yet also a gift all at once. I have always been naturally drawn towards global literature as a teacher: books that are set in different cultures and, more importantly, books that present different perspectives on the world. I believe that exposure to global literature is a powerful way in which students can learn to think critically as well as gain direction and personal insight for their futures in a global world. This is especially true for students that have little experience of diversity in their environment.

Because of my own lived experience of perceiving things differently, thinking differently, and being open and accepting of differences, I feel that as a teacher I can challenge my learners in ways in which they may not have been challenged before and enrich their learning experience. By using global literature texts that appeal to my students' interests and abilities, I expose them to different lives, get them to think independently, learn respect for others, and prepare them to participate more responsibly in the world. I can help them move towards deeper understandings of differences and to step beyond stereotypes and generalizations.

In order to engage the children in what Peter Johnston (2004) has called "dialogic interactions," I work throughout the year on teaching them how to listen carefully to each other, ask questions, build on each other's ideas, and disagree with each other in a respectful way. The children control their conversations and I, their teacher, act as the facilitator. Engaging in book club conversations in and of itself is different from instruction in other classes where students' goals are often to prove that they are the "best," often by dominating class activities to get adult attention and praise. Initially, it is very unnerving to my students to be in book club groups. They are accustomed to giving the answer they think their teachers want in order to get the coveted grades. Learning for them is often regurgitating what the teacher has taught them. In the interactions around books, that are a staple in our classroom, there are no right or wrong answers. The students are accountable to each other for their learning and success, not to the teacher. They learn to establish and maintain supportive relationships. They have to learn that unless they listen to others, they will not get an audience for what they have to say. I aim to create a context for respectful and mutual exchange of ideas in a very safe and non-judgmental space. The students are learning about people outside their own cultural group, and to do this, they have to work through differing perspectives of their own community. Through reading global books and talking about them, they are building their capacity to imagine someone else's life and point of view.

Books for Oliver

I began this chapter with a description of a day, late in fall, when my fifth graders were engaged in conversations around *Books for Oliver*. The class had selected the book because it is set in Africa and they love the stories that I tell them about my childhood and life in Africa. The book is about Oliver, a boy who lives with his family in the highlands of Kenya. Oliver is excited about school and the new school year, but he and his parents worry about how they will afford to buy his textbooks. None of my students has been to Africa, and what knowledge they have about Africa is limited and stereotypical. My hope was that while the setting and situation of the protagonist was alien to them, my students would identify with a child who is their age and goes to school just like them. My goal for that literacy event was that my students would gain multiple levels of understanding: they would get to explore how some of their ideas and beliefs were the same as that of the main characters and yet, how they were also so different. As they listened to the story, I hoped they would experience how fundamental and key ideas about life are interpreted in different ways in the world.

Following our discussions, the students wrote reflections in their journals centered on *Books for Oliver*. They were clearly moved by the story and had a strong sense of empathy for Oliver. Their journal writing explored the situation, behavior, and relationships of a child who was just like them but so different in so many ways. Maya (all student names are pseudonyms) wrote, "I felt bad when he saw the other kids with books. Once I felt bad when I didn't have something and everybody else had it."

The students identified with Oliver as a student, and with his hopes and desires. They felt the pain of his challenge. Daphne wrote in her journal, "If I was Oliver, I would feel scared and embarrassed. I would be scared because I did not have my books and everyone else would. I would feel embarrassed because I could not be able to learn with the other students...I got the same reaction Oliver did when he got books! I was happy, glad, and excited that he got new books!" Sophia empathized with Oliver's determination, writing: "You can tell that Oliver really wants to learn. He wants to succeed and have a bright future, and he won't give up until he is in school learning."

The students' questions and comments expanded their ways of thinking and understanding. By seeing and trying to come to grips with a new and different experience, they explored what they know or have heard about other people and other countries. Henry, for example, wrote: "The first feeling I had was a little happy for Oliver because he had such a good (yet simple) life, because when I think of "People in Africa" I think poor people with dirt huts, small and cramped. The next feeling I had was sadness that he didn't have any books for school." My students also puzzled over the differences in their own experiences of schooling and learning and Oliver's. Jeremiah reflected, "They love school. It is like winning the lottery for them and kids in America usually don't want to go to school. Which is really amazing!" David was thinking along similar lines: "What makes me upset is that sometimes kids in the U.S. don't want to go to school but have to because it is the law."

Just like in our discussion, the written reflections showed the students' thinking taking a turn towards social justice as they began to tackle the issue of poverty and the ethics and morality of having so much when so many others are deprived. Elise reasoned, "His life is hard. He is poor and they should get money because they are hard working." The students felt the interrelatedness of the human experiences and were challenged to seriously examine themselves and the contrast in their situations and environments. Katherine was moved by the difference: "I feel very sad about how their life is there and how lucky we are to live in a place like this." Henry reflected on some harsh realities: "I honestly don't think it is fair that in America we don't need to pay for our school books but in places like Africa a lot of other people can't even afford one single book." Raj pondered the future as well as the present: "I hope Oliver gets a good job so his kids can have a really good life, because I bet his kid will be just like him." Kelsey drew a powerful lesson for herself and all of us from the story: "So maybe next time you go to the store and want something, think about kids in different countries and remember what situation they could be in."

The students identified with Oliver as a student, and with his hopes and desires. They felt the pain of his challenge. The students' questions and comments expanded their ways of thinking and understanding. The students also puzzled over the differences in their own experiences of schooling and learning and Oliver's. By seeing and trying to come to grips with a new and different experience, they explored what they know or have heard about other people and other countries.

As I look back on my students' journal entries and remember our conversations, I am pleased with their written and oral responses. They have responded to my invitation to read critically. Instead of parroting literal answers to questions from the text, they are struggling with their thoughts and exploring and defending positions from different points of view. They are challenging themselves by unpacking their own privileged positions. They are tentative and learning to accept ambiguity. They are acknowledging each other's perspectives and positions. They are willing and open to changing their minds. They are developing their own questions as they go along, and they are offering tentative solutions. While I facilitate their work through my questioning, my students are doing their own thinking and actively creating their own knowledge.

Bindi!

To enable the students to consider multiple perspectives, my students and I read global literature that comes from many countries (India, Vietnam, China, Mexico, South Africa, and Japan, to name a few) throughout the year. I purposefully integrate this literature throughout the entire year, rather than containing it to one-time period or project. I want to support my students' "habits of mind" (Beach, Thein, & Parks, 2008) to grapple with multiple perspectives, to consider their own roles and responsibilities as global citizens, and to develop critical perspectives over time and across multiple genres. The students' natural curiosity about different cultures and how people live differently is rich ground to start looking at perspective and cultural diversity.

Later in the school year, my fifth graders and I read a short article by Indian writer Milan Sandhu (2005) from *Highlights Magazine* titled "Bindi!" Raj, an Indian American student in my class, had found the article in an issue of the magazine that he was reading and shared it with me. I was excited because usually Raj tried very hard to fit in with his mainstream peers. He rarely opened up about his cultural identity in class. As I passed out copies of the article to everyone, I invited Raj to speak. He shyly explained to us that many women and girls in India wear a bindi or a dot on their foreheads. He has seen his mother, aunts, and grandmothers wearing them. The class was immediately curious and they bombarded Raj with questions: "What does the word 'bindi' mean?" "How do they make bindis?" "Why do they make/wear bindis?" Poor Raj was at a loss because he himself did not know the answers to these questions!

We decided to read the article in our small groups to find out more and then discuss what we had read. Some of our misconceptions were revealed right away. Daphne wondered: "Do you think they carve them on their forehead?" Alexandra countered: "Why would they do that?" "I bet that would bleed," commented Rebecca. We read on and discovered that bindis are either stickers or marks made on the forehead by tinted powders. My students were intrigued by the fact that bindis can match outfits and be a fashion statement.

The questioning and talk, however, slowly led the class to a deeper exploration of Indian culture and religion as we read about why bindis are worn. Kelsey speculated, "Do I have a third eye?" We began to unpack the Hindu belief that there is an inner core within each of us that is the seat of concealed wisdom. It is the center point wherein all experience is gathered in total concentration; it is our third eye and that spot is marked on the forehead by the bindi. "Wow! Is that where my soul is then?" asked Henry. A debate ensued about what the soul might be and whether it is the same as or different from the third eye.

There were not hard and fast "answers," but we reached a level of understanding that went beyond just knowing facts. John wondered, "What else do they believe?" We brainstormed how we can discover more about the beliefs and peoples of the Indian Subcontinent. There were rich side conversations exploring gender roles, customs, science, and medicine, including, "Can anyone wear a bindi?" (Stephanie). "Men used to, but they don't anymore." (Tom) "Why?" (Stephanie). "Why do they/did they have the tradition of applying blood to the forehead?" (Jason). "How is it cooling?" (David). The talk was a process of discovery as the students evolved in their thinking about something that appeared to be peculiar and exotic to them at first, but is in fact the norm for people in its cultural context. We ended the class with Raj promising to bring us some bindis to try on and the students excitedly discussing what each of them was going to research online about India.

Sadako

This work, of course, is not without its challenges. It does not always proceed in an expected way. Sometimes I feel confident in the meaning we are producing together, yet other times I can feel uncertain. As Kelly explored in Chapter 8, when I taught *Sadako* (Coerr 1977/1999) I experienced some frustrations at some points in our exploration of the text. Kelly discusses the tensions that arose for me as I tried to teach from a critical literacy perspective, while also being open to the full range of students' responses. *Sadako* is a historical fiction text that I choose to read aloud to my students because it is a simply told story that is very relatable and deeply moving. It presents realistic characters in an authentic setting, which makes it very engaging. What makes the book really special in my mind is that despite its simple storyline, it actually deals with a complexity of issues, including, family, friendship, ambition, suffering, and war. Whenever I share the book, it elicits a variety of responses in my students. As always, my goal as I read aloud is that the text and the experience will promote deeper understandings and multiple perspectives. It's important for me to have my students experience how different characters deal with life problems, to develop empathy, and then to share their developing ideas and perspectives, while respecting the opinions of others.

The initial response of my students to the book is usually a deeply personal and emotional one. They express their pain and sadness at Sadako's situation and connect with her at a human level. As we process these feelings, I want them eventually to move from a purely emotional level to a more analytical level of thinking; however, this particular set of students remained engrossed in Sadako's illness and tried to assign responsibility for what was happening to her, mainly on Sadako herself. I felt the discussions were rich in the sense that my students were creating their own understandings, while grappling with difficult and scary themes of illness, death, and loss. As Kelly described in her chapter, it was challenging for the students to move beyond the character to a more contextual understanding of the issues the book presents.

I felt frustrated, more with myself in the way that the lessons were unfolding, than in my students. Facilitating critical literacy discussions is always a delicate balance. I do not want to lead my students, or evaluate their thinking in any way, or create situations where they would be responding to questions in ways that they thought I wanted them to respond. I want them to think for themselves. In this case, I realized that my students' background knowledge, of the war and the atomic bombing of Japan, was sketchy. Even though we had had some introductory discussion of the historical background of the story, they really needed more support if they were to engage in a more analytical and critical questioning and exploration of the text to tackle the broader contextual issues of power and war.

I prepared a reading of a nonfiction first-person testimonial from a survivor of the Hiroshima bombing. It was after we read that piece that the students started placing the story of Sadako in its historical context. As Kelly documented, they gradually moved to a broader discussion of the ethics of war, offering multiple perspectives and takes on the choices that were made, or could have been made, and what the possible effects might have been. Raj's comment, "Well, we killed innocent civilians" created a good deal of heated conversation. Students' reaction ran the gamut: shock, consternation, anger, embarrassment, guilt, outrage, agreement, and denial. I finally felt like we got to where I wanted to be: having my students think not only emotionally but also analytically for themselves.

Nevertheless, it was challenging to maintain the balance: to ask the questions and yet give the students the space to think freely for themselves. Many times during the course of those discussions, I felt frustrated at the way the discussion remained centered on one topic, yet I had to pull myself back continually, worrying whether I was probing too much, leading my students with my own agenda, inserting myself too deeply in their conversations, and interfering with the thinking of my students.

Despite these challenges, or perhaps because of them, I remain steadfast in my belief that this kind of teaching is vital. As Möller (2012) argues:

As educators, we must take the risks of exposing children to literature that contains historical and contemporary social justice themes, providing material that will draw out their opinions and attitudes and allow them to add layers of meaning in a trusting atmosphere where they have peer and adult guidance as needed. (p. 34)

While it may be risky, it is a risk that I believe I must take. As I create opportunities to promote critical thinking and expose students to new and different ideas that disrupt their ways of thinking, I need to be considerate and careful. To be successful, we have to build trust and respect as key pillars of our teaching. The culture of the classroom has to be such that everyone's points of views and beliefs are valued, each student can listen and be heard, everyone is accepted and people are free to disagree at times and say what they think or feel without being put down or hurt in anyway. My experience has been that rich and productive discussions around books only happen when the teacher has invested time and effort into building such a classroom community.

Pursuing Critical Literacy Teaching with Global Literature in a Time of Common Core

While the Common Core Standards have become a charged issue, I welcome their focus on a deeper level of learning. The emphasis on using evidence from texts to present careful analyses, well-defended claims, and clear information is what I have always worked on with my students. Rather than asking students questions they can answer solely from their prior knowledge and experience, the standards call for students to answer questions that depend on their having read the texts with care. That has always been an important aspect of my teaching because critical literacy and critical thinking are based on careful interpretation of texts. There are many positive aspects to the Common Core Standards, but what is of concern to me, as to many others, is what seems to be an enormous emphasis on "assessment," which translates into standardized testing. There is value in testing but not when it is overdone and used as a tool to link student performance to teacher accountability. More and more, I see schools, teachers, students, and parents caught up in the pressures of getting the right test scores. The cost of this is going to be high in terms of stress and anxiety on the part of the students and teachers, as well as in terms of time. I'd rather have students and schools spend more time on teaching and less time on testing.

Making the Unfamiliar Familiar

Sometimes we think that young children have limited capacity to think about complex situations. This is far from the reality. The reality is that exposure is everything. When exposed to different experiences through powerful literature texts, I find my affluent students become endlessly curious and very quick to express concerns about their perceptions of unfairness, as well as their empathy for others. They only need to be presented with alternatives to their privileged ways of thinking and behaving; they only need the encouragement to imagine the world beyond their immediate life experiences. I have found that creating the spaces to read global literature about the wider world and then taking the time to talk about meaningful issues can allow my students to become more powerful and more purposeful, more informed and intelligent, more aware, and more free in their thinking. Global books, and talking about these books, inspire this re-envisioning.

My passion for global literature and my way of thinking and being brings an interesting dynamic to the classroom. I am always making the "unfamiliar familiar" to them because of who I am. At the same time, by bringing the world to my students through offering them opportunities to read global texts, I am also challenging them in their thinking. We travel the world through our reading, and as we do, we look at it together with new eyes and new understandings. To do this successfully, I need to build community and trust and while that takes time, the end result is that my students feel secure and encouraged to actively seek out views, norms, and situations that are different from their own. They are open to exploring them, both to try and truly understand their own selves, as well as to see the humanity of others, which to me is the essence of critical literacy.

In a safe, inclusive classroom environment that promotes inquiry, reading global children's literature that has multicultural settings and characters can be an exhilarating experience for both teachers and students. Not only can it take us on new and wonderful global adventures, but more importantly, it can also be a powerful way to dispel negative stereotypes. Global literature teaches children tolerance and respect for others, creates pride in different cultural heritages, and encourages empathy by showing children how human emotions and feelings are universal. By providing opportunities where children have the time to talk and reflect, and to explore ideas, teachers can use quality global literature to engage students, move them forward in their thinking, and teach them about the world.

All teachers are keen to motivate students to read and engage with texts; however, taking a critical literacy approach and using global texts changes the dynamics of learning in fundamental ways in the classroom. I believe teachers need to start by rethinking the role of literacy and focusing on teaching students to use literacy to analyze our social world as a whole and form their own opinions and judgments. They have to develop their expertise and comfort level in using global literature in the classroom. This provides students with the opportunity to be exposed to different ways of life, helping them develop empathy and tolerance of others' differences. The foundation of acceptance, tolerance, and understanding for others should be developed within the safety of the classroom, so building a classroom community based on trust, caring, and respect is a first priority. Equally important is developing a repertoire of instructional approaches that focus on careful scaffolding of classroom discussions. When we ask students to push past the traditional boundaries of reading and writing and confront social, economic, or political issues through the use of global literature, we have to make sure that we as teachers do the same first. We have to be engaged in, critique, and look at situations from multiple perspectives to help our students develop a lens in which they view literature, life, and an ever-changing world in a more analytical, reflexive, and critical manner. I believe this is the most valuable lesson we can teach our students.

References

Beach, R., Thein, A. H., & Parks, D. L. (2008). *High school students' competing social worlds: Negotiating identities and allegiances in response to multicultural literature*. New York, NY: Routledge.

Dozier, C., Johnston, P., & Rogers, R. (2006). *Critical literacy/critical teaching: Preparing responsive teachers*. New York, NY: Teachers College Press.

Freire, P. (2004). *Pedagogy of the oppressed*. New York, NY: Continuum International Publishing Group.

Johnston, P. (2004). *Choice words: How our language affects children's learning*. Portland, ME: Stenhouse.

Lewison, M., Flint, A. S., & Van Sluys, K. (2002). Taking on critical literacy: The journey of newcomers. *Language Arts, 79*(5), 382–92.

Möller, K. J. (2012). Developing understandings of social justice: Critical thinking in action in a literature discussion group. *Journal of Children's Literature, 38*(2), 22–36.

Short, K. G. (2012). Story as world making. *Language Arts, 90*(1), 9–17.

Children's Literature, Media, and Materials

Coerr, E. (1977/1999). *Sadako and the thousand paper cranes*. New York, NY: Penguin.

Larkin, J., Rambo, E., Brown, D. (2007). *Books for Oliver*. New York, NY: Mondo Publishing.

Sandhu, M. (2005). Bindi! *Highlights for Children Magazine, 60*(6), 8.

10

RE-ENVISIONING READING INTERVENTION AS SOCIAL ACTION

Maggie Naughter Burns

Five years ago, I left the elementary classroom after 13 intense, gratifying, and sometimes frustrating years to take a position as a Reading Specialist in a new school building. I made many adjustments as I transitioned into this new role. Working with a new staff and different students posed a welcome challenge. Changing small groups every 30 minutes, instead of having the same students all day long, was doable. One of the most difficult aspects of this change was the loss of the opportunity to build a classroom community with the same students over time; however, I focused on building that same sense of community in the small group settings. It was different but exciting all at the same time.

When my district decided to pilot a Response to Intervention (RTI) program in our school, my experience as a reading specialist changed dramatically. Working from the premise that many reading difficulties can be addressed with high-quality, focused instruction, RTI programs are informed by a multi-tiered design to identify reading difficulties and provide proper instructional support to students. As one of two reading specialists in the building, I was encouraged to be on the "RTI Team" and provide my "expertise." Unfortunately, the way I understood "RTI" and the way our district perceived "RTI" were two very different things.

I mention my understandings and beliefs about RTI here because they reflect a common theme that repeats itself throughout this chapter: the constant challenge to my belief system as I comply with district mandates. I call this "the dance." Over my years as a classroom teacher, I had sometimes lost my practice and myself as I struggled to comply with district mandates that promised a "balanced" approach to literacy instruction that valued the professionalism of teachers but at the same time offered a pacing map, a basal series, and a requirement of "fidelity." With the RTI initiative, I felt the same constraining expectations were looming again. When the initiative was presented, my heart fell. Once again, I was engaged in the ever-present "dance" of compliance to mandates and a broader view of literacy education. This time, however, I was fortunate enough to be a part of the global literature inquiry group. This group provided support and guidance as I grappled with engaging and motivating a particular third grade RTI group of African American boys. Learning from these boys and from the collaborative nature of the teacher inquiry group took me down a path in my teaching I would have never imagined possible. The journey helped me to re-envision my teaching and see literacy as a true social practice, rooted in the experience of the students, and oriented toward social action. For a moment, I found a way to reconcile the district mandates and students' needs. For a moment, I was able to witness student success that came about from their interests and ideas. For a moment, I was able to feel like a successful teacher.

In this chapter, I present a series of significant vignettes that capture the complexities of the teaching and learning I experienced during the time I spent in the inquiry group. They encompass both my transformative experience working with a reading group of four inquisitive boys, as well as my attempts to work with colleagues in my school. They contain my false starts and disappointments, as well as my moves forward and successes. I also include a discussion of the challenges I continue to face as I keep participating in this complex "dance" and as I keep trying to re-envision the reading intervention setting as a place for social action.

Re-Imagining Texts and Teaching within RTI

Vignette 1. *A group of third grade African American boys enters the Reading Room, laughing and talking. In their classrooms they are considered "problematic." In the Reading Room, I find them compliant and pleasant to work with. They begin to read from a familiar text and I listen to them.* Rakim (all student names are pseudonyms) *says, "This book is boring." I suggest choosing another book. He rolls his eyes and sighs, "None are really interesting to me." I ask, "What would be interesting to you?" Rakim states, "I really don't know, but I want to learn about something. These books are baby books."*

In this moment, I felt like I had been hit with a ton of bricks: whomp! This comment prompted some much needed reflection on how I was engaging my students in the Reading Room. The students' reading scores were well below grade level; however, they were not interested in the texts offered in the reading program I was using. My goal was to increase their reading proficiency, but it was difficult doing so when the books in this reading program did not interest them. The students and I were all going through the motions and complying with what was offered in the lessons; however, the motivation and engagement was lacking. Each week on Friday, I was charged with conducting "progress monitoring" on all my RTI groups in an effort to ascertain if the intervention was working or not. This "progress monitoring" consisted of giving the students a one-minute probe, marking their mistakes, and recording their score on a computer program that generated a graph to show their progress. The students were made aware of the need for their graph lines to slope upward. In fact, it was suggested to the teachers they offer the students the responsibility of graphing their own progress, even the struggling students, publicly, in the classroom.

The graphs of these boys' reading progress were flat lining. My suspicion was that it was a question of motivation and engagement, not a skill deficit. Everything I had learned in my master's program was being challenged with this initiative. The one thing I knew for sure and what research supported without question was that students need a skilled teacher, well-versed in current research and practice, to meet their diverse needs (Allington, 2008; Johnston, 2010). Was I truly doing that? Was I best serving these students? Their response to the texts we were reading were at best "compliant," just like me. How could I get them to the next level while growing them as readers and writers?

Initially, I was hesitant to join the inquiry group because of what I perceived as these instructional constraints of my job. How would I be able to use global literature with my struggling readers during my daily half hour with them? Given the expectations of my job, could I pursue teaching in alignment with the focus of our inquiry group? The group, however, helped me broaden my perspective on teaching and learning. This occurred not only in terms of deepening my knowledge and understanding of global literature and the many and varied ways to use it across grade levels and curriculum but also in terms of opening up the sense of isolation many teachers feel in general. The sense of urgency and worry associated with the adoption of the Common Core and the new teacher evaluation system was minimized for me with the exposure to other teachers, schools, and perspectives I may not have experienced had I not stayed with the group.

Vignette 2. Energized and inspired by the inquiry group, I attempt to raise more awareness of global literature within my elementary school. I create a "wall of global literature" outside the Reading Room. I gather book jackets of approximately 25 global texts that I had in my personal library and hang them outside the reading room. I use Velcro tabs so that students and teachers can interact and examine them. I then create a survey asking teachers and students to share their understandings and perceptions of global literature. I invite students to choose books from "the wall" to read in their classrooms and share their thinking on the wall next to the book jackets. When I meet with teachers I make sure to mention "the wall," my lending library, and talk a bit about one or two of the books. I thought this wall can be a bridge into using more relevant and interesting texts with students. I have such a feeling of excitement about this "wall of global lit"!

Well, it looked really good. However, no one bites. Not one teacher asks for a book. Not one student fills out a survey. Every time a class is outside the Reading Room waiting to go to the Library, I encourage interaction with the material. No one is interested.

During this time, my reading teacher colleague reminded me that "change is a process." She encouraged me to keep the display up and made her own attempts at promoting the literature. Nonetheless, one teacher said to me, "I just can't add one more thing to my day, Maggie. I already have a selection of books I use in my classroom." Another one said, "These books are a bit edgy. I don't know if my parents will be okay with me reading them to the kids." Still another one said, "That version of Cinderella will be very confusing to my students. It's very different than what they know."

Even though I was disappointed in the teachers' responses, I made attempts to use global literature in my reading groups, mostly to promote relevant writing. The writing that the students did in response to these texts was rich, had voice, and reflected their own personal lived experiences. The students' regular classroom teachers, however, were concerned I was not having the students respond to specific prompts. Their focus and curriculum was not reflected in the type of engagements I was promoting.

I felt very defeated and arrived at one particular inquiry group meeting in tears. I was slowly realizing the power of the culture of compliance. This new position as Reading Specialist opened my eyes to how compliant and fearful we all were as teachers. With a different vantage point, I had come face to face with the culture I had lived for almost 15 years. Compliance came first. Most often, there was time for nothing else. How could I become more of a change agent and help teachers and students see that there was a way to be compliant but also more instructionally relevant? I would have to do it myself. My inquiry group was extremely supportive. Each member quietly listened and offered suggestions for how I could support our goals to incorporate more global literature as well as challenge this culture of compliance with a more student-centered approach to literacy in the intervention setting. The conversation helped me to not only open up to things I may not have thought of on my own, but more importantly, it enlightened me to the power of listening. The group had listened and because of that they were able to make informed suggestions. Maybe, I thought, if *I* listened more to *my* students, my instruction could be more relevant.

I reflected on the feedback and suggestions from the group as well as my feelings of constraint, and I realized that there was a lot more within my control than I had thought. Over time, I realized that although I did not have the same kind of control over my curriculum that others in the inquiry group had, I did have control over the decisions I made within my school's reading program. I had choices within my implementation of the Fountas and Pinnell Leveled Literacy Intervention (LLI) System in terms of the texts, the delivery, and the approach. Upon examining the texts included in the intermediate LLI Kit, I found there were many that reflected multiple perspectives, cultural differences, and social action.

I decided to make some changes. First, I decided to choose texts that reflected global perspectives and that matched my students' reading levels. Next, I decided to listen more and talk less. When I did talk, I focused on asking more open-ended questions in an effort to get the students thinking about the text. Lastly, I decided that I would respond to students' questions with questions in an effort to construct a possible answer in collaboration with them, instead of giving over the information.

Armed with my new perspective, I was eager to see how my third grade boys would respond to a particularly compelling text (Morrow, 2013) describing one man's efforts to bring books to kids in rural parts of Colombia, South America.

Vignette 3. *I begin the lesson with a book introduction. "Today we are going to read a text that is a bit different from the others we have been reading," I state cautiously as I hand out the books to each student. "This is a non-fiction text about a man named Luis Soriano who brings books to children in rural communities in Colombia, South America on his two donkeys, Alfa and Beto. The text is called, "Alfa and Beto: The Biblioburros." All four boys look up at me. Rakim responds, "This is real? It really happened?" I reply, "Yes, this is a true account of what Luis Soriano does every day of his life." The boys immediately open the book and begin to read. Trying to remain true to my intentions, I don't say another word and observe and listen.*

The boys are reading and reacting verbally and non-verbally to the text. Jamal's mouth drops open and his eyes widen. Rakim blurts out, "What!!!?.... Where is this?.... Wait a minute. He rides a donkey!" Shaking Michael's shoulder, Eric exclaims, "He broke his leg!.... Wait until you get to this page and it tells you how.... You have to get there.... Are you there?" I watch the boys engage and encourage each other to keep reading to find out more. They are keyed into each other in a way I have not witnessed before. Usually they are looking to me to confirm or explain aspects of the text. Now it is like I am not even there. They continue to question the text out loud, to each other, confirming, refiguring, and debating. I feel like an intruder! It is as if they are constructing their understandings with each other with no thought or need for approval.

I am awestruck. They look to me with their own sense of awe. I hesitate, then ask, "What else are you thinking?" They wonder, taking turns without interrupting each other: "How do people live without school or books? How come some kids don't get to go to school and learn to read? Where is Colombia, South America? What is it like? Does Luis always ride the donkeys to get the books to the kids?" I do not reply immediately after each question since there is another question on its tail. Then I wait.

Michael asks, "Do we have time to read it again to see if we missed anything?" He had never asked this before. I can only utter, "of course!" They are riveted by the diversity of the culture and the economic context. They stop on certain pages and examine the pictures. Eric states, "See here, there are no houses. It's like the country, but it looks different." Jamal adds, "Look at the rocky roads the donkeys have to walk on…maybe they tripped and that's how Luis broke his leg." Rakim reminds the other boys, "It tells us right here how he broke his leg, see?" I do not interrupt, or try to explain anything until they ask it of me. I remain an observer allowing them to move through the text independently and with each other.

Our inquiry group had opened me up to some new ideas about how to work within what I perceived as confines; however, I was slowly starting to realize the confines were of my own making. Making the choice to follow the sage advice of my fellow inquiry group members, all seasoned teachers, facilitated a learning experience for my reading group they had never had before. I opened up, and therefore the students opened up. I quieted down and listened and they shared more of their thinking. Understanding more of their thinking helped me to structure a more meaningful and engaging experience with the text as we moved forward. Suddenly, I felt more like a teacher and less like a drill sergeant.

Inspired by the boys' enthusiasm and their questions, I began to incorporate a range of resources and texts beyond the LLI Kit. I realized I needed to include multigenre texts and resources in order to support their inquiries. The next time we met, I presented the boys with two online resources. The first was Google Earth. In this mini-geography lesson, we used the site to find South America, Colombia, and other small towns in this country. The boys wanted to explore the location of Colombia in relation to our city. Even though none of us had much experience with Google Earth, we negotiated the site together. The boys took turns using the mouse and navigating the site. We zoomed in to see the countryside and get a greater sense of Luis's travels.

I also brought in a video I found on Luis and his biblioburros. This made the text even more real to them. The video includes many images that are part of the text but that are presented in real time. The students heard Luis speak in Spanish, with subtitles in English. They asked me to slow the video down so they could read the subtitles. They also asked me to replay it because they did not want to miss anything. They were riveted by the landscape, the language, and the differences in the experiences of the children and lifestyle in rural Colombia.

Their interest and enthusiasm helped sustain me as we created this curriculum together in response to their questions and wonderings. I worried about making sure the resources and texts I was presenting the students were authentic, engaging, and supported their purpose, which was also evolving. I had truly never taught by responding in real time and in collaboration with the students. As scary as it was to me, it was also invigorating, challenging, and exciting. We all looked forward to every session and what it would bring up for all of us. We problem solved together and moved forward each day. The boys also read other versions of the text and became more aware that Luis was well known enough to have picturebook authors (Winter, 2010) write about him. They became more and more inspired by Luis.

Vignette 4. *Rakim looks me straight in the eye and says, "Mrs. Burns, these kids…they don't seem to have much, not even a school. That's pretty sad. It seems like these kids are really poor." Eric adds, "What do they do during the day if they don't have school? It doesn't even look like they have a playground or anything either." I explain, "Their country is very poor and it is hard for these small rural communities to build and maintain a school. Luis knows how difficult it is for children in these communities to get access to books, that is why he is doing this work."*

Rakim states, "We have to help. Can we send our books to him to give to the kids?" Eric jumps in, "Yeah, we can get our old books and books we have at home and we can get books we already have read here at school and collect them for Luis and then send them to him! Then the kids will have more books!" Jamal responds excitedly, "We could have a book drive and ask all the kids at school to bring their books and maybe we could ask the principal if he could help us buy some books for the kids. We have so many books here at school Mrs. Burns! Can we send the books to Luis?"

I am amazed by their compassion and thoughtfulness, but know we probably cannot send books to Luis. I explain, "Boys, I am so impressed by your ideas to help Luis and give the kids books. I think it is a fabulous idea, but it will cost a lot to send heavy books to South America. We may have to find another way to help Luis. Can you think of something else we might do to help?" Eric asks me, "Can you email him and ask him what he needs?"

After our conversation, I emailed Luis's organization and received a prompt response that they accept monetary donations so that Luis can buy the supplies he needs for the library. I also found another video of Luis giving a tour of the library and his school that he manages when he is not delivering books and shared it with the boys.

Vignette 5. *"Luis wrote back!" Rakim exclaims. "That is so cool. So, he needs money. How can we make some money for him, guys? What can we do?" Eric shouts, "We can have a penny harvest! Like we did last year, remember? We can get those jars and collect pennies then roll them and send the pennies to Luis for the books. Everyone always has pennies." Jamal interjects, "Pennies, that's only one cent. We need more than that. How about quarters? Most kids have quarters and our moms usually have quarters…." Michael says, "Dollars would be too much. My grandma hangs on to her dollars. People these days…money is tight, but quarters might work. What do you think, Mrs. Burns?"*

I tell them I think they have a great idea, adding, "Let's start thinking about all the things we will need to do in order to have this fundraiser." Jamal asks, "Can we email Luis back and let him know we are having a fundraiser for him?" Eric interjects, "Wait, let's see how much money we get then let's send him an email telling him everything."

During the following weeks of RTI, the boys were involved in a myriad of engagements centered on their social action project. They had conversations and debates over how to proceed with their fundraiser: how to get the word out, how to collect the money, how to keep people interested. Once they solidified their plan, we made a list of action steps to help them stay on track and meet deadlines. I witnessed a growing sense of agency in all four of them. They were walking taller and happier, they had a sense of purpose, and they were moving forward. My sense of agency as their collaborator was growing as well. I liked this new role of listener, facilitator, coach. We were all working together to help others and everyone was benefitting. The way the boys talked to each other was also changing. They were less competitive and more trusting. They noticeably checked in with each other as they moved forward in the project. Our reading group became structured around our action items, which the boys prioritized, in order to make the most of our time together to complete them. My fear and concern about creating the curriculum as we experienced it was replaced by a sense of accomplishment each time we checked an item off our list.

A Social Action Project Promotes Authentic Literacy Practices

Many of the engagements the students instigated as part of this project involved reading and writing. Three such engagements specifically involved getting the word out about their project to the principal and the student body.

Writing a Script

The first engagement involved crafting a "script" to read at our school's Morning Program to present the project to the school community. The boys worried that if they were to just talk off the cuff, they would forget some important information. They brainstormed information they should include in the presentation. They considered reading the book about Luis to the audience, providing information about Colombia, and sharing how Luis traveled on his donkeys to distribute the books. The boys quickly realized, however, that they would have a limited amount of time and they were confused about how to pull together the information into a script. I introduced the concept of "audience" to the boys and invited them to consider who they were writing the "script" for. Once they wrapped their heads around the idea of "audience," they began to work together more collaboratively to create their script, debating what to add or take away, what to say, and how to say it. The conversations were lively and enthusiastic. They wrote their draft on poster paper and revised it together. Then they asked me to type it on the computer so they could practice. The boys were very much aware that they were known as "struggling" readers in their school, even telling me they had to work on their "fluency" if they were going to speak at the Morning Program. Even though they worried about possibly embarrassing themselves in the presentation, they were more concerned that any problems in their reading might result in raising less money for the children in Colombia. We decided we would use our RTI time to practice. This process was not always smooth or easy, but the kinds of literacy practices we were engaged in were authentic and were for a particular purpose; this purpose made all the difference.

> Vignette 6. Rakim says to me, "I want to practice out loud and have you listen to me. Maybe then you can help me fix my mistakes." I offer, "What if I record you and you can all listen back to the recording and share with each other how you thought the reading sounded? We can use our fluency card to help us stay on track." The boys all agree they would like to be recorded. We begin practicing at the beginning of each of our sessions using the fluency card as a guide.
>
> When the students hear themselves they are stunned. They begin to comment on their own reading and the reading of each other in less than complimentary ways. They urge the speaker to "speak louder" and "read faster" and "try harder." They are impatient and frustrated with each other. I can hear the exasperation in their voices. I sense them becoming more self-conscious than they have been. They cast their eyes down as they respond to each other and Rakim starts rolling his eyes after their practices.
>
> I decide to address the negativity. I ask, "How does it feel when someone gives you a negative comment about your reading?"
>
> "It feels bad and makes me not want to practice anymore," says Eric.
>
> "I feel bad telling these guys to sound louder, but we have to be good for the school. We want to do a good job," Rakim says, looking down at his script. "It's frustrating!"
>
> I ask the boys, "Have you ever heard of feedback?"
>
> They all nod their heads no. I explain the concept of feedback to the boys as one that is more supportive and less critical. I suggest to them that they listen to each other then share something they liked about the reading with the reader first. After they have complimented the reader, I encourage them to offer the reader a suggestion for improvement, giving the reader the reason why. I offer the fluency card again as a resource and aid for this feedback. We practice the script and use the feedback loop. I write COMPLIMENT and SUGGESTION FOR IMPROVEMENT on the white board as a reminder for all of us to start with the positive.

The combination of audio recording, reading, and giving feedback prior to the public presentation brought the student's performance to another level. They immediately began to improve their parts in the script. The reading became more automatic. Each time they practiced they became more fluent, expressive, and confident. Each time they gave feedback, they made sure to begin with the positive, look the speaker in the eye when they spoke, and use the fluency card as their guide. Each time they read they had an authentic sense of purpose. More importantly, they were happier, less anxious, and more positive about their progress. Every day Rakim was sure to remind us all, "We just keep getting better every day." They adopted a true "can do" attitude that seeped out into their day. Their teachers commented on their more positive attitude. They were more engaged in their classrooms. They were happier in school.

Composing an Email

Once the script was complete, the boys realized they had not asked the principal for permission to engage in the fundraising and felt they should ask him. One of the boys asked if they could use my email account to send an email from the group to our principal. They then began to craft this email. One of the boys suggested using their script as the email since it had all the important information in it. I supported their decision as they attempted to do this. When they read it over, though, they felt it did not sound right. This gave us another opportunity to discuss the concept of "audience" and how different audiences require different writing. We talked about how writing to the principal in an email was different than writing a script to present to the student body. Rakim said, "He is the boss of the school. We have to be even more respectful…we also have to convince him that this is a good idea." Eric stated, "it can't be as long as our script, because he is a busy man." The boys decided to use the script as a guide, and began to craft the email. As they worked on both pieces, they worked to choose their words carefully, they reread their writing before they wrote more, and they listened to what each other had to say. It was truly amazing how empowered the boys felt as they created these writing pieces together in a collaborative way. What added to this feeling of empowerment for them was the validation the principal gave them when he immediately responded to their email and followed up with a visit during their RTI time to discuss the project with the boys.

Creating Posters

The boys also wanted to create posters to advertise their project. They felt the posters would serve as important reminders for students to bring in their quarters. The boys requested I print out various size pictures of quarters for them to place on their posters. They thought a big quarter as a visual would also help the student body remember to bring in their quarters. The concept of "audience" came up again. Eric noted, "We can't put everything we wrote in our script on the poster…there has to be less words." Jamal said, "We HAVE to put *Quarters for Colombia* on our poster… that has to go on." Michael added, "Let's put 'bring in your quarters for Luis and the kids in Colombia.'" Eric added, "It's different than a script. It has to give important information but not tell EVERYTHING."

The boys debated on the wording for their posters and agreed on a standard tag line of "Quarters for Colombia." They each made a mock-up of a poster they wanted to create and engaged in conversation using the structure of the feedback loop, without my suggestion, to revise their posters. They asked if they could have some friends help them make posters as well. They were concerned with getting posters on each of the three floors of the school building in all the most trafficked places. We dedicated two times at the end of the school day for poster making. They edited their poster mock-ups and reminded their friends of correct spelling and capitalization during our poster making sessions.

Persevering Through Obstacles

The boys had built up great momentum and dedication to their project but had yet to present the idea to the student body. Unfortunately, state testing presented a barrier for a two-week window during our planning and action step period. This was very frustrating to the boys and to me as our school climate became hyper-focused on the testing schedule. The boys were on a positive trajectory with this social action project. They were engaging in real-life literacy experiences for a real purpose. They were becoming aware of the reasons to write for various purposes; they were considering their audiences for these purposes; and they were growing a sense of agency as thinkers, contributors, and citizens. They had begun to see themselves as change agents. Their increased confidence and motivation was contagious. I was worried this momentum would be compromised with this loss of time. Would we all be able to get back on track?

Fortunately, we were. With purpose comes resilience and motivation. The boys arrived back after their two-week hiatus ready to work. They walked in, flipped the chart paper back to their action list, took out their scripts, and asked me to cue up my phone so I could record them practicing their script. Now it was May. We had less than two months of school to raise money for Luis and there would be many activities and celebrations during that time. We had to get going.

Vignette 7. *Finally, it is our time to present at the Morning Program. The entire elementary school, grades K-5, has gathered in the school gymnasium to celebrate the social and academic achievements of all members of the school community. The boys, excited and nervous, stand in front of students, teachers, parents, and community members ready to present a social action project they designed after engaging with an inspiring text in their reading group. They have spent the past few weeks crafting their "script," making and labeling collection jars, and creating reminder posters to present to the student body who, they are certain, will help them realize their goal. Large plastic jars line a large folding table, while a Prezi slide show projected on a wall behind them helps illustrate their points.*

The boys begin to speak to their peers about raising money for children in rural Colombia, South America, who have no schools or books. They smile as they take turns passing the microphone to each other as they proudly explain their project to the school community. When they are done speaking, they excitedly hand out the jars to each class that will be used to collect money for their cause.

Over the next few weeks, the boys became the "go-to" for students' questions about their fundraising project. Their teachers asked them to explain the project in more detail to their classrooms. The boys brought the book about Luis and other versions of it to their classrooms to share with their peers. They showed the video to their classes. They asked me to explain the "feedback loop" to their teachers and they wanted their other teachers to utilize the practice of audio recording in their classrooms. The boys were noticeably confident as they checked and collected the jars and prepared to count the quarters on the last day of the fundraiser.

Vignette 8. *The boys meet with the principal to share how much money they have raised.*

Rakim:	*Mr. Smith, you are not going to believe how much money we raised for the kids in Colombia!*
Eric:	*We have so many quarters…*
Jamal:	*It was hard to count them all…it was a lot.*
Mr. Smith:	*Well, how much money is it?*
Rakim:	*Can I tell?*
Michael, Eric, and Jamal:	*Sure…sure.*
Rakim:	*Four hundred dollars even!!!! Can you believe it?!*
Mr. Smith:	*Wow! Boys, you really did it. You should be so proud of yourselves! You are helping so many kids to read. How do you all feel?*
Rakim:	*Great! So great! I can't wait to tell my grandmother!*
Eric:	*I can't believe how much we got. Can we tell the kids at the next Morning Program?*
Mr. Smith:	*Sure. Do you want to write up another script?*
Jamal:	*No, we just want to say it.*
Rakim:	*We just want to say what we did and how much money we raised. Can we just have the microphone and do that? We don't have to say as much as we did the first time. We just want to thank the kids who brought in all that money.*
Mr. Smith:	*Sounds great to me.*

This group of third grade boys came to me in February with little sense of agency or identity as readers and writers. Thinking about others and taking action to help those less fortunate empowered these students to think beyond themselves. While they were doing this, the constraints and compliance we all felt initially fell away as we all realized the possibilities within and before us. The teaching and learning became less restrictive as purpose and intention drove our work.

Vignette 9. *It is June. The boys stand in front of the entire student population at the outset of the monthly Morning Program. They are smiling from ear to ear, dancing back and forth from one foot to the other, and anticipating their big announcement. The moderator introduces them at the outset of the program, "Today we have our third grade boys back to report on the results of their Quarters for Colombia fund drive to raise money for books for kids in Colombia, South America. Boys."*

Rakim takes the microphone, clears his throat, looks down, looks at the other three boys, and then at me, smiles nervously, and pauses, "We just wanted ya'll to know that you helped us raise $400 in quarters for the kids in South America!" A round of applause ensues and the boys raise their hands in the air in victory. They stay in their places after the applause ends. The moderator comments on their success and shakes each one of their hands. The boys leave the stage beaming.

I am constantly searching to find ways to remain positive and to see the possibilities and lessons through my life experiences. My chosen profession, teaching, provides a constant challenge to this innate human desire. When a teacher goes to work, she will engage with a varied host of individuals all trying to find their way. Our public educational system does not always consider our students first. Our teachers, as a reflection of this, get caught up, in "the dance." I got caught up in "the dance." These boys, this project, and my inquiry group, helped me to step out of "the dance" and re-envision the possibilities for my own teaching and more importantly, the learning of my students. That June, the boys and I all felt happy, successful, and embodied a sense of purpose we had not felt before at school. As a side note, each student increased their fluency and went up a reading level during the course of this project. Their writing stamina increased, as well as their awareness of proper grammar, spelling, and punctuation.

If I had not opened myself up to my inquiry group and took the time to reflect on my practice, my students, and our real purpose, this experience would have been much different. This experience was a gift to me. I was able to see, if I had the courage, I could step away from the culture of compliance swirling around me to truly focus on the lived experiences and human desires of my students.

With that said, I must admit there are many things I would do differently. I cringe when I read over this chapter and think, "Another teacher is going to notice what I missed here" or, "I should include this piece because teachers will think I forgot to do this or that…" I have to stop myself and know that nothing is perfect. These experiences, and these lessons, provide feedback for the next experiences and lessons. One of the most important takeaways at this point, to me, is to be mindful of what I say, how I say it, and when I say it to students and teachers alike. Listening is something I continue to work on, as it has become a way to learn the most about people.

Continuing "the Dance"

It all sounds so inspiring, and it was. However, the challenge of remaining positive, of seeing the possibilities in students and in the learning, remained and has
continued to elude me since that June. I took the lessons I learned and moved
forward, but it was not easy. I still have to do "the dance." I have to trust district
initiatives made in the name of strengthening our structures so that all teachers
and students are supported. I am able to see now how this process of change takes
time, and I continue to work on my patience.

After that June, our inquiry group members continued to stay in touch, but
we did not meet as formally or as consistently as we had before. We took a pause
in our meetings as our grant ended and we were all feeling overwhelmed with
the impending changes in our respective districts. The RTI plan in my district
morphed yet again and with that, more changes to our schedule, our instructional
delivery, and our focus. As my school district grappled with the complicated
process of implementing many new required initiatives, I once again became
enmeshed in the culture of compliance. This was a tough place to be after having
such success the year before with the third grade boys. There were many tasks we
were charged with as reading teachers that went beyond instructing the most
struggling students. It was overwhelming to say the least. Without the support of
the inquiry group, I was a bit lost. I needed the validation of my belief system, if
it was only monthly, from professionals who shared that belief system and could
support me as I worked to actualize it. Compliance took most of my time. I
found it difficult to be a good listener, a coach, a collaborator. I found myself
trying to get the tasks charged to me done so I could spend more time doing
those things I valued; however, there never seemed to be enough time. The year
moved very quickly. Finally, something happened to snap me out of it.

> Vignette 10. *Three fifth graders enter my reading room. My back is to them as I
> call up their class list on my computer. I turn to see them sitting at the reading table.
> Now their backs are to me. They turn to meet my gaze. I give them the low-down:*
> *"So today I will be giving you three passages. You will read each one for one
> minute. At the end of a minute, I will tell you to stop. We will then go to the next
> passage, which you will read for a minute, then I will tell you to stop. Then we will
> begin the last passage. If you come to a word you do not know, I will tell it to you.
> While you wait for your turn, you may read a book that you have brought or choose
> one from the table. Please make every effort to remain quiet as I test your classmate.
> Each one of you deserves the best conditions so you do your best. Are there any
> questions?"*
> *The students shrug and begin looking at the books. I call the first student over to
> my computer. As I get ready to begin, I glance back at the other two students. One
> of the students, a girl, is just sitting at the table looking at the board. She does not
> have a book. She has not chosen a book. I say, "You need to be reading quietly*

while I give Shaveh this test." She looks at me blankly. I say again, "Did you bring a book with you?" Another blank stare. I ask, "What is your name?" She continues to look at me. Now I am frustrated and concerned with the time this is taking. One of the other students pipes in, "Mrs. Burns, she does not speak English. She probably does not understand you." I hold up a book. "Why don't you have a book in front of you?" She looks at me again and holds up her right arm, which is out of my line of vision. There is a cast on it up past her elbow. I stop, get up, and go sit next to her. "Hi, I am Mrs. Burns. What is your name?"

I can't even believe I have done this. I am so bent on getting these probes complete, a task I loathe, that I forget about being human! I am so disappointed in myself, but more concerned at this point with this unfamiliar English Language Learner student sitting in front of me. I make an attempt to talk to her and convey my apologies. The other student present is able to translate for me. We sit for a few minutes while this young girl explains, through the student translator, how she broke her arm.

Later, the translator explains to the young girl what we will be doing with the passages. She looks at me and says in English, "I don't know a lot of English." I smile and assure her of my help in the task. Yes, I have to conduct this one-minute probe even though she knows very little English. We stop after she makes 10 errors. She asks if she can borrow one of the picturebooks she has seen on the table. It is called Golden Domes and Silver Lanterns *(Khan & Amini, 2012). I ask her what she likes about it. She says, "It reminds me of home." She takes the book.*

Is it really because I do not have the inquiry group that I have struggled since the close of that year with my third grade boys? Is it because I do not have that sounding board, this more objective view, these varied experiences to draw from in my times of doubt and confusion? Do I truly need other outside professionals to help me remember my intentions and beliefs about learning and kids? I say yes. I say, for me, I need a group of trusted professionals to bounce ideas off of, to ask advice, to investigate new texts, approaches, and engagements. I need a structured, scheduled time, and committed teachers who want to take this time so I can develop and evolve.

My dissatisfaction with the issues that surround compliance often distracted me from the true work I needed to do with my students. It made me feel powerless, afraid to try something new, and constricted. Even as I grappled with issues of equity and social justice as it relates to the system of education and the practice of teaching, I realized that my students also grapple with a curriculum that marginalizes them and an educational system that makes assumptions about them and their families. I decided I needed to move beyond my own paralysis and provide my students with experiences that supported their thinking, their learning, and ultimately their evolution as human beings. Focusing on equity and social justice issues in the intervention setting provided me a way to bring more critical thinking and action into my teaching.

Even though I have not engaged students in another project like "Quarters for Colombia" again, my teaching has incorporated various engagements and texts that

I might not have even considered before I joined the inquiry group, especially with English Language Learners. Our school has one of the highest English as a New Language (ENL) populations in our district. These ENL students come from many Spanish speaking countries, the Middle East, and Southeast Asia. Their cultures are as varied as their English proficiency. Many students are victims of war, or are refugees, or have experienced extreme poverty and oppression. They often do not want to share their experiences and tend to assimilate by adopting more American ways. Working with the ENL students can be challenging due to the language barrier; therefore, picturebooks and drawing became valuable teaching and learning tools. To further engage and motivate the students, I create opportunities for students with more proficiency to translate for others with less. Taking a risk with these students and stepping out of the traditional ways of working in the intervention setting has enlivened my teaching again. It is certainly not a perfect process, but I continue to tweak, reflect, and create new ways of working with students despite my discomfort and fear of acting out of compliance. Had I not learned so much from the boys in the "Quarters for Colombia" project, I would not have been able to allow myself to teach in these more responsive ways. That experience has moved me forward, although it is a rocky road.

We are never done learning as teachers. Every day is an opportunity to learn more about our students, ourselves, and our practice. That is the gift that keeps us moving forward. I am grateful to have had this opportunity to reflect and learn about myself and my students through writing about this experience. It has brought me to another level of awareness that I hope will positively impact my students and bring more social justice work into my intervention setting.

References

Allington, R. L. (2008). *What really matters in Response to Intervention: Research-based designs.* New York, NY: Pearson.

Johnston, P. J. (Ed.). (2010). *RTI in literacy: Responsive and comprehensive.* Newark, DE: International Reading Association.

Children's Literature, Media, and Materials

Khan, H. & Amini, M. (2012). *Golden domes and silver lanterns: A Muslim book of colors.* San Francisco, CA: Chronicle Books.

Morrow, P. (2013). Alfa and Beto: The biblioburros (abridged version). In I. C. Fountas & G. S. Pinnell, *RED leveled literacy intervention student test preparation booklet* (pp. 19–20). Portsmouth, NH: Heinemann.

Winter, J. (2010). *Biblioburro: A true story from Colombia.* New York, NY: Beach Lane Books.

11

LEARNING IN THE INQUIRY COMMUNITY

A Letter to Maggie

Simeen Tabatabai

Dear Maggie,

I know that you will understand what I am talking about when I say that teaching can be exhausting. A teaching life is taxing: emotionally, intellectually, and physically. With my 25 or so students, plus any number of adults that can be present in my room, there are hundreds of interactions that are going on at any one point in time in my classroom. As I interact with my students (individually, in groups, and/or whole class), they are also interacting with each other, the texts we are reading, and their responses to them. Within these interactions are the building blocks of educational experiences and individual learning. Only teachers who inhabit these spaces can know how challenging it can be to navigate them productively.

I think of you, Maggie, whenever I think about how important it is for teachers to support each other to move forward and be productive in the challenging work we do as teachers. As I learned more about you and your work, I realized that yours was a distinctive voice in our inquiry group that has reiterated for me the ultimate goal of teaching: fulfilling the needs of our students. Your passion for doing your best and your compassion for your students moved me powerfully every time.

You teach in a high needs/high risk environment, which is the opposite of where I teach. There is an extreme contrast between the socioeconomic situations of our students. The work you do with your students, despite the challenges that you face, is amazing. You shared with us the "Quarters for Colombia" project that your students Rakim, Eric, Jamal, and Michael did after reading "Alfa and Beto: The Biblioburros" (Morrow, 2013) with you in class. In your own words, "This text instigated a change in this group that I could have never imagined." Your belief in the potential of your students, your faith in their ability to learn, and your advocacy on their behalf is truly admirable. Even more remarkable is your confidence in yourself as a teacher and how you have chosen to make decisions that are based on your beliefs and professional judgment.

You know, there was a time when I would have given anything for a chance to work in an urban, high-needs school district like yours. That was many years ago, when I had just moved to the U.S. and earned my teaching degree and certification. We know that even though our schools serve an increasingly culturally and linguistically diverse student body, the majority of current and prospective teachers are white monolingual middle class women (Darling-Hammond & Bransford, 2005). I thought I would be the perfect person to bridge that gap in my small sphere. I felt that I was well suited, being a minority myself, to counter negative stereotypes and to serve as a role model, mentor, and cultural translator for students from diverse backgrounds. I could relate to my students' cultural backgrounds and hold high expectations of their academic abilities and potential. I knew I was uniquely prepared because of my life experiences to design culturally relevant learning experiences for my students and to build trusting relationships with students and families.

As life and luck usually have it, when I was looking for an opening and was offered a job, it wasn't in the urban setting that I wanted but in an affluent and suburban school district, with a majority of white students. I had to accept the job offer, despite my many reservations and reluctance. I had no choice. I needed the job and there was nothing else out there. I remember coming back from work and complaining daily to my very patient husband that I didn't think I was well suited for the position that I was in. I had nothing to offer my wealthy, white, mainstream students. They lived in a different world. I was unhappy and dissatisfied. I distinctly remember the moment one day when, as I was going on and on, my husband raised his head from his book, looked at me and said quietly, "Don't underestimate yourself. If nothing else, the least you will do is disturb the waters for them a bit." I stared at him dumbfounded. My whole thinking about my work and teaching life changed in that moment because of that one comment.

I realized how I was limiting myself by being focused only on what I could do academically, emotionally, and socially for culturally diverse students. I had never considered the potential gains for white students of having teachers from different backgrounds, cultures, or ethnicities. Because my worldview and thinking didn't mirror theirs, maybe the insights I had to offer them were as valuable, if not more so, than the ones I could give students who identified with me? I went back into my classroom the next day with a new perspective and energy, and I found my work becoming amazingly rewarding. Even though my experiences and thinking often do not resonate immediately with my students, I can open doors for them to explore and understand issues and realities of life that might not be their lived experience. Their exposure to me is their exposure to a new and different way of seeing things.

Maggie, I see your experience as a mirror image to mine. You are a white teacher teaching minority students. We both teach across cultures. In our discussions, you have shared the shifts in your attitudes, beliefs, and disposition as you have grown and developed as a culturally responsive teacher. We have both changed and grown in similar ways as teachers. You hold high expectations for your students and carefully scaffold their learning to move them ever forward towards success. You know they can succeed when they are given the chance. You are a passionate advocate for your students because you understand the social, economic, and political inequalities that they face in their schooling. I respect you for being a fighter, Maggie. Despite many challenges, you are fighting for your students' learning.

The global literature inquiry community brought us together, and we connected because we both love the challenge of teaching and the work we do. To teach and learn is an incredibly complex and exciting process. I know you understand when I say that I feel blessed to have the opportunity to be a teacher. I have deep beliefs about how children learn, just like you do. And a big part of my beliefs is that I myself have to constantly keep on learning. I am continually striving to understand in new and different ways how my learners learn. Reflection on my practice is very important for me. How can one teach without really thinking about how learning takes place? I am always learning and shaping and reshaping myself as a teacher. I always hope to continue to do so.

You know, it is because of this belief in lifelong learning, and to stay current in my field, that I have always worked hard to maintain my connection with my own teachers and professors. Over the years, I have taught education courses for the Literacy Department at my Alma Mater, taken doctoral classes, and participated in research. When Kelly invited me to join the global literature inquiry community and came into my classroom to conduct her research, I was thrilled. I remember walking for the first time into the small café where our inquiry community met, feeling just a little nervous. I looked at you and the group around you, sitting at a table in the corner—Kelly, Krista, Heather—smiling faces, welcoming hand waves. I walked towards all of you. I knew Kelly, of course. She was my teacher, and I had learned so much from her over the years. Krista and I had taken some courses together in the past, but you and Heather were new to me. I remember thinking: Would these people listen to what I had to say? Would they help me expand my thinking? Help me feel that I was part of something bigger? Would they become part of a community of learners with me? Would they take me on a journey with them? After quick handshakes and hugs, we settled down to introductions.

Very quickly, I found out that "Yes!" you were all indeed my fellow travelers. You were colleagues, and supporters, and co-teachers and mentors…you were listeners and learners with me. I looked forward eagerly to our meetings that followed. Our core topics were always our teaching of global literature and how we navigated critical literacy in our classrooms. However, inevitably our discussions would go off on tangents and then the topics of our conversations would range far and wide: student issues, curriculum, Common Core, budgets, policy, administration, testing, teacher evaluations…

There were incredibly rich discussions every time we met and shared our teaching and thinking. I learned so much from each member of the inquiry group. Some of that learning is easy to talk about, like sharing ideas about books and lessons, creating learning events, or ways of assessing students' learning and so on. Some of my learning, however, is more difficult to put into words. For me, the inquiry community became an invaluable tool of reflection about my own teaching through experiencing the teaching lives of my colleagues as all of you shared them in our conversations. There were so many points of connection, even though we all work in very different teaching environments. I also saw what super teachers you all were, how deeply you cared about the work you did, how deeply you cared about children and learning. I was able to discuss and share my concerns with you and discovered that you had similar concerns. I could express my views and be listened to in an open-minded manner. Very quickly we developed relationships that were based on respect, empathy, and understanding. In this way, we could focus in our conversations on exploring our common goal of educating our students academically and emotionally. Thanks to the members of the inquiry community, I was able to process, reflect, and understand my teaching and my students at a deeper level.

As I reflect on why the inquiry community became such an important part of my teaching life, I realize how important it is for teachers to have support from each other. Teaching can be tough, especially in these trying times of rapid flux. So many people today, who have never actually set foot in a classroom, seem to think they know how to solve the problems of education. How can they know what teachers need to be successful? These concerns came to the surface in our inquiry community meetings as we talked about our work and the constant pressures created as a result of the implementation of the Common Core, and the high stakes testing and teacher evaluations. We all agreed that teachers need support. We need to know that our colleagues and superiors have our backs. We need them to listen to us, and value us, value our experiences, and give us honest and fair feedback on our teaching.

Maggie, Kelly, Krista, and Heather, I am inspired by your talent and dedication. You shared your unique experiences, backgrounds, insights, and worldviews with me, and you helped me grow as a learner and teacher. Thank you for sharing. Thank you for teaching me through what you brought to our discussion table. Thank you for the support and collaboration. Thank you for listening, and thank you for talking. Thank you for being there.

Simeen

References

Darling-Hammond, L. & Bransford, J. (Eds.). (2005). *Preparing teachers for a changing world: What teachers should learn and be able to do.* San Francisco, CA: Jossey-Bass.

Children's Literature, Media, and Materials

Morrow, P. (2013). Alfa and Beto: The biblioburros (abridged version). In I. C. Fountas & G. S. Pinnell, *RED leveled literacy intervention student test preparation booklet* (pp. 19–20). Portsmouth, NH: Heinemann.

12

LEARNING IN THE INQUIRY COMMUNITY

A Letter to Simeen

Maggie Naughter Burns

Dear Simeen,

Teaching is an extraordinary profession. It offers the teacher not only the opportunity to constantly learn about myriad subjects and instructional approaches, but most importantly, it gives the teacher the gift of learning more about herself, through her teaching experiences with the students she meets on this journey. I am not certain of any other profession that allows for and expects this type of personal evolution. Maybe some teachers do not see it this way, but when I talk with you about your teaching and your goals, this idea of personal evolution immediately comes to mind. I feel it is how we are linked and why we enjoy discussing our craft so much.

Simeen, you represent to me diversity, culture, and a very different life and teaching experience from my own. Your voice carries with it a tone of compassion, intelligence, and understanding, shaped by a lifetime of living in other countries besides the U.S. Your dedication to providing your students multiple perspectives of all kinds through the text choices you make, and the person you are, helped me to see myself as a teacher and a person in a very different way. This shift, I feel, has had a positive impact on how I view not only my students but also people in general. This shift was the reason I was able to carry out the "Quarters for Colombia" social action project with my third grade students. You, Simeen, gave me the courage to ask, "what are you thinking?" and helped me to grow my patience so I could truly hear my students' answers and use them to drive their learning.

My experience as a person and a teacher has been one similar to that of your students. Growing up, I did not consider myself privileged, but I was. I, like your students, existed as you put it, "cocooned...in [my] comfortable reality, with critical thinking around identity, privilege, and power, not a central aspect of [my] schooling experiences." I have never traveled abroad or ventured too far away from the city I grew up in.

I wish I had had a teacher like you. A teacher with such diverse life experience that truly wanted to know, "what are you thinking?" and "why are you thinking that?" A teacher that presented me with diverse, rich, culturally sensitive stories and texts that challenged my worldview and perceptions about race, class, and culture. A teacher who constructed a classroom rooted in "dialogic interactions" that allowed ideas and thoughts to expand, grow, and change. You say in your chapter, "Knowledge and understanding of others makes us question our own assumptions about how the world works and can lead to deep and lasting changes in our beliefs. Changing our beliefs is often the first step in changing our behaviors and actions to change the world." The questioning of assumptions is at the heart of your teaching.

When you spoke about your work using *Books for Oliver* (Larkin, Rambo, & Brown, 2007), "Bindi!" (Sandhu, 2005), and *Sadako* (Coerr, 1977/1999), your goals, all rooted in this idea of critical thinking and questioning, were always driving your instruction. Your instruction, to me, is rooted in your life experiences before you came to the school, and since. I hear how your students, as they question their perceptions and owned ideas, shape how you address your teaching, your text choice, your stance, as their collaborator and coach. You and they are evolving with every encounter.

Your discomfort during your exploration of *Sadako*, was in response to your students' needs and responses. You added to the curriculum as you were in it with the intention of closing gaps in understanding the students were offering you. You chose additional texts that you hoped would bring them to a deeper understanding of the themes in the main text as the learning unfolded. These deliberate choices you have made to maintain "a delicate balance" when facilitating critical literacy engagements, is quite impressive. On top of all this, you speak with great concern about not wanting to judge, lead, or evaluate your students so they respond in a way they think you may want them to. Stepping away from that culture in teaching of the "right" and "wrong" answer to promote this deeper thinking is very difficult in this age of testing and accountability. But you do it, and because you do, you actually get the students closer to the realization of these new standards. You are all evolving with each experience and each text. You and they are really changing the world. They may never get another teacher just like you, but they now are more than aware that other ideas, cultures, experiences, and people unlike them exist, impact the world, and matter.

I think it is a bit ironic how you felt the inner city setting was the appropriate place for you, based on your life and teaching experiences up to that point, and then you ended up in the suburbs. Whenever we met in our inquiry sessions, and as I write this letter to you now, I am certain it was part of some divine plan that you ended up where you did. Those students need you and you need them in some way. I feel our students bring things up for us that we need to face in our professional and personal lives. I also think we do that for each other as teachers. This is such a human profession.

Your teaching and your experience brought a lot up for me, Simeen. When I met you and the other members of our group, I was so in awe! Aside from your welcoming smiles and kind and compassionate natures, you are all so intelligent. My definition of "intelligent" includes a big space for being open to new ideas and the belief that we are always learning and evolving. Each one of you embodies those ideals, and although I did not know you at first, I felt I was in the presence of individuals that felt the same way about teaching and learning.

I had become a bit lost and needed to be reminded of why I became a teacher, and you all helped me to remember who I was and what I valued. Simeen, you in particular with your mantra of "what are you thinking" helped me to construct an inquiry project with my third graders I could have never imagined. You taught me the value of silence when students were brave enough to share their ideas. You taught me the value of teaching for "dialogic interactions" by positioning the students and myself as collaborators. You taught me to have patience with myself during the uncomfortable times in our engagements when I had to create the curriculum in the moment, in response to student needs, interests, and questions. This is not the standard "plan and implement" type of teaching we are used to, but when done with the students' needs in mind, can be so invigorating and rewarding. Simeen, I heard your voice, and the voices of Krista, Heather, and Kelly, all cheering me on, as I navigated unchartered territory with my students. I was truly out of my comfort zone but remained steadfast, because of the support of our group. The collaboration and camaraderie of our group kept me moving forward.

If I had not had you all, if I had not heard about your own experiences, if I had not had the opportunity to discuss my fears, my practice, and my ideas with you all, I would not have been able to carry out the "Quarters" project. This group gave me my legs. It helped me to step out of the often oppressive culture of education as it exists in schools and to pursue my teaching in a way that was best for my students. The boys graduated last June. They still talked about that project and what they did for the kids in Colombia. They still have a strong sense of pride and accomplishment from that experience. You were an integral part of that journey for them, and for me. I am truly grateful to you and our group for that gift.

Things do not always go as we wish in our classrooms, schools, and school districts. We, as teachers, will have to negotiate many changes over the coming years. We must remember, despite how we may perceive these changes, our students matter the most. Second to the students are our co-workers. As we share and collaborate, we can lift each other to new understanding and ideas. That is what you all did for me. You showed me a path, actually a few different paths, to choose from. You supported me through my worries and fears, and you offered advice and tweaks along the way. Through all that, I learned to trust myself, my evolving belief system, and, most importantly, the students, who in the end, showed me the way. Thank you Simeen, and Heather, and Krista, and Kelly.

Yours,
Maggie

Children's Literature, Media, and Materials

Coerr, E. (1977/1999). *Sadako and the thousand paper cranes.* New York, NY: Penguin.
Larkin, J., Rambo, E., & Brown, D. (2007). *Books for Oliver.* New York, NY: Mondo Publishing.
Sandhu, M. (2005). Bindi! *Highlights for Children Magazine, 60*(6), 8.

13

ENGAGING IN LOCAL INQUIRIES AND CULTIVATING GLOBAL VISIONS

What Did We Learn?

Kelly K. Wissman

When we first began meeting as an inquiry community—our conversations often darting from uninspired Common Core modules to confounding teacher evaluation schemes, from misguided Response to Intervention interpretations to the specter of "coaches" filling out checklists in the backs of classrooms—it was often the beauty of picturebooks that shifted and focused our attention to what was possible, meaningful, and purposeful. Literature and art, stories and color, narrative eloquence and exquisite illustrations captured our attention and imagination. These books, and the richness of the voices and experiences housed within them, provided a kind of anchor within a very unstable and often confusing educational time. Over time, the books continued to play a key role in grounding our conversations and inquiries, yet the connections we made to each other and to the work of the inquiry community also took on a primary role. While navigating this complicated and often contradictory landscape of policies and practices, we often found that taking the time to listen, consider, ponder, and reflect with a group of educators engaged in like-minded inquiry brought a sense of clarity and renewed purpose. As the teachers' letters to each other in this book attest, these realizations were often hard-won and fleeting, sometimes emerging after considerable strife and sometimes tears, but the work of it, the commitment to it and to the group, was sustaining.

Since those regular monthly meetings, we have stayed in touch and continued our teaching with global literature in similar and in new ways. The educational landscape is continually shifting, yet the grand initiatives that were just beginning when we started meeting are now more familiar and somewhat more attuned to the needs of students and teachers. At the same time, though, the larger world continues to be embroiled in violent, destructive acts that fill media outlets with images of refugees forced from homes and candlelit memorials to lives lost to terrorism. Across the Middle East and Europe, vulnerable children flee violence and strife with their families in the hopes of finding safe harbor, even as rhetoric by politicians in the United States carries traces of the ethnocentrism and fear that once led to the internment of Japanese Americans during World War II. In the United States, Muslim Americans face increasing instances of discrimination, while state-sanctioned violence against Black men and women has necessitated a social movement in which what should be self-evident must be named and reaffirmed again and again: #BlackLivesMatter.

In these times, it seems essential to return to the lessons that books and art can teach us, to embrace complexity, to live in spaces of possibility while coming to know others and ourselves more deeply. As Rosenblatt (1982) contends, literature can play a part in "aiding us to understand ourselves and others, for widening our horizons to include temperaments and cultures different from our own, for helping us to clarify our conflicts in values, for illuminating our world" (p. 276). Global literature, as we have found, has much to offer as we try to make sense of these difficult and often unnerving times; reading global literature together and coming together to talk about it has even greater potential.

Teaching with Global Literature: Four Principles

Throughout this book, we have considered how students took up opportunities to claim books and their own responses to them as evidence of their active participation in and shaping of the world around them. We also explored the complexities and challenges of doing so within educational settings not always ideally suited for these kinds of inquiries and within the broader social context in which young people navigate a range of discourses about what it means to be an American, a reader, and a member of the global community. At times, these movements and relocations were smoother for some students than for others whose identities and ideas remained a bit more fixed. For the teachers, too, reading global literature was often a dynamic act that created new and compelling entry points for how they interacted with their students and the insights they gained from them, for how they envisioned their own purposes within their classrooms.

We have written about the teaching of global literature in a range of suburban and urban contexts, with English Language Learners and "struggling" readers, across multigenre texts and close analysis of picturebooks, through thoughtful journal entries and clear calls for social action. As I look across the four teachers in the inquiry group and across the time I spent in their classrooms, I see four shared principles related to teaching and learning with global texts:

1. Choosing Meaningful, Substantive Texts to Connect, Captivate, and Challenge
2. Grappling with Multiple Perspectives
3. Cultivating Classrooms as Communities of Inquiry
4. Reading Within and Beyond the "Four Corners" of the Text

I see these as very much interrelated principles and as principles that can be adapted across various grade levels, across urban and suburban schools, and across the work of grade level teachers, literacy specialists, and English as a New Language teachers. Within the diverse classroom contexts we explored in the book, text selection was certainly key and cannot be underestimated, yet the texts worked in tandem with the creation of educational spaces that welcomed multiple perspectives, valued a spirit of inquiry, and nurtured responsive and relational readings of the world. An interesting, compelling text about a real world problem (Morrow, 2013) catalyzed Maggie's boys from "compliant" students to fully engaged readers, writers, and speakers for social justice. A story of a brave, intelligent, emerging bilingual boy in Malawi who brought "electric wind" to his village (Kamkwamba, Mealer, & Zunon, 2012) inspired Heather's students to reach higher. Reading across multiple genres within Simeen's classroom prompted students out of insulated ways of thinking and nurtured powerful moments of discovery and connection. Giving students an opportunity to ask "what matters" to characters very different from themselves and to inquire into the effects of war encouraged students in Krista and Toni's classroom to connect deeply with texts and to build on their emotions to provide incisive analyses. From dreaming up and bringing to fruition a social action project designed to provide books to children far away, to telling deeply textured stories of immigration, loss, and hope in response to global picturebooks, the students across all four contexts continually read not just "within the four corners of the text" but often beyond those corners and beyond the four corners of their classrooms.

I should note, though, that finding global texts of any kind, let alone captivating, high quality, and current ones, was a challenge, as many school and classroom libraries lack a range of up-to-date, non-stereotypical global texts. Our grant funds certainly helped us supplement these materials in important ways; however, we stand with others raising insistent calls for the inclusion of diverse books within classrooms and libraries (e.g. Möller, 2013; Yokota, 2015). In addition, as we have explored, simple access to texts is not enough. Teachers need time with each other, time with librarians, media specialists, and authors, and time with the books themselves to make thoughtful and informed decisions about incorporating global texts within their classrooms.

Promising Pedagogical Practices with Global Literature

Across the four teachers' classrooms, rich student engagements with global literature resulted from extensive planning and thinking about pedagogy. They came from conversations within inquiry group meetings, planning discussions with co-teachers, reading professional texts with a sense of openness and discovery, and maintaining a sense of what might be possible, even within challenging contexts. There is no doubt that this work takes time, requires expertise, and flourishes with the support of others engaged in like-minded inquiries. Some dimensions of it include:

- wide-ranging study of children's literature;
- careful thinking about how to surround that literature with nonfiction, multigenre texts;
- thoughtful arrangement of classroom resources to promote discussion;
- opportunities for students to respond to the books across multiple sign systems;
- considered attention to local, state, and national standards;
- purposeful development of a teaching stance of listening and openness; and
- an embrace of the sometimes uncomfortable feeling of not knowing all the answers or how students will respond to particular texts.

This list captures only a fraction of the intellectual work involved in teaching global literature from a critical literacy and teacher inquiry stance. Despite its shortcomings, however, it does suggest, like so many scholars of teacher inquiry communities and teacher learning before us have documented, that the deprofessionalism and deskilling of teachers, the "one and done" models of professional development, cannot suffice within these complex times (e.g. Cochran-Smith & Lytle, 2001; Lieberman & Miller, 2011; Simon, 2015). Instead, we need intentional communities of educators coming together to discuss practice, engage in inquiry, and transform teaching and learning.

Within my own teaching of global texts in my teacher education classes, the stories and examples I share from the classrooms and students of Maggie, Simeen, Krista, and Heather are often the most resonant and influential. These stories help preservice and in-service teachers not only imagine but also *see* what might be possible in their own contexts. At the same time that my teacher education students and I delve deeply into global texts, I also underscore and try to embody the class as a place of inquiry in which they, too, can inquire and take on multiple perspectives and consider action, just as their students might. Creating these opportunities to "dwell" (Sumara, 1996) in texts is not always easy. I often encounter some impatience from teachers who understandably seek immediate or discrete "lessons" to implement into their classrooms and that explicitly meet Common Core State Standards. My students are sometimes perplexed when we explore texts that challenge notions of American greatness or engage in response activities that raise more questions than they answer or create art in response to a picturebook that would be very difficult to assess within current measures of reading comprehension. At other times, they are intrigued and inspired to stay within these contingent and fluid learning spaces, grasping their possibilities for their own future teaching. What I hope also stays with them, in addition to the books and pedagogical possibilities, is the awareness of how important it is to find support for this kind of teaching within a community of educators.

Seeing Anew: Asking, Listening, and Pausing

Within my visits to the teachers' classrooms, I witnessed how important it is not only to have high quality global literature available in classrooms but also to create contexts for meaningful engagements with that literature. When Simeen asked her students, "What are you thinking?", rich reflective conversational spaces were opened where students wrestled with their own responsibilities as members of a global community. When Maggie listened to the questions her students asked about a young man's efforts to bring books to kids in rural Colombia on donkeys, an idea for a social action project was born. When Krista paused in a read aloud and waited for students to share their responses, a range of deeply personal, philosophical, and analytical perspectives about war and its consequences filled the room. In asking, listening, and pausing, each teacher nurtured valuable, purposeful, and intentional engagements with books.

There is, of course, much more work to be done. As we look back on the teaching and learning documented in this book, we sometimes cringe at a language choice, a perspective unexplored, an essential reading forgotten, a path not taken. What now seems self-evident and clear from this distance, did not seem so at the time. Yet, we remain hopeful for what still might be as we consider how students engaged with global books. Within an educational context where engagements with global literature were purposeful and meaningful, the students in Heather's classroom found themselves in the books and found themselves as readers, thinkers, citizens, and scholars. When her students asked, "Where are *our* books?!" after they were forced to go without global picturebooks during a period of high-stakes testing, they brought into sharp relief the injustices already manifesting within their own educational histories. Within that question, asked adamantly and assuredly, the students recognized the power of reading and the value of educational inquiry tied to their worlds and to the broader world. They made a claim to "our books" as an educational birthright. They were critical readers of their worlds.

Heather's students, I would argue, offer all of us a call to action. As teachers, teacher educators, policy makers, parents, and citizens, we need to listen to the desires and hopes of students to read and write texts that are socially meaningful and that support critical inquiries. As critical literacy teachers and scholars, we need to acknowledge that these requests for books and stories also demand something of us. They demand our own embrace of the hurt and marginalization that underlay these calls, that we recognize how rarely children's books within classrooms serve as mirrors to our diverse world, and that we work with a renewed sense of urgency across multiple contexts to promote more expansive visions of the purposes of the English Language Arts. The students call us to reimagine our pedagogical spaces as ones that nurture inquiry, that "disturb the waters," and that promote a sense of belonging, even as they also call us to articulate clearly why these texts and spaces are fundamental, not extraneous to, a humanizing education within a globalized world. Heather's students, exhausted from days of testing, remind us that to pursue critical literacy teaching with global books often means to be confronted by the seeming intractability of unjust educational policies, practices, and curricula, but that we can and must raise questions about the way things are, plainly and insistently. They encourage us to resist the "rationalist underpinnings" (Janks, 2002, p. 9) of critical literacy and to embrace the fundamentally human and embodied nature of reading, interpreting, talking, and writing about texts that challenge, inform, and inspire. Above all, the students call us to embrace the hope and sense of possibility that they continue to bring to classrooms as they seek texts and teachers who will open the world to them. We must rise to their challenge.

It is our hope that this book leaves you inspired and curious, hopeful and clear-sighted, ready to take on the promise of teaching with global literature and ready to see where your students' inquiries take you.

References

Cochran-Smith, M., & Lytle, S. L. (2001). Beyond certainty: Taking an inquiry stance on practice. In A. Lieberman & L. Miller (Eds.), *Teachers caught in the action: Professional development that matters* (pp. 45–60). New York, NY: Teachers College Press.

Janks, H. (2002). Critical literacy: Beyond reason. *The Australian Educational Researcher, 29*(1), 7–26.

Lieberman, A. & Miller, L. (2011). Learning communities: The starting point for professional learning is in schools and classrooms. *Journal of Staff Development, 32*(4), 16–20.

Möller, K. J. (2013). Considering the nonfiction CCSS nonfiction literature exemplars as cultural artifacts: What do they represent? *Journal of Children's Literature, 39*(2), 58–67.

Rosenblatt, L. M. (1982). The literary transaction: Evocation and response. *Theory Into Practice, 21*(4), 268–77.

Simon, R. (2015). "I'm fighting my fight, and I'm not alone anymore": The influence of communities of inquiry. *English Education, 48*(1), 41–71.

Sumara, D. J. (1996). *Private readings in public: Schooling the literary imagination.* New York, NY: Peter Lang.

Yokota, J. (2015). What needs to happen? *Reading Today, 32*(6), 18–21.

Children's Literature, Media, and Materials

Kamkwamba, W., Mealer, B., & Zunon, E. (2012). *The boy who harnessed the wind.* New York, NY: Dial Books.

Morrow, P. (2013). Alfa and Beto: The biblioburros (abridged version). In I. C. Fountas & G. S. Pinnell, *RED leveled literacy intervention student test preparation booklet* (pp. 19–20). Portsmouth, NH: Heinemann.

14

TEACHING CRITICALLY WITH GLOBAL TEXTS

Insights for Teacher Preparation and Professional Learning

Cheryl L. Dozier

> *"Education is the most powerful weapon which you can use to change the world."*
> —Nelson Mandela

In this luminous and insightful book, Kelly, Heather, Simeen, Krista, and Maggie explore the complexities, celebrations, and tensions of introducing their students to global literature and engaging with their students in rigorous and thoughtful ways. This important work shows the range of ways the authors opened minds and hearts to help students explore worlds beyond their immediate contexts and experiences. Our world is complex. Our world is ever changing. How we prepare children for their world matters. Their world demands a critical, contemplative, and mindfully engaged citizenry. Throughout this book, Kelly, Heather, Simeen, Krista, and Maggie share their engagements with global picturebooks as they open doors and possibilities "to nurture empathetic, critical, and hopeful readers of the world who encounter global texts as mirrors, windows, sliding glass doors, and maps, and who construct new worlds of understanding as they engage with the books and with each other" (this volume, p. 37-38). The authors did not choose a "sanitized" or scripted path for their exploration. Instead, they chose a path to examine and wonder together. They became co-learners alongside their students (Cambourne, 1995) and did not shy away from more challenging and tentative spaces.

The deliberate and intentional community Kelly created with the teachers provided a space for reflection, reconsideration, and support as together they explored ways to expand the worldviews of their students. In turn, the classroom communities Heather, Simeen, Maggie, and Krista constructed provided spaces for students to learn from both the intentionality as well as the richness of the explorations of global picturebooks. Together, they became empathetic as they examined and expanded their worldviews. The teachers first lived in a community honoring and valuing global picturebooks with Kelly and then created their own communities where *their* students honored and valued global picturebooks. At the heart of all of the communities was learning to listen carefully, build on one another's ideas, question or disagree in a respectful manner, consider multiple perspectives, and move beyond holding the one true answer. In these communities, learners grappled with issues beyond a peripheral way, oftentimes inspiring action. As Linda Christensen (2000) reminds us, "To become a community, students must learn to live in someone else's skin, understand the parallels of hurt, struggle and joy across class and culture lines, and work for change.... For that to happen, they need a curriculum that encourages them to empathize with others" (p. 2). All of the teachers built communities where *all* voices mattered, and children knew their thoughts, musings, and wonderings were significant.

These communities were built while all four teachers navigated a range of constraints in their particular contexts. All four held to their firm convictions that this work mattered enough to transcend restrictive mandates and an imposed curriculum. They chose to widen the curriculum in a time when many of their districts were narrowing the curriculum. At a time when teachers were expected to follow scripted modules, these teachers paused, reflected, and put their learners front and center of their responsive teaching. In the current era of scripted programs, increased testing, and constricting curricular mandates, teaching takes bravery. And, the teachers in this book are brave. The teachers' resilience in the face of daunting regulations resonates through the pages of this text. Their explorations were expansive and generative in a time where many educational mandates feel restrictive or reductionist.

For all, their collaborative work in the global literature group created spaces for possibilities. They believed in the power of the children in their classrooms and held a firm belief that all children can learn. Their questioning centered on *how* to bring all learners into the conversation, not *if* learners could engage in the conversations. Each teacher believed in children as intellectuals, as learners who could—and would. Their collaboration offers numerous insights and opportunities for exploration within teacher preparation and professional learning.

Exploring our Teaching Selves

Teaching begins by exploring the teaching self. As Cole and Knowles (2000) remind us, "We teach who we are" (p.188). All four teachers in this book held deep and abiding convictions about the importance of lifelong learning and engaging in communities of learners. These community spaces honored their teaching identities. All believed in the transformative spaces of teaching and learning. Simeen, in her letter to Maggie, shared her deep conviction about her need to "constantly keep on learning" and continuously strive "to understand in new and different ways how my learners learn. Reflection on my practice is very important for me. How can one teach without really thinking about how learning takes place? I am always learning and shaping and reshaping myself as a teacher. I always hope to continue to do so" (this volume, p. 131). Maggie and Heather wrote about the importance of the inquiry community during times of unrest in their buildings. Both Krista and Toni named themselves as avid and voracious readers. For all, the learning community mattered in profound ways as they gained strength and inspiration from one another.

Yet, as we learn from the honest and frank chapters in this book, even with their firm convictions, this work was not always easy. Throughout the book, all four veteran teachers shared tentative moments, moments where they questioned or abandoned their visions, moments of exasperation, moments of self-doubt. Their monthly meetings, where they actively engaged and questioned one another, provided encouragement for their continued exploration.

As teacher educators, we must come to understand who our teacher candidates are, find their zones of proximal development, and then support them as they imagine or reimagine their teaching selves (Warford, 2011). Like most of the teacher preparation programs across America, the teachers I work with at the University at Albany are primarily white females (Ladson-Billings, 2009) who enter teaching with at least 16 years as students and learners. Given that prospective teachers' experiences as students form the foundation of their values and beliefs as teachers, teacher educators can help future teachers examine their values and beliefs through writing literacy autobiographies where teachers unpack and examine their literacy histories. Literacy autobiographies, filled with literacy artifacts—favorite children's books, writing samples from elementary school through college research papers, notes and letters to and from family members, awards, diplomas, eulogies written, wedding toasts, and family recipes—highlight celebratory as well as challenging spaces in teacher candidates' literacy histories. After reflecting on their literacy autobiography selections, teachers consider how their beliefs, values, and experiences impact their teaching lives, instructional practices, and instructional decision-making. The literacy autobiographies provide a framing for conversations as teachers consider where they saw themselves in texts (or did not), where they "felt" like learners or where they became disenfranchised. Prospective teachers also look across artifacts to notice where their artifacts were located. Some write primarily about school based literacies, while others write of literacies beyond the school walls. Some embrace their schooling experiences and want to emulate favorite teachers or powerful moments. Others who felt disenfranchised use this reflection to name their wish to never treat students as they were taught. By opening up spaces for intentional reflections, we invite teacher candidates to examine their teaching and learning lives. These reflections matter for how future teachers will teach their students.

In the literacy specialist courses I teach, we also read "White Privilege: Unpacking the Invisible Knapsack" (McIntosh, 1990), a disconcerting article for many teacher candidates. While this article provides a space for teaching critically and for considering identities and whiteness, some students resent this exploration. Some question why we need to consider privilege, while others question the relevance of an article written decades ago. Still others are struck by the article's timeliness as we continue to face racial injustices. I intentionally use this article in the capstone practicum course, though, to help us pause and consider what we take for granted. To teach critically for an informed and engaged citizenry, we must be willing to confront difficult spaces and examine our intellectual unrest.

An exploration of our teaching selves helps us to examine where we are positioned and where we position ourselves. Some reflections are celebratory, while others remind us of difficult memories or moments. When we grapple with these tensions and uncertainties, when we look at and through our discomfort, we live the possibilities for navigating challenging conversations with our learners.

The Texts We Choose

Text choices matter. The texts we choose for our classrooms can open doors, help children grapple with the complexities of the world, and introduce them to worlds they do not yet know—or they can marginalize or exclude children. In her TED Talk, *The Danger of a Single Story*, Chimamanda Ngozi Adichie (2009) illuminates how impressionable we are in relation to the stories we read and hear. Through her captivating talk, Adichie reminds us that representations, or lack thereof, impact how individuals view the world. She also reminds us, as we work to select culturally responsive texts, to move beyond a single story to illustrate an entire culture. In her blog, Debbie Reese (2007), a Nambe Pueblo Indian woman, also writes about the importance of teachers helping children "develop an ability to identify racist, biased, and outdated information" (para 4). Likewise, Tschida, Ryan, and Ticknor (2014) remind us it is our responsibility to choose a range of texts to disrupt historical and cultural narratives, since often our prospective teachers have read books or experienced classrooms where "historical events and figures take on mythic status and where a few surface facts often stand in as common sense for the complete historical record" (p. 32). Just as we examine our teaching selves, so, too, we need to examine the text choices in our classrooms.

Throughout the book, the authors discussed the importance of global picturebooks to build learners' identities as learners work to understand their place in the world and to better understand the world in which we live. Kelly, Maggie, Simeen, Krista, and Heather recognize it takes time, care, and an openness to read through books and resources looking for stereotypes, bias, and to move beyond the single story. As Simeen writes, "By using global literature texts that appeal to my students' interests and abilities, I expose them to different lives, get them to think independently, learn respect for others, and prepare to participate more responsibly in the world. I can help them move towards deeper under-standings of differences and to step beyond stereotypes and generalizations" (this volume, p. 105). Debbie Reese (2007) writes in response to a comment on her blog post, "Our country, our children, so desperately need honest instruction and honest books about American Indians, but we're so hung up on and attached to feel-good stories.... Questioning all those feel-good moments and traditions feels like an attack on those who hold those traditions dear." Bumping against the "feel-good moments" and traditions can be challenging. As we learned from the authors of this text, it takes care and conviction to challenge previously held assumptions.

Teacher educators, teachers, librarians, and literacy coaches are gatekeepers. To choose mindfully, *we* must be engaged readers and read widely to recommend books. As Janks, Dixon, Ferreira, Granville, and Newfield (2014) remind us, no text is neutral. Therefore, we must also consider where, in our coursework and in our teacher preparation programs, we ask students to explore and consider texts for their future classrooms. In which specific courses and practicum experi-ences do we help future and current teachers move beyond their current comfort levels and expand their understandings about texts in deep and nuanced ways? Where and how do we help teachers move beyond simply building their class-room libraries around their favorite childhood books?

In our courses and in professional development sessions, we can invite teach-ers to reflect on the books they have selected to share with students and consider the social issues students have the opportunity to discuss based on those choices. A careful exploration of books, like the exploration Kelly and the teachers engaged in, helps teachers become more intentional in their choices as they decide what the books they have selected offer for their learners and *how* they might use them in their classrooms.

In one school, after numerous professional development sessions I conducted related to expanding classroom libraries, selecting books based on learners' inter-ests, and finding books to engage learners, several teachers expressed concern that students were not reading at home. One fifth grade teacher commented, "We ARE their [students'] literacy diets." This comment caused us all to pause. First, we questioned, how we can fully know what our students are reading outside of school? Second, we wondered, within our classrooms which books are we choos-ing to immerse our students in? Do the children in our classrooms see themselves in the texts we make available? Do the books in our classrooms invite them into worlds they have not yet experienced? Are there enough text possibilities in our classrooms? As teacher educators Tschida, Ryan, and Ticknor (2014) write, "We encourage our students to think about the messages they want to send to their students with and through books and how meaningful teaching with thoughtfully selected texts can help them expand and question these messages" (p. 30). If most texts children select and read are from classrooms, it is our moral imperative to examine the books, materials, and resources we are "feeding" our students.

Within our teacher preparation programs and as literacy coaches, we want to help teachers reimagine their text selections and see the importance of moving beyond random selection of books, to become more thoughtful, intentional, and to draw from knowing their learners to select literature where students see themselves. In a rural community, where I recently began working with a literacy coach, we explored the resources the teachers currently use and have access to in their bookroom and in their classrooms. I asked, "Where do your students see themselves in the books in your classrooms?" I also shared the following quote, "Books are sometimes the only place where readers may meet people who are not like themselves, who offer alternative worldviews" (Tschida, Ryan, & Ticknor, 2014, p. 29). After a long pause, a spirited conversation ensued. The teachers responded they routinely pick books off the shelf and read them aloud straight through without discussion. Within their busy days, they had not previously considered the range of texts offered in the classroom or the impact their choices could have on their learners. The teachers' honest conversation and their previously unexamined instructional practices, make the work at the heart of this book all the more powerful.

With a current emphasis on close reading, Lehman and Roberts (2014) reminds us to ask, Is the text worth reading closely? What do we gain by reading texts more than once? What patterns do we notice? What new understandings do we develop through our close readings? What new ways to do we begin to see the world? The texts the teachers chose in this book merited close examination, leading to a deeper and more nuanced exploration. Maggie noticed Michael's transformation and deep engagement when he asked, *"Do we have time to read it again to see if we missed anything?"* We do not ask this question when texts do not matter.

How do we support future teachers to fall in love with language, with books, with words, so their close readings will engage and enchant their students? As we share books with our students—read alouds, mentor texts to explore craft features, possibilities for guided reading or literature circles—we can share the range of ways we read texts closely to savor the author's craft, to examine text structures, to see the world in broader or more nuanced ways. Kelly and the authors in this book engaged in "numerous and layered readings of multiple texts to construct meaning, make connections across texts, and consider the complexities of the human condition" (this volume, p. 69).

Much like Heather moved away from her "throwaway" books to incorporating award-winning picturebooks, the authors of this book have led me to reimagine, reconsider, and question the books I use within my teacher preparation courses. To help our literacy specialist candidates select books that "elicit connection, emotion, or interest amongst my students" (this volume, p. 42), I need to look across the texts I have chosen and recommended as read alouds, mentor texts, and texts for inquiry groups to examine what my choices say about my intentions as a teacher educator. When I am working with children throughout the tutorials, what do the books I am recommending to the teachers say about my choices? If book choices and text selections are unexamined, where will students engage in conversations to develop a more expansive worldview? Likewise, if book choices within teacher preparation programs are unexamined, where will teacher candidates have opportunities to engage in conversations to expand their worldviews?

Exploring Multiple Perspectives through Inquiry

All four classrooms in this book were active communities of inquiry. The authors valued and believed in the importance of children asking questions. They actively sought ways for the children to become question posers, and not simply answer questions asked by teachers.

The teachers' belief in children constructing their own understandings was rooted in hope. As hooks (2003) contends, "As teachers, we believe that learning is possible, that nothing can keep an open mind from seeking after knowledge and finding a way to know" (p. xiv). Explorations, some big and some small, were led by the learners. The teachers supported their students' emerging questions and the sometimes messy and seemingly chaotic learning environment. They trusted their learners, believed they had something important to say, and opened up spaces for students to explore and grapple with these emerging questions. Student questions formed the basis of classroom inquiry.

In our teacher preparation program, we, too, have discovered the power of inquiry when our graduate students engage with learners in inquiry communities in the capstone practicum course. Like Maggie's reading group, the communities in our graduate courses sometimes begin with fits and starts as the teachers step back, and students take the lead. Recently, a group of three fifth graders developed an inquiry exploring if zoos were "good or bad" for animals. Given how passionate all three were about their topic and their views, conversations during inquiry time were lively. Mark and Brendan (student names are pseudonyms) initially believed zoos were "wonderful," "excellent," and created a "safe" place for animals to live. Noah disagreed, noting zoos placed animals in cages when they truly belonged in the wild. During their inquiry, Mark and Brendan read about research conducted in zoos and how zoos breed endangered animals. Noah read about cage sizes and animal environments. Each brought their research to the inquiry group and cited how and why *their* positions mattered more.

The conversations shifted when they learned about a 28-year-old polar bear, Arturo, in a zoo in Argentina. All three read about Arturo's plight, reviewed articles on the conditions of the Argentinian zoo, read petitions for Arturo to be moved to a Canadian zoo, and debated the benefits and disadvantages of a 28-year-old bear being moved across two continents. One day Brendan noted, "I thought it was an easy choice. But, while I think he'd be happier in Canada, I'm not sure an old bear could survive the trip." Each afternoon they shared their research with their families.

All three wrote letters to the zookeepers in Canada and Argentina, signed a global petition, and developed an expanded vision for their world. The teachers were excited to watch their once quiet students examine multiple perspectives and articulate their developing, and ever-changing, perspectives. As Mark said, "I thought zoos were all good until I read about Arturo. Now, I worry about the animals."

Throughout the inquiry, the graduate students helped Noah, Brendan, and Mark make their learning "visible," much like Krista did when she hung students' favorite quotes throughout the classroom. In the practicum, the boys often returned to add to or revise their charts, Post-it® Notes, and recorded questions, comments, and musings. During the Family Presentation at the end of the semester, as they shared their inquiry, Brendan commented, "We've changed." And, indeed, they had.

Their often contentious early conversations became more respectful. Over time the three listened to one another and moved beyond absolutes. The inquiry supported the boys to move beyond one way, one truth, one perspective. Just as the students in Heather, Maggie, Krista, and Simeen's classes grappled with tentative understandings and initial absolute positions, so, too, did the learners in the practicum course.

As our graduate students engage with their learners through inquiry, we support them to ask: Whose voices are missing? Whose voices are privileged? We ask our graduate students to consider these questions throughout their coursework—questions that often stop our teacher candidates in their tracks. For teacher candidates to teach critically, we want them to grapple with these questions throughout the teacher preparation program so they will, in turn, engage critically with their future students.

We learn from Heather, Krista, Simeen, and Maggie how important it is to create inquiry communities where the learners lead, where examining and exploring multiple perspectives opens doors for expanding our worldview. By experiencing these communities in their coursework, we foresee teacher candidates will create spaces to learn from and with their learners in their own contexts.

Imagining the Logic of Learners

When we listen, we learn. All of the teachers recognized the centrality of questions to honor and validate learners as the teachers come to understand how children imagine the world. Through these more open and open-ended conversations, the teachers built on their students' first draft thinking (Mercer, 2000) and learned from their learners, all the while engaging in and modeling respectful discourse. All are genuinely interested in their students' responses. They did not seek a known answer. Instead, they were coming to know their learners, how their learners viewed the world, and how learners considered and contemplated.

The global books Krista, Maggie, Simeen, and Heather read with their children provided a springboard for newly emerging understandings. Their classroom conversations were built on trust—trust in teachers and trust in one another. In these spaces, learners offered tentative understandings, asked questions that could lead to discomfort, and came to examine circumstances and situations more carefully.

Throughout the book, we read powerful examples of the teachers intentionally learning from their students, including during more challenging moments. The teachers suspended judgment, as they sought, first, to imagine the logic of their learners (Dozier, Johnston, & Rogers, 2006) to understand why students viewed a book, a situation, a conversation, in a particular way. They slowed down the conversations in their classrooms and asked, "What are you thinking?" "What else are you thinking?" "I want you to start thinking about how they are represented [in this book]." These questions created the spaces for powerful conversations and deep engagement.

When Maggie began to listen more intently to her students, she discovered they shared more of their thinking with her and with one another. As Maggie came to better understand her learners, she developed more engaging experiences based on their expressed interests. Both Simeen and Krista shared their struggles over the portrayals of war in the books they read. Through their observant listening, they learned how their students interpreted the texts and the experiences of those portrayed in the picturebooks. Heather came to see her students Zuleyka and José in new ways through her careful listening. While both Zuleyka and José presented challenges, Heather did not stop there and place blame on the learners. Instead, she uncovered their unique perspectives and learned from them. Heather found books of interest where her students could connect and respond emotionally.

None of the teachers shied away from difficult conversations. When we engage in difficult conversations, there will be ruptures as we learned in Krista and Toni's class. There will be unfulfilled conversations as Simeen shared. But, instead of stopping or shutting down these conversations, each teacher guided her students to continue to explore, to continue to grapple, to continue to examine assumptions and understandings. Because each teacher trusted that the process of exploring disruptions and grappling mattered for their learners to articulate their developing understandings, each teacher created spaces for students to live in grappling and disruptive moments. In doing so, their students articulated their developing understandings.

We have much to learn from Kelly, Simeen, Maggie, Krista, and Heather for teacher preparation. What are the ways we help our preservice teachers imagine the logic of the learners? Where do we provide spaces for our prospective teachers to grapple with and explore tentative understandings? Krista, Maggie, Heather, and Simeen took the time to nurture initial and sometimes stumbling attempts, to understand where learners were, as their students tried to see outside themselves. Heather wrote, "The intense engagement that global literature offers my students helps them see themselves as a valuable, indispensable resource in understanding and interpreting the text" (this volume, p. 51). In teacher preparation programs, we, too, can explore powerful texts, provide a safe and generative space for inviting emotional responses to texts, and expand dialogic spaces as we connect with our students and imagine their logic as learners.

Providing Time and Space

During each meeting, Kelly provided time and space within the inquiry community to explore tentative understandings. The teachers had time to question each other, to wonder together, to support one another. All attested to the importance of time—time to dwell in the texts they were discussing, time to come to know themselves and the texts in new ways, time to reconsider, time to reflect, time to engage in sometimes uncomfortable conversations, time to help students challenge their assumptions, time to savor the author's language and craft, time to explore multiple texts in multiple genres, and time to challenge interpretations. Understandings gained during their monthly conversations legitimized the importance of this work. In their letters to one another, the teachers focused on the strength they gained from one another and the compassion they showed when they explored new territories or experienced challenges in their home districts.

Within our teacher preparation programs, we need to be sure to create time and spaces for explorations, for challenging assumptions, for grappling, and for disrupting previously held assumptions. This complex work is not possible if our prospective teachers have not experienced for themselves the rich and nuanced ways students share their developing understandings. As Kelly reminds us, access to rich and engaging books is only a start, "Teachers need time with each other, time with librarians, media specialists, and authors, and time with the books themselves to make thoughtful and informed decisions about incorporating global texts within their classrooms" (this volume, p. 140).

The dedicated time the teachers had for their inquiries made a difference. The teachers looked forward to their continuing development as professionals and for the friendships they developed with one another. In teacher preparation programs at UAlbany, we work to begin these intentional communities in hopes of sustaining them. In the past two years, we have invited recent graduates to come together to discuss their instructional practices, engage in inquiry, and focus on teaching and learning. These Early Career Conversations are meant to sustain the learning communities begun in the literacy specialist program. These meetings, held three to four times each year, are opportunities to listen to graduates explore topics that matter to them as they navigate their new classroom contexts. As one recent graduate shared, "I need to come home to re-engage and to rethink what matters. It's hard to do this when I'm so rushed in my school. I come to these meetings to stay current. I love being back."

Agency and Activism

Maggie's students became deeply engaged when they discovered *Alfa and Beto: The Biblioburros* (Morrow, 2013), a text that opened the door to making a difference. Once the door was opened, they sought to learn more—from other books, from videos, from one another. They were empowered and needed to share their learning with their school and asked, "How come some children don't get to go to school?" which led to, "How can we make a difference?" Maggie stepped back, provided support when needed, and let the learners take the lead. In doing so, the students developed a school-wide strategy to raise awareness, conducted a fundraiser, and sent four hundred dollars for students in rural communities in Colombia, South America for much needed resources. Following students' leads for activism provides opportunities for deep engagement.

In teacher preparation, if we want to help the teachers move beyond thinking about issues to taking action, we need to provide opportunities for our students to engage with learners as they seek to make changes. During a writing practicum in our literacy specialist program we invited elementary students to take action by writing a letter to their principal about a change they wished to see in their school. At both schools where the practicum takes place, students wrote about their wishes for playground equipment, anti-bullying messages, class pets, and school wide gardens to feed the hungry.

During each semester, a large number of students wrote about their desire for more books, books to complete series, and books by a wider range of authors. Juliet shared her request with her principal, "I think that we should have more opportunities for wider selection of books. Did you know that some people like to read different genres of books? You might wonder why I want different books. The reason is I am not able to go to the public library that often." Olive wished for a visit from her favorite author since "Her books are very inspiring. Each book has a lesson in it that the kids could learn from." Keith's request was borne out of frustration when he couldn't finish an entire series. If money was an obstacle, Keith offered the idea of interlibrary loan, "The librarian could get it for free by inter-library loans (borrowing a book from another library then giving it back after a bit). Thank you for reading this and I hope you can help our readers finish their series."

Janae asked for additional library time. Ben inquired about more help to check out books since it took "forever" during library, and he wanted to read his books right away, while Renee requested an after school reading club because she felt she did not have enough time to read in schools. Marie knew more books would mean the need for more shelves and suggested holding a book drive to earn money. Izzie's request, "I would honestly love to have newer books" reflected the experiences of students enrolled "for five long years and the books get old quick. As you can see, we really want new books. Can we please get newer books?" Students' voices mattered. Their letters led to librarians interviewing students to learn of their requests, more shelves ordered, and an intentionality as student choices were now included in text selections.

Throughout this book, we have seen the power of global picturebooks to transform teachers' and students' lives. The specificity of the students' requests to their principals speak to the power and impact of the texts that surround us. Through students' engaged actions, we see how deeply and intently text choices matter.

Conclusion

Building communities is at the heart of this book. In these communities, teachers explored together and built trusting relationships. The teachers moved beyond their comfort levels to explore differences. During their monthly conversations together they did not shy away from unpacking and examining their discomfort. When teachers engage in inquiry, explore global literature, examine multiple perspectives, consider their roles and responsibilities in an ever-changing world, they, and their learners, cannot look away. Once students expand their understandings, it is hard to turn back—and why would they?

In the opening chapter, Maggie shared, "*It's hard to see straight.*" It is a tumultuous time in our field to see straight. And, clearly, the teachers in this book "see straight." They see straight to the hearts and minds of their learners. In doing so, they guide and support learners to move outside themselves to develop empathy, to question one another, to see the power of their voices to make changes, to come to see the world in new and expansive ways. This book makes us hopeful and makes us want to explore what is possible. Like bell hooks (2003), all of the teachers sought "to illuminate the space of the possible where we can work to sustain our hope and create community with justice as the core foundation" (p. xvi). Every learner deserves this. The learners in Kelly, Maggie, Simeen, Krista, and Heather's classes live it.

References

Adichie, C. N. (2009). *The danger of a single story* [video speech]. Retrieved from www.ted.com/talks/chimamanda_adichie_the_danger_of_a_single_story

Cambourne, B. (1995). Toward an educationally relevant theory of literacy learning. Twenty years of inquiry. *The Reading Teacher, 49*(3), 182–90.

Christensen, L. (2000). *Reading, writing, and rising up: Teaching about social justice and the power of the written word*. Milwaukee, WI: Rethinking Schools.

Cole, A. & Knowles, J. G. (2000). *Researching teaching: Exploring teacher development through reflexive inquiry*. Boston, MA: Allyn and Bacon.

Dozier, C., Johnston, P., & Rogers, R. (2006). *Critical literacy/Critical teaching: Tools for preparing responsive teachers*. New York, NY: Teachers College Press.

hooks, b. (2003). *Teaching community: A pedagogy of hope*. New York, NY: Routledge.

Janks, H., Dixon, K., Ferreira, A., Granville, S., & Newfield, D. (2014). *Doing critical literacy*. New York, NY: Routledge.

Ladson-Billings, G. (2009). *The dreamkeepers: Successful teachers of African American children*, 2nd ed. San Francisco, CA: Jossey-Bass.

Lehman, C. & Roberts, K. (2014). *Falling in love with close reading: Lessons for analyzing texts—and life*. Portsmouth, NH: Heinemann.

McIntosh, P. (1990). White privilege: Unpacking the invisible knapsack. *Independent School*, *49*(2), 31.

Mercer, N. (2000). *Words and minds: How we use language to think together*. London, England: Routledge.

Morrow, P. (2013). Alfa and Beto: The biblioburros (abridged version). In I. C. Fountas & G. S. Pinnell, *RED leveled literacy intervention student test preparation booklet* (pp. 19–20). Portsmouth, NH: Heinemann.

Reese, D. A. (2007). A Native blogger in pursuit of educating about American Indians. Retrieved from www.alsc.ala.org/blog/2007/11/a-native-blogger-in-pursuit-of-educating-about-american-indians/

Tschida, C. M., Ryan, C. L., & Ticknor, A. S. F. (2014). Building on windows and mirrors: Encouraging the disruption of "single stories" in children's literature. *Journal of Children's Literature*, *40*(1), 28–39.

Warford, M. K. (2011). The zone of proximal teacher development. *Teaching and Teacher Education*, *27*(2), 252–8.

AFTERWORD

Peter H. Johnston

Not long before his death, Urie Bronfenbrenner (2005), one of the architects of Head Start, observed, "To a greater extent than for any other species, human beings create the environments that shape the course of human development" (p. xxviii). In other words, who our children become individually and collectively and the societies they build are shaped by their daily lives in school today. Schooling cannot simply be an institution for passing on the culturally accumulated academic tools. We must have a bigger vision than that.

The teachers whose voices we have heard in this book have a bigger and growing vision. They want children to develop academically to their fullest potential but also to live in a just and caring manner. They have brought this vision within reach by providing critical examples of classroom practice along with the personal, professional, and relational backstories that made their practice possible in spite of myriad institutional constraints. These are not the usual air-brushed examples that invite unrealistic expectations of perfection, simplicity, and linearity. Rather, they are ordinary examples from ordinary classrooms in which teachers work with courage and persistence in the face of their uncertainties, discomfort, and moral tensions.

These powerful stories offer hope, not just for teaching and teachers but also for the future of society. Their examples suggest that because of engagements with global literature, students develop, among other things, better relationships, more productive identities, a stronger sense of agency, and a diminished likelihood of stereotyping. Perhaps more importantly, they develop a stronger sense of equity and justice and a critical awareness of their own role in its production. Though these teachers often doubted they were doing enough, there is ample evidence to show the value of the teaching they are doing, both in the book and in other forms of research.

Consequential Decisions and Cascades of Consequences

The decisions these teachers made collectively and individually are networked in important ways so I will pick a nonlinear and recursive route through what I see as the most important decisions.

Engaging Minds

First, they chose beautifully illustrated books with engaging narratives, narratives that would invite students into the places and the mental lives of the characters. Second, they took steps to ensure that students would be willing and able to do so—providing multigenre companion texts, along with inviting, open-ended questions. Let me explain why these first two decisions, focusing on engagement and inviting children into characters' minds, are so important.

The careful choice of texts, along with invitations and support to ensure student engagement, is critical because engagement, per se, has positive consequences. Students who are more engaged in school have more friends, make better decisions, feel more in control of their lives, are happier, and are less likely to be lonely, or to engage in anti-social behavior (National Research Council & Institute of Medicine, 2004). Pressures in schools including testing, the need to cover particular "content," and definitions of "close reading" act to limit students' attention to the "four corners of the text," and work to push teachers toward teaching strategies that do not engage students. But when students are not meaningfully engaged, they do not think or act strategically. In our own work on engaged reading (Ivey & Johnston, 2013), albeit with older students, we have found that students who are fully engaged in their reading, read strategically and share the strategies they are using with their peers. Because they are engaged, they also find that they cannot help but talk with their peers about the books they read. In the process, they develop strong, supportive relationships along with broad changes in their identities, their moral development, and their happiness. This talk among peers begins the development of a community with relationships of trust and agency.

Such conversations among students pattern themselves after the teacher-supported conversations during read alouds, and are particularly important. Books and conversations in which students are able to imagine themselves into characters' minds are especially important. We know from experimental research that children who are engaged in conversations that require the use of mental verbs (e.g. feel, think, imagine) and mental state language (e.g. sad, confused, anxious) become more socially cooperative, misbehave less, have better self-regulation, better social skills, larger friendship networks, and better moral development (Johnston, 2012). We know that these same sorts of transformative changes, in children (and adults), also result from engagement with the mental lives of characters in narrative texts (Bal & Veltkamp, 2013; Busselle & Bilandzic, 2009; Johnson, 2001; Lysaker, Tonge, Gauson, & Miller, 2011; Mar & Oatley, 2008).

In fact, some researchers have linked such literary experiences with the development, indeed, the evolution of human consciousness (Sumara, Luce-Kapler, & Iftody, 2008). Sumara and his colleagues argue that it is by imagining the consciousness of others that we become aware of our own consciousness (not the other way around) and that these experiences also expand our repertoire of possible interactions. These researchers define "literary experiences" as interactions in which a person "expands her or his own conscious awareness through thought experiments about how characters create and interpret their self-consciousness" (p. 233). These are exactly the conversations taking place in these teachers' classrooms, conversations that expand students' ability to imagine themselves into others' minds—their social imaginations. Children with stronger social imaginations tend to engage in more pro-social behavior (Deković & Gerris, 1994; Slaughter, Dennis, & Pritchard, 2002) and they are more likely to be accepted by their peers (Parkhurst & Asher, 1992). In other words, just as with these teachers' inquiries, experimental research shows that engaging children in literary experiences that expand their social imaginations produces a cascade of powerful consequences.

Thinking Communities: Expanding Minds and Valuing Difference

A third curricular decision was to set aside time and arrange for students to engage in extended dialogic thinking together, listening to each other, hearing and constructing multiple perspectives, and building on each other's ideas. Committing large segments of time to these practices requires teachers to understand how important the practices are. Indeed, this sort of experience produces another cascade of consequences. Certainly older students who have engaged in dialogic interactions in English classes understand and recall their readings better and attend more carefully to literary elements in the texts they read (Nystrand, 2006). As children think together, they also come to understand how to interact in ways that foster learning. Experimental studies have shown that developing this ability to think together, among other things, expands children's willingness to listen to and consider others' ideas, their reasoning ability, comprehension, expressive language, confidence, and also, predictably, the quality of their interpersonal relationships (Trickey & Topping, 2004).

When Heather's students recognized the absence of "our books" during testing season, they were likely not only missing the books themselves but also the literary experience that includes the interactions anchored in the books. In other words, they likely missed the intellectual community with all of its relational and intellectual significance. They knew when they were engaged in developmentally productive interactions and when they were not.

A fourth important curricular decision evident in the teaching in this book is the decision to put students in control of their learning, building a sense of agency. This is linked, of course, to efforts to ensure that students are engaged. In their interactions around the books, the teachers did not offer answers to the students' questions. Instead, they sustained uncertainty, particularly the uncertainty generated by multiple perspectives. The teachers did this by asking open questions, and not offering or judging answers but instead asking for students to explain themselves to each other. Sustaining uncertainty is what makes possible the extended engaged thinking together that allows students to develop a sense of agency in knowledge construction.

Building children's comfort with uncertainty also has some important side effects, including the ability to keep an open mind on a topic, a reduced tendency to stereotype, and a more positive view of difference and ideas that challenge the status quo (Kruglanski, Pierro, Mannetti, & Grada, 2006). This is what social psychologists refer to as a reduced need for closure. Its opposite, a high need for closure, is increased when people are put under pressure of time or accountability testing.

A fifth important instructional decision is choosing books with characters whose lives and circumstances invite understanding of difference, stretch and challenge students' experiences, and invite consideration of moral dilemmas. This is the most difficult curricular commitment—to choose global literature—because it requires providing the necessary supports to ensure that students are willing and able to engage these very different lives and contexts and to come to value the necessary intellectual and moral discomforts. These teachers collaboratively developed the expertise to deploy multigenre (particularly informational) texts, conversations, questions, stories and analogies that would invite this engagement. It is a difficult balance because the teachers need student communities to take up residence in the minds of characters whose lives, cultures, and experiences are significantly different. The goals of these communities are deeper understanding of self and other and of the complexity of humanity. In the process, students build a positive connection between feelings of discomfort and imbalance and the satisfaction of deeper understanding.

A sixth and final important decision is the use of multimedia texts. It is not only that the illustrated books, being shorter than "chapter books," make it possible for students to encounter a wide range of characters, narratives, and contexts from which to construct meaning. The multimedia nature of these texts requires "transmediation"—the juggling and transforming of meaning across multiple sign systems which is also demanded in their use of role play, music, and art. Transmediation contributes to students' analytic conversations and complex language functions (McCormick, 2011). That there is less evidence for the value of such practices than for other decisions the teachers made, is a testament to our historically limited view of reading and of learning.

The thread that holds together this last set of priorities (three through six) is a valuing of difference. Students come to recognize that differences in perspective produce dialogic interaction, differences in sign systems produce transmediation, differences in culture and character stretch minds and, ultimately, expand consciousness.

Transforming Selves

Children construct their understandings of self within social relationships with peers, teachers, and book characters. When these relationships are positive, it is more likely that students develop a stronger sense of relatedness (Furrer & Skinner, 2003; Goodenow, 1993), which, along with a sense of autonomy and competence, is a fundamental human need (Ryan & Deci, 2000). In fact, each of these needs appears to be met in these dialogic classrooms in which students are engaged with literature in ways that demand deep and transformative thinking.

In this context, consider the transformation of third grader José who had claimed an identity as "hyper" until playing the role of Dr. Martin Luther King Jr. in a re-enactment of the lunch counter sit-ins in Greensboro. He was helped to get into Dr. King's mind in several important ways. First, the anticipation guide produced a dialogic tension between doing what the law requires and doing what is morally right—a space of moral uncertainty. Second, viewing movies of civil disobedience training helped students to understand the emotional control demanded by nonviolent protest. Third, videos of the protesters included talk about protesters' "feelings of solidarity and pride" when they were jailed for their efforts to change unjust laws which help the children build their social imaginations and their emotional self-regulation while offering possible selves into which they might choose to grow. As the teachers apprentice these children into our shared humanity, these are important understandings and capacities.

Kelly, like the others, worries about whether teaching is "somehow 'less' critical if a tangible action does not occur." In this context, we should not ignore the fact that two years later students remembered José for his role, and likely remembered the significance of the role he, as Martin Luther King Jr., played in changing inequitable laws through civil disobedience. It seems likely that José remembers it too and would act as necessary. In October of 2014, high school students in Colorado engaged in civil disobedience to protest proposed curricular changes in their Advanced Placement U.S. History curriculum (www.bloomberg. com/bw/articles/2014-10-09/colorado-students-protest-moves-to-change-ap-history-classes). The changes they protested would have replaced material that would "encourage or condone civil disorder, social strife or disregard of the law" with materials that would only "present positive aspects of the United States and its heritage." Those high school students recognized the curricular change as a social and intellectual step backwards, a willful lack of interest in considering the errors of the past and the means through which they were addressed. I suspect that their concern is not unlike these students protesting the loss of "our books." Although the present book has provided examples of children taking action, Kelly, Maggie, Heather, Simeen, and Krista sometimes might have to wait a while to witness larger social action from their students. Nonetheless, the seeds have been planted.

When we look for the results of the planting, we might remember Eleanor Roosevelt's (1958) statement to the United Nations on the tenth anniversary of the Bill of Human Rights: "Where, after all, do universal human rights begin? In small places, close to home—so close and so small that they cannot be seen on any maps of the world…."

"Small places, close to home." Consider Zuleyka's transformation from an unhappy person excluded from the classroom community to a contributing community member with a strong sense of agency through her identification with the narrative of a strong woman who accomplished her goals against the odds. It is not insignificant that she became a role model for her younger sister as "one of Ms. O'Leary's best students." It might have been otherwise. Neither are her changed relationships with other students insignificant—relationships that will affect the selves and relationships those students construct as well. These students find in books, and among peers, possible selves they might construct and some consciously recognize those sources of self-transformation.

Teacher Learning Communities

Much of what I have said about the learning communities in these classrooms can be applied to the teachers' learning community. Their uncertainties led to conversations that, in turn, led to relationships of mutual respect, support, trust, and consciousness about teaching, and action. Just as for the children, the teachers' transformation is an ongoing process as they challenge themselves and their students to learn and grow. Indeed, teacher and student transformations are intimately linked (Ivey & Johnston, in press) and these teachers' journeys help us to understand the ways teachers and students are transformed and transformative within the relational engagements of their learning communities.

Rock climbers, perched precariously high on a rock face, recognize that in order to move forward they have to let go of one handhold. Sometimes a climber is struck by fear of falling and becomes "frozen to the face," unable to let go and face the uncertainty of the next handhold. These teachers, with each other's help, are facing their uncertainties, letting go of old practices and moving forward. In the process, they are able to see new handholds and, emboldened by what they have already accomplished, and with each other's support, to reach out again. Their collective stories and analyses provide the rest of us with numerous handholds and, with their support and with each other's, individually and collectively, we, too, can improve our practice, the lives of children and the future of society.

References

Bal, P. M., & Veltkamp, M. (2013). How does fiction reading influence empathy? An experimental investigation on the role of emotional transportation. *PLoS ONE, 8*(1), e55341. doi:10.1371/journal.pone.0055341

Bronfenbrenner, U. (2005). *Making human beings human: Bioecological perspectives on human development.* Thousand Oaks, CA: Sage Publications.

Busselle, R., & Bilandzic, H. (2009). Measuring narrative engagement. *Media Psychology,* 12(4), 321–47.

Deković, M., & Gerris, J. R. M. (1994). Developmental analysis of social, cognitive and behavioral differences between popular and rejected children. *Journal of Applied Developmental Psychology,* 15, 367–86.

Furrer, C., & Skinner, E. (2003). Sense of relatedness as a factor in children's academic engagement and performance. *Journal of Educational Psychology,* 95, 148–62.

Goodenow, C. (1993). Classroom belonging among early adolescent students: Relationship to motivation and achievement. *Journal of Early Adolescence,* 13, 21–43.

Ivey, G., & Johnston, P. H. (2013). *Social processes of engaged reading and engaged classrooms.* Paper presented at the Literacy Research Association, Dallas, TX.

Ivey, G., & Johnston, P. H. (in press). Engaged reading as a collaborative, transformative practice. *Journal of Literacy Research.*

Johnson, S. (2001). *Emergence: The connected lives of ants, brains, cities, and software.* New York, NY: Touchstone.

Johnston, P. H. (2012). *Opening minds: Using language to change lives.* Portland, ME: Stenhouse.

Kruglanski, A. W., Pierro, A., Mannetti, L., & de Grada, E. (2006). Groups as epistemic providers: Need for closure and the unfolding of group-centrism. *Psychological Review,* 113(1), 84–100.

Lysaker, J. T., Tonge, C., Gauson, D., & Miller, A. (2011). Reading and social imagination: What relationally oriented reading instruction can do for children. *Reading Psychology,* 32(6), 520–66.

McCormick, J. (2011). Transmediation in the language arts classroom: Creating contexts for analysis and ambiguity. *Journal of Adolescent & Adult Literacy,* 54(8), 579–87.

Mar, R. A., & Oatley, K. (2008). The function of fiction is the abstraction and simulation of social experience. *Perspectives on Psychological Science (Wiley-Blackwell),* 3(3), 173–92.

National Research Council & Institute of Medicine. (2004). *Engaging schools: Fostering high school students' motivation to learn.* Washington, DC: The National Academies Press.

Nystrand, M. (2006). Research on the role of classroom discourse as it affects reading comprehension. *Research in the Teaching of English,* 40(4), 393–412.

Parkhurst, J. T., & Asher, S. R. (1992). Peer rejection in middle school: Subgroup differences in behavior, loneliness, and interpersonal. *Developmental Psychology,* 28(2), 231.

Roosevelt, E. (1958). "In your hands." Speech delivered at the Tenth Anniversary of the Universal Declaration of Human Rights. Retrieved from www.un.org/en/globalissues/briefingpapers/humanrights/quotes.shtml

Ryan, R. M., & Deci, E. L. (2000). Self-determination theory and the facilitation of intrinsic motivation, social development, and well-being. *American Psychologist,* 55, 68–78.

Slaughter, V., Dennis, M., & Pritchard, M. (2002). Theory of mind and peer acceptance in preschoolers. *British Journal of Developmental Psychology,* 20, 545–64.

Sumara, D., Luce-Kapler, R., & Iftody, T. (2008). Educating consciousness through literary experiences. *Educational Philosophy & Theory,* 40(1), 228–41.

Trickey, S., & Topping, K. J. (2004). "Philosophy for children": A systematic review. *Research Papers in Education,* 19(3), 365–80.

APPENDIX

Children's Books and Professional Texts Essential to Our Inquiries

Children's Literature

Heather's Recommendations

Seeds of Change: Planting a Path to Peace	Jen Cullerton Johnson
The Boy Who Harnessed the Wind	William Kamkwamba
Golden Domes and Silver Lanterns	Hena Khan
Richard Wright and the Library Card	William Miller
Tomás and the Library Lady	Pat Mora
Mama Miti	Donna Jo Napoli
Planting the Trees of Kenya	Claire Nivola
Sitti's Secrets	Naomi Shihab Nye
When I Was Young in the Mountains	Cynthia Rylant
Grandfather's Journey	Allen Say
Wangari's Trees of Peace	Jeanette Winter
A Day's Work	Eve Bunting

Simeen's Recommendations

The Land I Lost	Quang Nhuong Huynh
Water Buffalo Days	Quang Nhuong Huynh
Blue Jasmine	Kashmira Sheth
Sadako	Eleanor Coerr

The Circuit	Francisco Jiménez
Voices from the Fields	S. Beth Atkin
Journey to Jo'burg	Beverley Naidoo
Becoming Naomi León	Pam Muñoz Ryan
Voices in the Park	Anthony Browne
Baseball Saved Us	Ken Mochizuki
Shin's Tricycle	Tatsuharu Kodama
Faithful Elephants	Yukio Tsuchiya
Migrant	Maxine Trottier
Books for Oliver	Jim Larkin
Inside Out and Back Again	Thanhha Lai

Krista's Recommendations

World War II Picturebooks

Baseball Saved Us	Ken Mochizuki
Boxes for Katje	Candace Fleming
The Bracelet	Yoshiko Uchida
The Butterfly	Patricia Polacco
The Cello of Mr. O	Jane Cutler
Faithful Elephants	Yukio Tsuchiya
The Greatest Skating Race	Louise Borden
Hiroshima No Pika	Toshi Maruki
The Little Ships: The Heroic Rescue at Dunkirk in WWII	Louise Borden
Mama Played Baseball	David A. Adler
My Hiroshima	Junko Morimoto
My Secret Camera	Frank Dabba Smith
Sadako	Eleanor Coerr
Shin's Tricycle	Tatsuharu Kodama
So Far from the Sea	Eve Bunting
Star of Fear, Star of Hope	Jo Hoestlandt
The Unbreakable Code	Sara Hoagland Hunter
The Yellow Star	Carmen Agra Deedy
Feathers and Fools	Mem Fox
Why War Is Never a Good Idea	Alice Walker
Playing War	Kathy Beckwith

World War II Novels

Title	Author	# of pages	Fountas & Pinnell Level
Aleutian Sparrow	Karen Hesse	156	N/A
Blue	Joyce Moyer Hostetter	197	S
The Book Thief	Markus Zusak	560	S
A Boy at War: A Novel of Pearl Harbor	Harry Mazer	112	T
The Boy Who Dared	Susan Campbell Bartoletti	192	S
Code Talker	Joseph Bruchac	231	X
Dawn of Fear	Susan Cooper	176	Z
Dear America: The Fences Between Us	Kirby Larson	320	R
Don't You Know There's a War On?	Avi	208	S
Elephant Run	Roland Smith	336	S
Four Perfect Pebbles	Lila Perl	144	Z
Hitler's Canary	Sandi Toksvig	192	U
The Journal of Scott Pendleton Collins	Walter Dean Myers	144	U
Journey to Topaz	Yoshiko Uchida	160	Y
Number the Stars	Lois Lowry	156	P
On the Wings of Heroes	Richard Peck	160	R
The Quilt	Gary Paulsen	96	Z
Sadako and the Thousand Paper Cranes	Eleanor Coerr	64	O
Shadows on the Sea	Joan Hiatt Harlow	244	P
Snow Treasure	Marie McSwigan	208	P
Soldier Bear	Bibi Dumon Tak	158	S
Someone Named Eva	Joan M. Wolf	200	U
Stepping on the Cracks	Mary Downing Hahn	224	S
T4	Ann Clare LeZotte	112	N/A
Under a War-Torn Sky	Laura Malone Elliott	288	O
Warriors in the Crossfire	Nancy Bo Flood	142	M
When My Name Was Keoko	Linda Sue Park	208	O
Willow Run	Patricia Reilly Giff	149	S

Professional Texts

Burns, T. J. (2009). Searching for peace: Exploring issues of war with young children. *Language Arts, 86*(6), 421–30.

Dressel, J. H. (2005). Personal response and social responsibility: Responses of middle school students to multicultural literature. *The Reading Teacher, 58*(8), 750–64.

Jewett, P. (2011). "Some people do things different from us": Exploring personal and global cultures in a first grade class. *Journal of Children's Literature, 37*(1), 20–9.

Martin, L. A., Smolen, L. A., Oswald, R. A., & Milam, J. L. (2012). Preparing students for global citizenship in the twenty-first century: Integrating social justice through global literature. *The Social Studies, 103*(4), 158–64.

Morgan, H. (2009). Picturebook biographies for young children: A way to teach multiple perspectives. *Early Childhood Education, 37,* 219–27.

Qureshi, K. S. (2006). Beyond mirrored worlds: Teaching world literature to challenge students' perception of 'other.' *English Journal, 96*(2), 34–40.

Saine, P. & Kara-Soterioa, J. (2010). Using podcasts to enrich responses to global children's literature. *The New England Reading Association Journal, 46*(1), 100–8.

Short, K. G. (2009). Critically reading the word and the world: Building intercultural understanding through literature. *Bookbird: A Journal of International Children's Literature,* (47)2, 1–10.

Short, K. G. (2011). Building bridges of cultural understanding through international literature. In A. W. Bedord & L. K. Albright (Eds.), *A master class in children's literature* (pp. 130–48). Urbana, IL: NCTE.

Short, K. G. (2012). Story as world making. *Language Arts, 90*(1), 9–17.

Smolen, L. A. & MacDonald, S. (2008). Adolescent literature and reader response: "It's about global awareness and social justice!" *The International Journal of Learning, 15*(10), 207–12.

Youngs, S. (2012). Injustice and irony: Students respond to Japanese American internment picturebooks. *Journal of Children's Literature, 38*(2), 37–49.

Ward, B. A. (2010). Engaging students with global literature: The 2009 notable books for a global society. *The New England Reading Association Journal, 45*(2), 43–56.

INDEX